Y0-EGG-114

The Hurling Time

by the same author

*

autobiography

TRIALS IN BURMA

THE JOURNEY OUTWARD

INTO HIDDEN BURMA

histories

THE GREAT WITHIN

BRITISH MERCHANT ADVENTURERS

THE LAND OF THE GREAT IMAGE

FOREIGN MUD

THE FIRST HOLY ONE

LAST AND FIRST IN BURMA

biographies

SIAMESE WHITE

THE GRAND PEREGRINATION

MARCO POLO

CORTÉS AND MONTEZUMA

travel

LORDS OF THE SUNSET

novels and romances

SHE WAS A QUEEN

SANDA MALA

THE DARK DOOR

QUEST FOR SITA

THE DESCENT OF THE GOD

THE MYSTERY OF DEAD LOVERS

drama

THE MOTHERLY AND AUSPICIOUS

WHITE OF MERGEN

LORD OF THE THREE WORLDS

The Hurling Time

MAURICE COLLIS

'That tyme was Syr Wylliam Walworthe made knyght in Smethe Fyllde, for that he slowe the Chefteyn of hem the whiche were rysers. And thys was called "the hurlyng tyme".'

GREGORY'S CHRONICLE
(*Gregory was Lord Mayor of London in* 1451)

FABER AND FABER
24 Russell Square
London

First published in mcmlviii
by Faber and Faber Limited
24 *Russell Square London W.C.*1
Printed in Great Britain by
Western Printing Services Limited, Bristol

To

THE HONOURABLE STEVEN RUNCIMAN

Contents

Illustrations

NOTE: *Chroniques de France*, from which many of the illustrations are taken, is a 14th-century manuscript in the British Museum. How far the faces are portraits is impossible to say. One can at least be sure that the costumes and arms are not anachronistic, as the manuscript is nearly contemporary with the events described.

MAPS

Introductory

When planning this book my first idea was to confine it to a detailed description of the peasant revolt in and about London during the first fortnight of June, 1381, and more particularly to what happened in the streets of London on Thursday, Friday and Saturday, the 13th, 14th and 15th of June, events which a Corporation report, written in the same year, declared to have been 'the most wondrous and hitherto unheard-of prodigies that have ever happened in the City',[1] and which afterwards were called 'The Hurling Time'.

On reflection, however, it struck me that the hurling time really began with the astonishing adventures of the English people in France from the battle of Crécy in 1346. Between 1346 and 1381 the English founded an overseas dominion and lost it. The ruling classes, raised to a pinnacle of celebrity by success, were deprived of all reputation by the disaster which followed. The psychological disturbance was immense. The general population which had followed their rulers enthusiastically when they were victorious, turned on them, adjudged them traitors and condemned them to death. Their escape was so narrow as to have seemed a miracle to writers of the day.

This sequence of events, which ended happily for the ruling classes after their hairbreadth escape, has the structural unity of a drama. I have attempted to reconstruct it from the original documents. Many historians have laboured in the field already; their

[1] Letter Book H. fol. CXXXIII (Latin). See Riley's *Memorials of London*, p. 449.

interpretations differ considerably. I have interpreted the sources as I have understood them, and in my presentation of their story have been mindful of the dramatic unity underlying the whole.

For a book of this kind, addressed to the reading public in general, footnotes giving reference or other comments have been considered distracting and unnecessary. This view, I think, is old-fashioned. People nowadays know quite well that an historical work without references is a waste of time to read. It is no better than fiction. The device of putting references and notes at the end of chapters or in an appendix instead of at the bottom of their page may please casual readers, but will only irritate the more careful, who instead of running the eye easily to a note below have to turn to another place. Convinced that the modern public demands references and likes them to be as handy as possible, I have given indication wherever necessary of my sources either in the text or at the bottom of the page.

The Start of the French Adventure

Since the conquest of England by the French duke, William, in 1066, the kings of England had had a dual role, as sovereigns of England and, on account of their various demesnes in France (first Normandy and then Aquitaine[1]), as vassals of the King of France. The possessions of the kings of England in France were not English possessions. Though they belonged to the King of England, he held them as a French duke. That was the way the feudal system worked.

By the fourteenth century, however, feudalism in its international aspect was growing incompatible with an increasing national consciousness. From the French angle, England was no longer regarded as a kingdom which a French duke had taken possession of, but as the country of a king whose possessions in France had become an undesirable anachronism. The growth of this view was natural and inevitable; in practice the English king, in his disguise as a French duke, was not a real feudal noble of France who could be controlled to the extent that other French nobles were controllable. His estates were in reality more like bits of France fallen under foreign rule, though they were administered by the local people like a French duchy. This was so evidently the case that the English themselves had begun to think of their king's demesnes in France as English possessions and even to feel proud of them.

[1] I use the word Aquitaine throughout for the area between the Loire and the Pyrenees called variously Aquitaine, Guienne and Gascony, or by its smaller divisions, Poitou, Limousin, Quercy and Perigord.

By 1330 only the ports of Bordeaux and Bayonne, and a strip of country in their vicinity, remained to the English crown, and of this remainder the French crown sought to dispossess it. The two countries began to face each other in what was approaching a modern way. With so irritating a *casus belli* their relations grew increasingly strained. There were two possible courses open to the then king, Edward III. The more obvious was for him to strengthen his forces in Aquitaine, resist further encroachment on his duchy, and if possible drive the French back. The other, far more ambitious, was to invade France across the Channel and strike at the root of French power. He resolved on the second course. To give it an air of legality and reason, sufficient to attract allies and avoid outraging the public opinion of Christendom, he put forward a claim to the throne of France, declaring that by descent he was the rightful heir, through his mother Isabella, sister of Charles IV, the previous French king, who had died without male issue. As Charles IV's nephew, he was the nearest male. (This claim was an afterthought, for in 1329 he had paid homage for his French possessions in the choir of Amiens cathedral.)

The French had already ruled out such a claim. Their lawyers held that a woman could not transmit title to the throne, since it was already the law that she could not reign. Charles's only child, a daughter, had been passed over in favour of Philip of Valois, his first cousin who had been crowned king in 1328 as Philip VI. It is characteristic of the transitional state of opinion (for feudal conceptions were only beginning to cede to national), that the French dismissed the king of England's claim to be king of France on the grounds of dynastic law and not because it was obviously preposterous on national grounds.

France in the fourteenth century was the most thickly populated and the richest state in Europe. Its inhabitants are said to have numbered twelve million, while those of England did not amount to four million.[1] The king of France could muster a feudal army many times greater than a king of England could lead across the Channel. His chivalry, enormously conceited, considered themselves the most formidable in the world. How then was it that

[1] This was before the Black Death of 1348 and the recurrent outbreaks of 1360, 1369 and 1375. By 1377, it is calculated, the population of England was not more than 2,200,000. (See *British Medieval Population* by Josiah Cox Russell, 1948.)

Edward thought he could make himself king of France by force? His revenue was small. At that time it was usual to expect the king of England to live as far as possible on his settled income and be chary of asking for supplementary grants from Parliament. His settled income was chiefly from crown lands and customs dues. The amount has been variously calculated, and may be given as an average of about £70,000 a year. It was supposed to defray the cost, not only of the Household, but of the whole administration. War was an extra it could not pay for. But Edward had no great difficulty in persuading Parliament to make him the necessary supplementary grants. Therein lay his strength. The English people wanted a war with France.[1]

In addition to being assured of financial support, Edward had other sources of strength. His army, though much smaller than what King Philip of France could put into the field, was a better fighting machine. It was not, like the French, a loose conglomeration of the armed forces of the great feudal lords, but a force of picked men serving for a fixed pay and the chance of loot. In each county there was a commissioner for raising recruits. A county as a rule had only to find about 500 men or less for an army of 10,000, the average size, to be mustered. In the nature of things such men were bound to be mostly volunteers. In addition to such county commissions of array, contracts were made with individual lords to raise contingents of mercenaries. The army which resulted was altogether a more professional body than the French army. It had more cohesion and its leaders were under more control.

Besides being easier to manage, the English army had the use of a weapon which the French did not possess. This weapon was the longbow. It had greater range, rapidity of discharge, and penetration than the crossbow used by the French. The peculiarity of the longbow was that it could not be adopted by anyone else. To learn how to manage it took years. The best archers had been practising from boyhood. The English villagers enjoyed shooting arrows. Archery was a sport, both a pure sport for its own sake and for the sake of hunting, particularly poaching. After the longbow's introduction from Wales some generations

[1] Besides an inclination for adventure overseas, the English peasantry had a dislike of the French as people who had conquered them in 1066. Their aristocracy had been displaced by Norman barons and their tongue demoted by Norman French.

back, it had been taken up enthusiastically by the peasantry whose character and ways it seemed to suit.[1] They had enough initiative, love of outdoor amusement and leisure to develop it into a weapon against which armour was not proof. The French peasantry had felt no similar impulse. If they had shown interest, they would have been discouraged by the nobility whose more rigid conception of chivalry would have precluded them from accepting archers as able to contribute as much to victory as knights.

Besides possessing the longbow the English had evolved new tactics to go with it, which they had tried out against the Scots at more than one battle. These tactics were quite revolutionary. The prevailing usage in Europe was the charge by armoured knights on horseback. No other way of winning a battle was recognized .Infantry was quite a subordinate element. Crossbowmen were only used for preliminary skirmishing. The charging knights were lords and gentlemen. A battle was a chivalric occasion, with a resemblance to a tournament. The new English tactics changed all this. The knights were dismounted and stood in close formation. Archers in large numbers were placed on their wings a little forward in wedges. Attack was awaited. The opposing cavalry could be counted upon to charge. They were met by the arrows. The few who reached the dismounted knights were killed or taken for ransom.

These tactics were not only a revolution in the art of war, but in ideas. A battle was no longer to be won by the charging knight. It wasn't a tournament. It was not chivalry. The archer's day had dawned. And the archer was a common man out of a village.

Such was Edward's second source of strength. He could not tell whether it would suffice to give him the victory in France, as it had against the Scots, but he was fairly confident that it would.

To cross the Channel in safety a fleet was necessary and also a place to land. Neither side had any regular navy. The English practice was to hire merchant ships. With men-at-arms and archers aboard they became warships of sorts. As to where to land, Edward spent large sums of money bribing the magnates in Flanders to allow him to come ashore in their territories. He also bought their promise to send contingents to his army, in spite of most of them being feudatories of the king of France. Besides

[1] Edward I, who foresaw its possibilities, had encouraged the population to take it up, but they would not have made a success of it unless they had found it very congenial.

paying them subsidies, he was able to bring pressure to bear since they depended on England for the raw wool, whose weaving was their main industry. His claim to the French throne also helped to bring them over, for if he was the rightful king of France they could not be accused of disloyalty to the existing king of France. Further, he made overtures to the Holy Roman Emperor, Lewis IV, who gave him countenance by recognizing his claim and also promised contingents.

This was the favourable posture of affairs in 1338/9. Nevertheless, Edward was setting out on a hazardous adventure, whose issue could not be foreseen. Had he used his money and archers for strengthening his hold in Aquitaine, the risk would have been much less. War might have been avoided. Differences were not so deep that negotiation could not have settled them. But he and his nobility, as well as the general population, wanted adventure. The slower, more moderate, policy had no attractions while the other promised loot and glory. Few, perhaps, really believed France could be wholly conquered, France the centre of European civilization, its area so large, its wealth so great, the fame of its martial chivalry so established. But some of it might be taken. There would be estates for the lords and chances for lesser people to make their fortune.

Edward himself embodied this adventurous spirit. He was an out-of-doors man, immensely fond of hunting and sports. He adored jousting and often won in tournaments. At the time he was only twenty-seven, athletic and handsome, with engaging manners. Though his army was so modern, he was a great traditionalist. Everything which we associate with the Middle Ages—knights and ladies, extravagant costumes, escutcheons, devices, tournaments, pageants—had his especial love. Early in his reign the legendary Round Table of Arthur was revived. He built for it the round tower on the top of the mound at Windsor Castle. In St. George's Chapel near by his knights of the Garter sat each in his stall under an emblazoned banner. The gay fantasy of his own appearance when accoutred for the lists is suggested by the motto he is known to have had on his shield: 'Hay, Hay, the Wythe Swan, by Gode's soul I am thy man.' With his cap of maintenance topped with a lion and itself on top of a helm, mounted on a great courser draped with trappings embroidered with gold leopards, he looked more an heraldic than a military figure. But he was not wholly absorbed in chivalric make-believe. For another device he chose the realist motto: 'It is as it is.' Froissart[1] has left us a picture of him in more sober clothes crossing the Channel with Chandos, destined to become the most celebrated knight of the period: 'He sat on the quarter-deck, wearing a surcoat of black velvet and on his head a black beaver hat which suited him to perfection. He was as merry as he had ever been in his life and told his band to play him a German dance, which Sir John Chandos, who was with him, had newly brought over. And for fun he made the knight sing to an accompaniment. Yet every now and then he would cock his eye at the look-out man on the mast-head.'

King Edward landed at Antwerp in July 1338 and spent the rest of the year in the Low Countries and Germany cementing his alliances. The Emperor Lewis appointed him his Vicar for the coming campaign. Not till September 1339 did he enter France. He took a few small places near the border and laid waste the countryside. King Philip, though he had mustered a feudal army, deferred battle on the advice of an astrologer. By the end of October Edward's money was exhausted and, his allies becoming lukewarm, he withdrew to Brussels in November. The campaign had been nothing more than a border raid. The French too had raided England. With a hired fleet of sea-rovers, aided by galleys from Spain under the Castilian admiral Egidio Boccanegra, they

[1] Froissart had not met King Edward at this time. It was not till 1356, at the age of eighteen, that he came to stay in England. Edward's Queen Philippa became his patroness. 'Elle me fist et créa,' he wrote afterwards. In the course of his life he became intimately acquainted with all the courts and leading men of Europe. No other chonicler of the period had so wide a knowledge of contemporary events. But his presentation of events is literary rather than academic. His chief aim is to create a picture of chivalric society, which he greatly admired. Cold reality did not interest him. He did not probe into motives or look closely into any man's mind. Despite its lack of focus, his vast canvas of high society in the fourteenth century is very revealing. He was certainly a man of genius. His writing is still so fresh that editions of his works continue to be saleable to the general public after six hundred years. No other chronicler of the period is readable nowadays except by students. In the quotations from him I sometimes translate from Kervyn de Lettenhove's edition of 1863 and sometimes give Lord Berners' translation, which was published in London in 1525. Lord Berners is not always quite exact, but his English is marvellous. It is not the English of the fourteenth century, but of the end of the fifteenth or beginning of the sixteenth. Yet the translator was so inspired by the original French, and himself had so remarkable a literary flair, that his English does not sound like Tudor English and seems perfectly wedded to his subject.

attacked numerous south-coast ports, Plymouth, Hastings, Southampton and others, and did some damage.

On his return to England early in 1340 Edward summoned parliament. The members, both lords and commons, agreed to grant money for the continuation of the war. But they were able to make a bargain. Edward had to consent to levy no taxes beyond what they granted. He did not always keep this promise, but that he had to give it showed that parliamentary authority was on the increase.

In June 1340 Edward left again for Flanders with a fresh army, stated by Froissart to have consisted of 4,000 men-at-arms (that is to say knights, esquires and their retainers) and 12,000 archers. The French had hired a large fleet to resist the invasion, including ships from Castile. But it did not attack on the open sea. When Edward approached Sluys, at that time the port of Bruges, he found it in harbour. What was more like a land battle took place. His archers first did great execution. His men-at-arms then boarded the French vessels. He won so complete a victory that for thirty years he had little to fear in all his many crossings of the Channel.

The campaign which followed, however, was as abortive as the first. Edward tried to take Tournai, the chief town on the French north-eastern border and very strongly fortified. He failed. His army was not suited for siege operations. A pitched battle was required to show what his archers could do. No opportunity of the sort was offered him. He signed a truce in September and returned home.

Crécy

Edward did not make another attempt for nearly six years. The campaigns of 1339 and 1340 had shown that operating against France from Flanders was ineffective. Large sums had gone to the magnates of the Low Countries, but they had proved unsatisfactory allies. A better prospect opened in Brittany, a ducal province of France, though more independent than most. The succession was disputed by two claimants, John de Montfort and Charles de Blois. They came to blows and by 1345 the duchy was divided between them. In the course of the struggle John de Montfort[1] had asked for and received English help. He now swore allegiance to Edward as rightful king of France and offered to assist him against King Philip.

Edward made his plans accordingly. These were more elaborate than before. The English expeditionary force would land on the Côtentin peninsula, a sixty-mile crossing from the Isle of Wight. Though the Côtentin is in Normandy, not Brittany, Edward had won over the local seigneur, Godfrey de Harcourt, Vicomte de St. Sauveur. As a diversion, Henry of Derby, later Duke of Lancaster, was sent with a small force to Aquitaine. There he exceeded expectations and rapidly recovered the greater part of the duchy which the French had overrun. His operations, which were approaching completion before the English army sailed for the

[1] The English connection with the de Montfort family remained close, for John de Montfort's son, John, who became duke of the whole of Brittany after the defeat of Charles de Blois at the battle of Auray (1364) with English help, was created Earl of Richmond by Edward III in 1373.

Côtentin, made French encroachments a less convincing excuse for invading France. Edward's invasion took on more plainly the appearance of an adventure, though cloaked by his claim to be France's rightful king.[1]

The invasion and the pressure exerted in Aquitaine were not the whole of Edward's plan of campaign. Despite his experience of the Low Countries' lords, he made a further arrangement for them to invade simultaneously from the north-east, aided by a contingent of English archers under Sir Hugh Hastings.

On 12 July 1346 the English army landed in the Côtentin at St. Vaast, eighteen miles east of Cherbourg. Edward had with him his eldest son, Edward, known in history as the Black Prince,[2] then a boy of sixteen. Besides the Earls of Warwick and Northampton who held the highest commands, nearly the whole of the fighting aristocracy of England was present. The exact size of the army is not known. The chroniclers are divided in their estimates. Specialists who have worked on the surviving pay rolls give various totals. About 15,000 is considered a likely number, 4,000 men-at-arms and 11,000 spear-men and archers. This was the army which fought at Crécy.

Between the landing on 12 July and the battle of Crécy on 26 August are only six weeks. At first sight it seems odd that an army landing near Cherbourg should be brought to battle at Crécy which is near Boulogne. It becomes stranger still when the invaders' route is noted—east to Caen and Rouen, south along the Seine to the suburbs of Paris, and north to Abbeville and Crécy, a total distance of some 350 miles. The explanation is that Edward set out eastwards to meet the Flemish force advancing westwards. On reaching Rouen, however, he found the bridge over the Seine had been destroyed. In search of another he marched up the west bank of the river. But not until he reached

[1] In 1340 Pope Benedict XII addressed a protest to Edward III on his assumption of the title of King of France. In the course of it he refers to the weakness of the claim at law, points out that Edward had already paid homage, warns him that the Flemings and Germans are using him to further their own designs and will drop him when he is of no further use to them, and ends by declaring that 'such title, lacking both profit and reason, may prove a poisonous root which in all likelihood will send forth fruits of sorrow and bitterness'. (Foedera II, ii, 1117.) But the Pope, living as he did at Avignon at this period, was thought to be over partial to the French king.

[2] Edward was never called the Black Prince during his lifetime. The term is first found in the Tudor chronicles.

Poissy, a few miles from Paris, on 13 August, did he succeed in crossing. Thence he wheeled north towards Amiens to meet the Flemish. His original intention presumably was, on effecting a junction with them, to return and perhaps besiege Paris. During the course of this long itinerary he fought only very minor actions. That he was able to reach the environs of Paris without being attacked in force was not as singular as it appears. The surprise of the invasion, the rapidity of his march, and the difficulty in mustering the French feudal array, account for it; Philip was not ready. But now sufficient contingents arrived and he was able to pursue the English as they went north. His plan was to reach the Somme first, destroy the bridges, prevent the junction with the Flemish, and then attack with his whole army.[1] The bridges were destroyed and Edward found himself shut in by the Somme. On 24 August, however, he managed to force his way across a ford a few miles below Abbeville. Over the Somme, he should shortly have been able to join forces with the Flemings, but on that very day, unreliable as ever, they began to withdraw towards the Low Countries.

It is not on record when Edward learnt of the defection of his allies. On 25 August, the day after the crossing, he marched nine miles north-east through the forest of Crécy and on the early morning of 26 August took up a position on the ridge between the villages of Crécy and Wadicourt. His action suggests that by now he had written off the Flemings, but was satisfied that without them he could beat Philip if he attacked, and that the right moment had come to await his attack. In the two campaigns of 1339 and 1340 he had sought to fight a pitched battle but Philip had held off. Now there was every sign that battle would be offered, for Philip was pursuing him evidently with that intent. It was a matter of selecting a suitable position and he had been lucky to find the very place. The ridge at Crécy was exactly right for a defensive battle. It was 2,000 yards long, a frontage not unsuitable for the size of his army. One flank would be covered by the village of Crécy, with the little river Maye below and the forest on its west bank. The other flank was at least protected by the village of Wadicourt, its woodland and cultivated fields, a

[1] The Chandos Herald has: 'He (Philip) thought to have shut in the English, as I think, between the Seine and the Somme and right there he thought lightly to give them battle.' (*Life of the Black Prince* by the Herald of Sir John Chandos, ed. Pope and Lodge 1910—line 226.)

shield against a turning cavalry charge. The ridge faced a valley, the floor of which was about a hundred feet below. The ascent to the ridge, though quite possible for the French cavalry, was sufficiently steep to slow them up, particularly on the western side. His archers would have a clear unimpeded view. Their effective range was 250 yards. For the whole of that distance the French knights would be exposed to the arrow shower. It was an ideal position, with a windmill in the centre, from the top of which he could survey all the field, and a convenient spot behind for the store waggons, horses and reserve. Indeed, his chief anxiety must have been lest Philip, when he saw the position, refused to attack.

We cannot tell exactly what information Philip had gathered about the English archers. He must have known, however, that his armour was not proof against their arrows. Nevertheless, he evidently believed they could be ridden down. The size of his army gave him added confidence. How large it was is not certain, but the general sense of all the chroniclers is that it was two or three times as large as the English. He had shown himself a cautious general so far. Throughout the long English march he had refrained from attacking before his army was fully assembled. But if he continued so cautious, his lords, who were longing to fight, would call him a coward. That Edward was tempting him to attack and had laid what was equivalent to a baited trap, cannot have entered his head. It was unthinkable that his gorgeous chivalry was no match for English villagers.

The French army reached Crécy on the afternoon of 26 August at 4 p.m. Edward had been on the ridge since dawn; his troops were well rested and had had a good dinner. The French were tired after their long march. Philip should have halted and postponed the battle till the morrow, and, indeed, such was his inclination. His lords, however, were too impatient to wait. Fearing perhaps that the English would slip away in the night, they insisted on an immediate attack. A body of crossbowmen, hired from Genoa, the best mercenaries of the sort, were sent ahead to engage the archers, who if harassed and distracted could the better be overridden. But before the Genoese got their range, the archers loosed on them a torrent of arrows. Dismayed they fell back in disorder, having suffered many casualties.

The French commanders did not appreciate the fatal significance of this initial reverse. The only missile troops they possessed had been put out of action. The knights would now have to charge up the hill without any missile support. But this prospect did not daunt them. Far from hesitating, their immediate reaction was anger that the crossbowmen were blocking the way. They galloped along the valley into the shattered ranks of the Genoese, slashing them with their swords, calling them traitors and cowards. (The French chivalry had, unlike the English, no feeling of comradeship for the foot soldiers.) This done, they put spurs to their horses and charged up the hill under the command of d'Alençon, the King's brother.

The English on the ridge were in three divisions or battles as they were called. The right, by the village of Crécy, was commanded by the Black Prince, boy though he was. His adjutants were Thomas Beauchamp, Earl of Warwick, Marshal of the army, who was thirty-three, and John de Vere, Earl of Oxford, of the same age. The left, by the village of Wadicourt, was under William de Bohun, Earl of Northampton, who was thirty-two. The centre, which was drawn back a little distance as a reserve, was in charge of King Edward himself, now thirty-four years of age. In accordance with the new tactics the men-at-arms, that is to say the nobility and gentry, had dismounted,[1] sent their horses back, and now stood in massed formations. The archers were placed on the wings of the two forward battles and projected from them as bastions do on a castle wall. This formation had the appearance of four wedges. They could shoot straight at charging horsemen and if the horsemen, seeking to reach the dismounted men-at-arms, entered between the archer-wings, they became exposed to a double enfilading arrow-shower.

D'Alençon's charge was directed against the Black Prince's battle. The steepest part of the slope was here. As soon as his

[1] In a defensive battle (the kind envisaged by the new tactics) men-at-arms were a more solid, coherent and active body if dismounted. Cavalry is an arm of the attack. Static cavalry is little use. The following were among the best known of the nobility and gentry who fought at Crécy: Thomas Beauchamp, Earl of Warwick; his brother John Beauchamp, who carried the Royal standard; Lord Cobham; Sir Thomas Holland; Roger Mortimer, first Earl of March; Lord Mohun; John de Vere, Earl of Oxford; Roger Ufford, Earl of Suffolk; William de Montagu, Earl of Salisbury; his brother John de Montagu; William de Bohun, Earl of Northampton; Sir James Audeley; Guy de Brian; Bartholomew Burghersh; Sir John Chandos; Sir Thomas Felton and Sir William Felton; Sir Richard Talbot and the Earl of Arundel, Richard FitzAlan.

knights were within range, the arrows struck them and they began to fall. But they did not falter and pressed on towards the men-at-arms. When this brought them between the wedges of archers the arrows came from both sides. Their horses, less armoured than they, made easy targets. Horse and man crashed down. By the time they were hand-to-hand with the English knights they were too reduced to be able to break into them. Pulled off their horses they were slain or made prisoner. D'Alençon himself was killed.

When the French command in the valley saw that the first charge had ended in disaster, they had no different manoeuvre to offer. They were wedded to the old-fashioned head-on charge, and could think of nothing better than to repeat it, again and again. There are alleged to have followed more than a dozen of such charges, each of which met the fate of the first. By the time they ceased to charge the flower of their chivalry was piled up dead in front of the English position. When darkness fell at 9 p.m. what remained of the French army melted away. English casualties were slight. No knights were killed.

Froissart has here one of his beautiful descriptive passages which Berners translates thus: 'Whan the nyght was come and that thenglysshmen hard no more noyse of the Frenchemen, than they reputed themselfe to have the vyctorie, and the Frenchmen to be dysconfited, slayne and fledde away. Than they made great fyers and lyghted up torchesse and candelles, bycause it was very darke; than the kyng avayled downe fro the lytell hyll where as he stode; and of all that day tyll than, his helme cam never of on his heed. Than he went with all his batayle to his sonne the prince and enbrased hym in his armes and kyst hym.'

Froissart is far from being the only man who wrote of these events. Moreover, as he himself declares, his narrative at this point is founded on the *Chronicles* of Jean le Bel, though he also made independent inquiries from surviving eye-witnesses. Yet his literary skill enabled him better to evoke the age. I will cite a few further extracts from him in the guise of Berners' prose, to supplement the outline already given.

First we have the snapshot of Edward landing in the Côtentin peninsula. 'The kyng yssued out of his shyppe, and the first fote that he sette on the grounde, he fell so rudely, that the blode brast out of his nose. The knyghtes that were aboute hym toke hym up and sayde, Sir, for Goddessake entre agayne into your shippe, and come nat a lande this day, for this is but an yvell signe for us. Than the kyng answered quickely and sayd, Wherfore, this is a good token for me, for the land desyreth to have me.'

Though Edward was claiming the French throne, he did not seek to win the good opinion of the French by refraining from ill-treating them. His march through Normandy to Paris had all the appearance of a plundering raid. Thus at Barfleur, a small unfortified port: 'The towne was robbed, and moche golde and sylver there founde, and ryche jewels . . . so moche rychesse that the boyes and vyllayns of the hoost sette nothing by good furred gownes.' The words suggest that villeins or serf peasants were in the English army. England's lowest class was getting its profit from the adventure. Froissart goes on: 'It was harde to thynke the great ryches that there was won, in clothes specially.' Besides looting, there was massacre and rape. At Caen, when citizens were being killed in the streets and women seized, an appeal was made to 'an Englysshe knyght with one eye called Thomas Holland'.[1] He intervened 'and saved many lyves of ladyes, damosels and cloysterers from defoylyng, for the soudyers were without mercy'. So much loot was taken that it could not be carried. The commanders had it collected and shipped back under strong guard to England. Prisoners worth a good ransom were also sent. Edward bought the most valuable from their captors as a speculation. Sir Thomas Holland was paid 20,000 nobles (£6,666) for two important French lords he had taken, the Comte d'Eu and the Sire de Tancarville.

The march continued in this fashion. Edward declared it a capital offence to burn churches, which suggests that drastic measures had to be taken to stop it.[2] An attempt was made to observe the code of chivalry, which protected the French nobility and their familes from violence. Thus Sir John Chandos, Edward's friend, saved the two pretty daughters of the Lord of Poix from being violated. But the invasion was a cruel visitation, the beginning of a long period of great suffering for the French people.

[1] This knight, aged twenty-six, son of Lord Holland, had in 1339 married Joan, daughter of the Earl of Kent and Edward III's cousin, and afterwards the Black Prince's wife (see page 98). He was one of the founder members of the Garter.

[2] Though Caen was much damaged, the two great churches built by William the Conqueror and his wife Matilda, the Abbaye des Hommes and the Abbaye des Femmes, the most splendid examples of Norman Romanesque which exist today, were unharmed.

'It was no marveyle though they of the countrey were afrayd, far before that time they had never sene men of warre, nor they wyst nat what warre or batayle ment. They fledde away as farr as they might here spekyng of thenglysshmen, and left their houses well stuffed, and graunges full of corne.'

On the morning of the 26th, when Edward had got his troops into position on the Crécy ridge, he went round on a hack to encourage them: 'The kyng lept on a hobby, with a whyte rodde in his hand . . . he rode fro renke to renke, desyringe every man to take hede that day to his right and honour. He spak it so swetely, and with so good countenance and mery chere, that all suche as were dysconfited toke courage in the seyng and heryng of hym. And whan he had thus visyted all his bataylS, it was then nyne of the day; than he caused every man to eate and drinke a lytell, and so they dyde at their leaser. And afterwarde they ordred agayne their batayllеs: than every man lay downe on the yerth and by hym his salet and bowe, to be the more fressher whan their ennemyes shulde come.'

Here we have Edward as the popular commander-in-chief who knew how to get the best out of his men. He is seen addressing especially the archers, on whom everything depended. Though a great enthusiast for the order of chivalry, in which archers had no place, he was sufficiently open to novel ideas to treat them as comrades in arms. His victory was due not only to new tactics but to a new attitude of mind.

While the English awaited the event with disciplined calm, the French came on to the field excited and in the utmost confusion. As Froissart has it: 'Ther was no man, though he were present at the journey, that coude ymagen or shewe the trouth of the yvell order that was among the French partie,' a fatal weakness, though 'they were a mervelous great nombre'.

A deft touch gives us a close view of d'Alençon, one of the bungling leaders of this disordered host. Froissart puts into his mouth a remark which reveals him in a flash. When the Genoese complained that after walking all day with their heavy crossbows they required a rest before starting to fight, the Count observed with withering sarcasm: 'A man is well at ease to be charged with suche a sorte of rascalles' and forced them to open the battle.

Just as we are let see for a moment the contemptuous face of a courtier knight, irresponsible and incompetent, so Froissart allows us a glimpse of the netherworld of the battle. The chivalry of France is piled up, dead, wounded or unhorsed and stunned, in front of the English line. No plundering during the battle was the order. The archers and the knights did not break their ranks, but 'also amonge the Englysshemen there was certayne rascalles that went a fote with great knyves and . . . they slewe and murdredde many as they lay on the grounde, bothe erles, barownes, knyghtes and squyers'. These spoilers are said to have been savage Welsh and Cornish spearmen, stationed behind the forward battles, who crept round to plunder the fallen French. It was the custom for the French lords to wear jewels in battle. The knife-men robbed the dead and stabbed any still alive through chinks in their armour, the easier to get at their valuables. When Edward heard of this afterwards, he was very angry. Some of the murdered French knights could otherwise have been taken prisoner and held for a big ransom. It was sheer waste to kill them for what they were wearing. But the knife-men knew their business. For fellows of their class robbery was far more lucrative and certain than ransom money.

It is quite remarkable how little the decisive part played by the archers was understood by the chroniclers of the day. The *Anonimalle Chronicle*, for instance, does not even mention them, nor does the *Chronicon Angliae*.[1] The Chandos Herald's metrical life of the Black Prince is also silent in their regard. Froissart is the only writer who shows that he fully weighed their achievement. In the later edition of his work he has the following (not found in the earlier edition used by Berners): 'I assure you that this day the archers of England gave great support to their side, for most men say that it was by their shooting that the affair was decided, though indeed there were many knights among the English who fought bravely.' But what really interested him (as it also did the other chroniclers and their readers) was the romantic side of the great battle, the gallantry of the Black Prince for example. The right wing which he commanded was the hardest pressed. Some of the French knights got through to it and there was hand-to-hand fighting. At one moment his adjutants thought it prudent to ask for help from the reserve. Edward's alleged reply 'Let the

[1] The *Anonimalle Chronicle* (1332–1381) written in French by a monk of St. Mary's Abbey York (ed. V. H. Galbraith, 1927). The *Chronicon Angliae* is now considered to have been written by the monk Walsingham of St. Albans, who later suppressed and altered some passages and renamed it the *Historia Anglicana*. Both are published in the Rolls series.

boy win his spurs', was evidently repeated up and down England and has become one of those famous historical sayings which the English public out of affection insists on preserving. Not unnaturally the exploits of the young Prince of Wales were given more space than the archers' shooting. His great reputation dates from Crécy. But if the archers did not get the headlines, they knew very well what they had done. And when they returned home, the villagers shared their knowledge. It was their longbow which had won the battle. *They* had overthrown the French chivalry.

But though the realities of Crécy disclosed chivalry to be a waning force, chivalric conduct was so bound up with romance that it continued to arouse as much interest as ever. Froissart had enough grasp to say what he did say about the archers, but his heart was with the knights; French, English or others, he was impartial. There was not much to admire on the French side at Crécy, except the epic valour of John, King of Bohemia. That he seized on and immortalized. King Philip had three kings with him at the great battle: James II, King of Majorca; the aforesaid King of Bohemia; and that king's son, Charles, who the previous month had been elected King of the Romans as a preliminary to his sacring as Holy Roman Emperor. All three men were romantic figures, but the King of Bohemia surpassed the others as the leading exponent of contemporary chivalry. Extremely restless and always on the move, he had been everywhere and done everything, except stay at home in Prague and govern Bohemia, which he found too dull a task. Among many other exploits he had led the Teutonic Knights against the heathen of Lithuania and Pomerania; claimed the Polish crown and taken Silesia; and, invited by the citizens of Brescia, entered Italy and ruled much of the peninsula for a while. Six years before Crécy he began to go blind, but continued to fight wherever fighting was to be had. When in 1346 King Philip asked for his help to resist the English invasion, he hastened to Paris with his retinue, accompanied by his son, Charles, the Emperor-elect. He was now fifty. His blindness had much increased and he could hardly see at all. Philip is unlikely to have expected more of the battered old paladin than the distinction of his presence, but John was to use the occasion as an opportunity for a great chivalric gesture. When battle at Crécy was joined, he was well back, no doubt beside King Philip. But he found it impossible to remain passive. For men of his athletic disposition it is hard to accept age and disability. He was overcome with a longing to prove that he was not so old and that his sight was not so bad as all that. On inquiring for his son Charles and being told he was fighting, he could restrain himself no longer. To sit out a battle like a dummy was a thing he had never done in his life. Froissart's story is that he said to his knights: 'Sirs, ye ar my men, my companyons, and frendes in this journey, I requyre you bring me so farre forwarde, that I may stryke one stroke with my swerde.' We may well suppose that they sought to restrain him. How were they to look after him, blind and old as he was, if he got mixed up in the press? But he insisted on going forward and they had to accompany him. 'And to the intent that they shulde nat lese hym in the prease, they tyed all their raynes of their bridelles eche to other, and sette the kynge before to acomplysshe his desyre.' The odd cavalcade advanced towards the ridge. They charged into the mêlée. King John had his desire. He struck a blow. Then he and his company were overwhelmed. 'The next day they were founde in the place, and all their horses tyed eche to other.' Edward sent back John's body on a litter covered with a cloth of gold, says the Chandos Herald. The chief honours were with the dead knight. King Philip had fled. King Charles had fled. So too had King James of Majorca. It had been left to him to uphold the honour of France. His action, at once so extravagant, senseless and magnificent, won the admiration of all Europe. It confused the plain truth that Crécy was the archers' day. John was good theatre but not quite real. His blind charge, though incomparably noble, was, like the chivalry it represented, a little nonsensical.[1]

There was no pursuit by the victors of Crécy. It was too dark, too late. Next morning in the mist some French reinforcements,

[1] The field of Crécy repays a visit because it remains almost exactly as it was six hundred years ago. The ridge, the valley and the forest, even the foundations of the windmill, are in place. The visitor is surprised to find in the village of Crécy a monument to King John of Bohemia. On it is a bronze plaque with a representation of the king charging, his sword drawn, a helm on his head. An inscription says—he gave his life for France. The monument was erected in recent years. In addition to this memorial there is a cross in the valley, supposed to mark the spot where he fell, though it is too far back, if it is true that he charged the English position. Colonel Burne in his *The Crécy War* states (p. 185) that in 1946 a party of Czecho-Slovaks from Prague journeyed to Crécy and held a memorial service at this cross on 26 August, the day of the battle. So the old knight's memory is kept green. But he is not now admired for what he was, a model of international chivalry, but has become a figure whom two countries claim as a national hero.

which had come up unaware that the battle was over, were easily destroyed. What was next to be done? The French army was no more. Could not Edward now advance on Paris and assume the crown of France? He perceived that he could not; he had won only a defensive battle; he had won because he had been attacked. He could, of course, march about the country, as he had already done, take small towns, rob, ravage, provoke another attack perhaps, but, if not, only wander on, leaving the strong walled towns in his rear and risk being cut off behind unbridged rivers, entangled in the country as the phrase went, to be surrounded at last, starved and have to surrender. There was the alternative of methodically storming walled towns and castles. But that would take years, even with the best siege appliances. Gunpowder was only just coming in. He had used two or three small cannon at Crécy, whose noise had caused some alarm. But such cannon could not batter down walls. He would have to depend on the usual old medieval methods—ladders, platforms, mining, catapults. These had not progressed in a hundred years, while military architecture had greatly improved. A fortified place was much harder to take than formerly. Starvation was left as the best siege weapon. But it was ludicrous to think of reducing all France that way.

Aware that though victor he had not vanquished France, Edward cast about how he could at least turn his great victory to some immediate advantage. The idea of seizing Calais took shape in his mind. He was near the town. There was no enemy force between him and it nor need he fear that Philip would soon be able to muster a new army. If he could take it he would have a permanent foothold in France, much nearer Paris than were his lands in Aquitaine, and only twenty miles from England. From such a bridgehead he could invade France at will. No need to depend on allies to provide a port. With Calais he would also have better control of the Channel. The French had used it as a base from which to prey on English shipping. Moreover, he could use it as a continental mart. English exports, instead of having to be shipped to ports in foreign lands, not always open and where dues had to be paid, would go to his Calais and be sold there free, or rather he himself would collect the customs. True, it was a strong walled town, but if he persevered it should be possible to reduce it. The decision was taken to beleaguer it at once.

The siege was even more arduous than he had anticipated. It

dragged on and on. He could not break in. But he could starve the defenders. The garrison occasionally received supplies by sea, however, and, by expelling children and old people, was able to hold out. Early in the siege the Scots burst into Northumberland, believing that with the army abroad they could penetrate deep into England. But the people rallied with enthusiasm to the support of the border magnates, Lord Percy and the Prince Bishop of Durham, who inflicted a crushing defeat on the invaders at Neville's Cross, taking King David Bruce prisoner.[1] Before Crécy Philip of France had written to the Scots saying that now was their chance and urging them to strike.[2] Had the raid been successful it might have obliged Edward to raise the siege and hurry home. Not till July 1347 did Philip attempt to relieve the town, when he appeared at the head of a new army. By this time the citizens were in the last stages of starvation. But he dared not attack the besieging English and, suddenly alarmed, withdrew in haste.[3] The town yielded on 3 August. Laurence Minot, whose ballads reflect the fierce national feeling which supported Edward in his French adventure, puts into the mouths of the townsmen who

[1] Henry of Knighton, Canon of Leicester, gives in his Latin chronicle a vivid account of this raid by the Scots and the resolute manner in which all classes came together to resist and defeat them. Froissart also has a good description, which contains the assertion that Edward's Queen, Philippa, then aged thirty-two, addressed the army of the northern lords before the battle. One of the earliest of English poets, Laurence Minot, celebrated the victory in a spirited ballad. His English is the northern dialect and differs somewhat from the midland dialect which Chaucer used and which developed into modern English. Here is part of the first verse:

*Sir David the Bruse said he suld foude**
To ride thurgh all Ingland wald he not woude;†
At the Westminster hall suld his stedes stonde,
Whils our King Edward war out of the londe.

(* should try. † turn back.)

[2] The French king's letter is given in Walter of Hemingburgh's *Chronicon*.

[3] See the letter from Edward III to the Archbishop of Canterbury preserved in Robert of Avesbury's *De Mirabilibus Gestis Edwardi III*. Robert was the Archbishop's Registrar. Edward had greatly increased the size of his army. If it numbered as much as 15,000 at Crécy (which is not certain) it now numbered 32,000. (Vide totals worked out (p. 152 of *Art of War in Middle Ages*, vol. 2) by Charles Oman from the extant acounts of Sir Walter de Wetewang, Treasurer of the Household.) Of this number, the largest any Plantagenet king had ever taken overseas or was to again, no less than 20,000 were archers. As Philip had not solved the problem of how to attack archers, one can understand why he went home.

came, as he states, with ropes round their necks to surrender the keys, the following:

> *'Thai said all: "Sir Philip, oure syre,*
> *And his sun, Sir John of France,*
> *Has left us ligand*[1] *in the mire*
> *And broght us till this doleful dance*[2]
> *Our horses that war faire and fat*
> *Er etin up ilkone bidene;*[3]
> *Have we nowther conig*[4] *ne cat*
> *That thai ne er etin, and hundes kene*
> *Al er etin up ful clene—*
> *Es nowther lenid*[5] *biche ne whelp—*
> *That es wele on oure sembland*[6] *sene.*
> *And thai er fled that suld us help.'**

The Six Burghers are still at Calais. Rodin, inspired by their story, has recreated them and they gesticulate in the square before the Hôtel de Ville, as they walk out with halters about their necks, on their way to placate Edward by offering themselves in place of the townsmen whom he wished to massacre. That a French romantic sculptor should find their story an inspiration and the French town they saved from massacre set them up as heroes, is more in the natural course than that we also should buy a casting of the same bronze and exhibit it in a London park. For the Six Burghers stand too in gardens by the House of Lords. Their presence here might be explained by our admiration for Rodin's

[1] *lying* [2] *plight* [3] *each one withal* [4] *rabbit* [5] *living* [6] *faces*

*Such was the English which some English people spoke at the time of the battle of Crécy. We find it difficult to read, partly on account of the spelling, and might find it more difficult to understand, if we heard it spoken in the accent of that date, which we cannot even imagine. The people who spoke English were the lower classes. The upper classes spoke and wrote in French. When Edward addressed the archers at Crécy, however, he must have spoken in English. Laurence Minot by writing in English, showed that he was writing chiefly for the lower classes. But English was beginning to displace French, another indication of increasing national consciousness. John of Trevisa, an Oxford don, in his English translation of *Bartholomaeus de Proprietatibus Rerum* (chap. xlii) says 'now the yer of oure Lord a thousond thre hondred foure score and fyve . . . in al the gramerscoles of Engelond childern leveth Frensch, and construeth and lurneith an Englysch . . . Also gentil men habbeth now moche yleft for to teche here childern Frensch.' The enmity with France must have seemed a good reason for dropping French.

art. But the main reason we bought the group is that we are still moved by the story. It is almost as if we wished to make amends.

The surrender of Calais is one of the best known episodes in our history. A close dissection of it yields, however, elements below the surface, not generally appreciated when it is read as a dramatic piece. What follows is an attempt to expose more of the realities of the occasion.

Edward had his case. The code of knighthood as understood at the time did not oblige him to spare the defenders of a beleaguered city if they neglected to surrender in time. Lords and the rich were spared if they paid a ransom. But the rank and file were unprotected, since they had not the wherewithal to pay. Edward had been held up by the defenders of Calais for nearly a year. He had incurred heavy expenses since his army had had to be so largely increased. Many of his men had been killed in the assaults. He had earlier on called upon the townspeople to surrender and according to custom offered them their lives if they did. They had refused because they believed their King would rescue them. Only when he failed them, did they decide to give up. In a parley from the walls they now offered to surrender on the terms which they had previously rejected. Edward replied that it was too late. Those who could pay a ransom would, of course, go free; the rest would be put to death.[1] He was doubly incensed with them, for not only had they resisted unreasonably long, but Calais men before the siege had been notorious for raiding expeditions against the English coast and preying like pirates on English merchantmen. Such was Edward's case.[2]

The merchant gentry in Calais, however, having fought and suffered along with the common people for a year, did not feel that they could hand them over to death while they themselves escaped. According to Froissart they replied to Edward that 'rather thanne to consent that the worst ladde in the towne shulde have any more yvell than the grettest of us all,' they would endure anything. They would never agree to surrender on such terms.

[1] According to Froissart, Edward's spokesman said: 'It is his (the King's) wyll . . . to ransome all suche as pleaseth hym and to putte to dethe suche as he lyste.'

[2] In addition to these considerations Edward had the practical reason of wishing to discourage other defenders of fortified towns and castles from holding out. If, continuing the war, he sought to conquer France by reducing its strong places, quick surrenders were his only hope of success.

Edward seems to have thought that the message was bluff. It was incredible that men, able to save themselves in the usual way by finding ransoms, would choose to share the fate of the general population. He would call their bluff. Accordingly he returned answer that if six of the richest burgesses came to him in the humiliating guise of condemned criminals, 'bare heeded, bare foted and bare legged, and in their shertes, with haulters about their neckes, with the kayes of the towne and castell in their handes,' and surrendered to him to do with them as he chose, he would spare the commonalty.

He would hardly have made this offer had he thought they would accept it. For one reason, he would be throwing away six of the biggest ransoms in the place by proposing to kill the six most competent to pay them. To hang the gentry and pardon their inferiors would, moreover, be a gross solecism. Public opinion in France would be so outraged that his own knights would not be safe, should any of them have to surrender one day. Nor indeed would English upper-class opinion in general endorse so topsy-turvy a procedure.

On receiving Edward's strange offer, the leading burgesses, one opines, might well have guessed that he would be unwilling, when it came to the point, to go to the length of his words. The story as related, however, insists that they took him seriously and resolved to make the sacrifice. Six of them, led by Eustace de St. Pierre, the richest merchant in the city, volunteered to be the six required and marched out in the guise of felons to surrender themselves. It is stated, however, that they were not entirely without hope that he might yield to entreaties for mercy, which sounds as if at the back of their minds they were not quite sure he intended to do as he said. They had a tearful send-off by the citizens and made so moving a spectacle when they arrived in the English camp that they were received with warm sympathy.

If, as I suppose, Edward did not expect them, his surprise on hearing of their arrival must have been great. It placed him in an awkward position. His bluff, instead of theirs, had been called. As he knew very well, it was out of the question to put the six burghers to death. His own people were already greatly distressed at the idea. 'In truth, there wasn't a lord or knight in the place who was not weeping out of pity,' writes Jean le Bel.[1] Neverthe-

[1] As stated above, Froissart founded the earlier part of his *Chronicles* (up to Poitiers 1356) largely on *Les Vrayes Chroniques* of Jean le Bel, who for years

less for him immediately to relinquish his agreed right to hang them would not do. An appearance of inflexibility had to be kept up for the moment. But opportunity for a graceful withdrawal was soon offered when Queen Philippa asked for clemency. He allowed himself to be melted and reprieved the burghers. In letting them off, he was obliged also to reprieve the rest, for the proposed massacre had been cancelled by the six burghers agreeing to surrender themselves. As they had carried out their side of the bargain, he had no alternative but to keep his. But what had occurred did not debar him from demanding ransoms. Accordingly, he detained the six burghers and, on the town capitulating, which it immediately did, also detained all burghers in it rich enough to pay a ransom. Pending payment, he sent them off, says Jean le Bel, to England. The *Anominalle Chronicle* adds that they were imprisoned in the Tower of London, a usual place for war prisoners to be detained while they were collecting the money for their ransoms.[1] As for the poorer inhabitants, they were treated with the greatest harshness short of massacre. They were all turned out of the town in the clothes they stood up in, says Jean le Bel. Their houses and property were confiscated. Reduced to beggary they were left to find in the countryside beyond what shelter and food they could. Jean le Bel adds bitterly that King Philip sent them no money or help. Calais was repeopled with English settlers.

The predicament of the townsmen who defended Calais helps us to understand the precarious situation of the lower classes at this time. They were not adequately protected by chivalry, the code of the noble knight. The rich class to which the six burghers of Calais belonged had the status of knights and squires.[2] But living in closer touch with the general population than did the knights of the nobility (particularly in this case when they had

was canon of Liège and had first-class sources of information. Froissart's account of the surrender of Calais follows Jean le Bel's very closely, though he embroiders in places.

[1] *Anominalle Chronicle*, Galbraith edition, p. 29, penultimate line. Ransoms were fixed very high and it often took a prisoner a long time to realize the sum demanded.

[2] Froissart makes their leader say when parleying with Edward's envoy at the walls: 'We are here within a small sorte of knyghtes and squyers.' As we shall see later the burgesses who represented the English towns in Parliament sat with the knights of the shire. Mayors and aldermen of London had the same status as the nobility.

shared the dangers and privations of a long siege), they were not satisfied that their honour was safe if they stood on what the code of chivalry permitted them. They saw that it was not enough to be noble knights within the meaning of that code. They felt that Edward, despite his Round Table, Knights of the Garter, etcetera, was not thinking as a true knight should in wanting to massacre the inhabitants. So much was this their view that, not only did they speak up for the commonalty as representative burgesses would normally do, but agreed to give their lives in support of the principle that the lower classes should not be treated in this way.

The more their action is considered the more revolutionary it appears. They were driven, no doubt, by feelings of pure humanity. They were not theorists. They were not arguing against chivalry. Their argument lay in what they did. And their deed had tremendous force. I daresay that it was as much discussed up and down the villages of England as the battle of Crécy. On reflection it must have seemed to the peasantry an extraordinary vindication of the natural rights of the common man. As such it will certainly have had an exhilarating effect and should be counted as one of several factors heralding the gradual rise to greater consideration of the lower classes.

The Black Death

Edward returned to England and paid off his army.[1] He and his son had become national heroes. The victory of Crécy and the taking of Calais, 'qu'on tenoit', in Jean le Bel's words, 'd'une des plus fortes villes du monde', were feats of arms without precedent. So brilliant did they seem that many thought of the campaign as decisive. But Edward was still a very long way from gaining the French crown. He could not even force Philip to recognize him as independent duke of Aquitaine.

A truce for a year, made on 28 September 1347, was discussed in a parliament held on 14 January 1348. Edward presided and asked the commons, who represented only the knights of the shires and the burgesses of the chief towns, to inform him what should be done when the truce expired. (If they advocated continuing the adventure, it would be easier to get subsidies from them.) The commons were quite willing for the King to continue winning victories and bringing home loot. The Rolls of Parliament report their reply as follows: 'Most dread lord, as to your war and the disposing of it, we are so ignorant and simple that we know not, and are not able to give counsel thereon. . . . May it

[1] As the matter of prices and wages becomes important later on, it is instructive to cite here the daily pay received by the various ranks. Oman gives it on p. 153 of his *Art of War in the Middle Ages*, vol. 2. The Black Prince £1; the ten Earls, and the Bishop of Durham 6s. 8d.; the 78 barons and baronets 4s.; the 1066 knights 2s.; the 4182 esquires and other men-at-arms 1s.; archers 3d. (with 3d. extra if they had a horse for transport); Welsh pikemen 2d.

please you to decide . . . with the advice of your council. . . . We will willingly agree to what shall be thus ordained.'[1]

At this stage the commons were fully satisfied that the nobility was competent to conduct the war to the profit of the realm. As we shall see, their attitude changed later and became more critical and less humble. Now everybody was pleasurably excited. The court and the nobility organized tournament after tournament. In 1347 and 1348 no less than nineteen were held under royal patronage, the King himself often appearing in the lists. Eight took place at Westminster in the space between the Abbey and the Palace and were attended by crowds of Londoners. Others were held at Windsor, at the royal manor of Eltham on the road to Canterbury, and at Canterbury itself. At the Eltham tournament in January 1348 Edward and his companions, twelve Round Table knights, wore mantles and garters with the new motto *Honi soit qui mal y pense*. The tournaments were the occasion of splendid banquets. Windsor chapel, too, was redecorated and the mythical St. George was brought in as colleague to the existing patron, the sainted king, Edward the Confessor, whose tomb at the Abbey was Westminster's great attraction.

While the lords were enjoying themselves in festivities of this sort, the gentry with their retainers were also in happy mood. Walsingham's *Historia Anglicana* has the following revealing entry. 'In the year of grace 1348 . . . it seemed to the English that as it were a new sun was rising over the land on account of the . . . plenty of goods and the glorious victories. There was no woman of any standing who had not her share of the spoils of Calais, Caen and other places across the Channel, such as clothes, furs, pillows and household utensils, tablecloths and necklaces, gold and silver cups, linen cloths and sheets. These were to be met with in houses throughout the kingdom. English ladies were to be seen going about proudly in French dresses.'

It may safely be assumed that the labouring classes had their share in all this. We have had a reference to the boys and villeins in the army turning up their noses at fur coats. There are many indications that the archers did well for themselves; on the morning after Crécy, for instance, when permission was given to strip the fallen French. The sack of Calais, after the inhabitants had

[1] Rolls of Parliament, ii, 164 (French). The translation here is taken from the document printed on p. 65 of *Illustrations of Chaucer's England*, ed. by Dorothy Hughes, 1919.

been turned out, was also very lucrative. The archers had their homes throughout England. Most villages must have had young soldiers returning with money and presents for their families. From this time, it seems, the country people began to dress in a way which the gentry thought was above their station. We even find a sumptuary ordinance, dated a little later, which was issued at the request of the commons (in the election of whose members the peasantry had no share) and laid down that 'carters, ploughmen, drivers, oxherds, cowherds, shepherds, swineherds, dairywomen and other keepers of beasts, threshers of corn and all manner of men engaged in husbandry, and other people who have not goods and chattels worth 40s, shall wear no cloth save blanket and russet, 12d the yard. They shall wear no girdles and shall have linen according to their condition. They shall live upon such food as is suitable, and then not in excess.'[1] This applied to the whole of the poorer part of the agricultural population, villeins included. It was found impossible to enforce the ordinance and it was withdrawn, an indication that gayer clothes were very widespread. A contemporary, Higden, the author of the annals called the *Polychronicon*, says, when discussing the English character, that the Englishman is never content to remain in the class to which he belongs. 'A yoeman arrays himself as a squire, a squire as a knight, a knight as a duke and a duke as a king.' These citations suggest that the English people, high and low, refreshed and excited by the victories and enjoying new comforts, were likely to press Edward and his lords, if pressure were needed, to continue raiding France.

But before that could be, a dreadful catastrophe supervened, which put an end to rejoicings and postponed further overseas adventures. The Black Death, for that was the monstrous apparition which was approaching, had, however, this peculiarity that, though the labouring classes suffered most from it, they suffered least afterwards. Indeed, the survivors were in better case than before. For the first time labour realized that it was a power, and used its power.

The Black Death was bubonic plague, a disease whose symptoms were buboes, inflammatory swellings in armpits and groin, with high temperature, collapse and speedy death, sometimes showing itself also in secondary symptoms of inflammation of the lungs. Since neither its cause nor cure was known, no one knew how to

[1] Rolls of Parliament, ii, 278 (French).

avoid it nor what medicine to take, factors which greatly increased its terror. That it was connected with rats was not guessed. Indeed, the full truth about it was not discovered until the beginning of this century, when it was traced to a bacillus endemic in a certain kind of rat. The bacillus caused epidemics from time to time in the rat world. A diseased rat infected the fleas it carried. When it died the infected fleas jumped onto other rats, bit and infected them. The rat epidemic grew in this manner and if exceptionally virulent spread over continents. When millions of rats fell dead, tens of millions of diseased fleas were stranded. Driven by the pangs of hunger they jumped on to what living creatures they could reach, and when the creatures were human beings transferred to them the deadly virus. Thus, the way to avoid plague was to keep out of the way of rats, particularly dead ones. Some exceptionally intelligent men may have had a glimmering of this during the Black Death, as may some in the seventeenth century during the Plague, also a bubonic visitation. But that it was fleas which carried the infection from the rat to human beings could never have occurred to anyone until the existence of bacteria was discovered.

Jean le Bel and Froissart make no mention of the Black Death, engrossed as they were with recording the deeds of knights, but other contemporary chroniclers do. One or two quotations will show what happened when it reached England. The writers surmise that it spread from India and that its route was from Constantinople to Genoa and Marseilles, and thence across France to the southern ports of England, which it reached in the summer of 1348. It was preceded by the news of its approach. On 17 August the Bishop of Bath and Wells ordered 'processions every Friday . . . in each church to beg God to protect the people from the pestilence which had come from the East into the neighbouring kingdom'.[1] But in fact it had already arrived in England, for on 23 August the Archbishop of Canterbury died of it. In Knighton's *Chronicon* we have under this year: 'The dreadful pestilence made its way through the coast land to Southampton and reached Bristol, where perished almost the whole strength of the town, as it were surprised by a sudden death.' Knighton was Canon of Leicester and he gives figures for that town, whose population was about 4,000. 'There died at Leicester in the small

[1] Quoted in F. A. Gasquet's *The Black Death*, p. 81 from Harl. MS. 6965 f. 132.

parish of St. Leonard more than 380 persons, in the parish of Holy Cross 400, in the parish of St. Margarets 700; and so in every parish a great multitude.' The *Chronicon Angliae of St. Albans* has: 'The plague was so violent that the living were scarce able to bury the dead. In the monastery of St. Albans more than 40 monks died in a short space of time,' out of some sixty, it is said. Geoffrey le Baker, a secular clerk in London, wrote in his *Chronicon*: 'Since cemeteries did not suffice, fields were chosen for burying the dead. Suits in the King's Bench and Common Pleas came to a standstill. A few noblemen died, but innumerable common people and a multitude of monks passed away. This great pestilence raged in England for a whole year or more, so that many villages were completely emptied.' And Robert of Avesbury, a canon lawyer and registrar of the Archbishop of Canterbury's court, records in his *De Mirabilibus Gestis Edwardi III*: 'In the newly made cemetery at Smithfield the bodies of more than 200 persons were buried every day, which is not counting those buried in other cemeteries.'

The total number of deaths is uncertain. The most favoured estimate is that one third of the population died. If the population before the plague was somewhere between 3 and 4 millions, as has been calculated, over a million persons, upper and lower class, must have perished. (There was no real middle class in England at this date.)

The upper class consisted of the nobility, the landed gentry, the higher Churchmen and the capitalists of the towns, or well-to-do merchants, with, at the bottom of it, some lawyers, clerks of the chancery and treasury, monks of education, a few doctors and men of learning, a small class, impossible to estimate, but conceivably amounting, men, women and children, to fifty thousand. As these people did not live in such close proximity to rats as the lower class, the percentage of deaths among them was less.

The lower class, except for the proletariat of a few towns, particularly London, was almost exclusively agricultural. At the top of it were farmers of freehold land, who employed some labour, but the bulk of it was included in four categories: those who owned or leased a small farm and cultivated it themselves; rural craftsmen; landless labourers who were paid wages to work the land or tend the animals of the upper class; and villeins, a distinct variety of peasant, who worked on the manorial estates of the upper class. Villeins differed from the rest of the agricultural population in two main respects: they were not paid wages and they were not free to leave the manor where they worked. Their status was something between that of a slave and a free man. The lord of the manor provided them with land, but they did not own it. They cultivated it for their own support like a leaseholder, but instead of paying rent had to work without wages for a stated number of days on the land in the manor which the lord reserved for himself. In some ways a villein led a sheltered life. His fellows helped him with ploughing and reaping, for the manor was a sort of co-operative unit. Villeins were more secure than small leaseholders or labourers. If they worked their allotted fields and put in their allotted hours on the lord of the manor's home farm, they were reasonably safe from want. But there was the one great objection. A villein was not free to go elsewhere. He could not take a job as a wage-earning labourer. He could not set up on his own. True, there were certain things he could do independently. He could make money by keeping pigs and cattle, selling eggs or honey, and use it to rise in the social scale by buying, perhaps, a piece of freehold property and so becoming partially free. But he was still tied to the manor. It was difficult for him to take advantage of chances that might come his way to rise in the world. He could better himself a little, but not much. The owner of the manor had more power over him than any lord had over a completely free man. He could not, for instance, take a dispute to the public tribunals, for he was subject in everything to the manorial court, where the lord of the manor or his representative presided.

It is not possible to say what percentage of the agricultural population was in villeinage and what percentage wage-earning labourers. Villeinage did not obtain throughout the whole country. It was rare, for instance, in the north. But it seems to have predominated in the home counties. For generations it had worked smoothly. But by the fourteenth century it had begun to be out of tune with the spirit of an age which was becoming less feudal and more nationalistic. The idea that all Englishmen were not free had started to seem odd to some people. Moreover, in the economic sense villeinage did not work quite so well as it used to. Villeins, less contented than before, were less industrious and efficient. Some lords found that it was better to let the villein commute his work days on their demesnes for a payment, a payment representing rent for the land he was provided with. This commutation turned the villein into a leaseholder. He at once became hard to distinguish from any free man who held land under a lease. The money he paid was used by the lord to hire free labourers to work the home farm. Thus the tendency for some time had been for villeinage to be slowly modified and very gradually subjected to the pull of ordinary supply and demand. But this had only gone a very short way.

The fleas which destroyed one third of the population were the cause of an economic upheaval. The supply of labour was immediately less than the demand. Such was the shortage that the standing crops rotted in the ground with no one to harvest them, domestic animals wandered without keepers, and ploughing and sowing for the following crop presented great difficulties. The competition to get labourers immediately drove up wages. We have seen that the archer of Crécy got 3d. a day. That was about what the free labourer got, something between 2d. and 4d. He now refused to work for less than 6d. or 8d. It was a wonderful experience for the working man. He was run after by his superiors, and able to sell his services to the highest bidder. Unfree labour, however, could not do this. Villeins working on the lord's demesne in lieu of rent had to continue as before. The spectacle of others able to benefit by the chance which had doubled wages increased the discontent which they already had for their lot. It did not escape them, moreover, that since the value of labour had increased, they were paying what amounted to more rent for their land by continuing to render the same services, though rent elsewhere had not risen. They became difficult to manage, and, where circumstances were favourable, those with fewer ties, such as the younger men, deserted the manors and, escaping through the forest to other villages, offered their services as free labourers. So keen was the competition among landowners that runaway villeins were engaged without inquiry. Such villeins might also enlist in the army.

While the lower classes benefited through the supply of labour being far short of the demand, the upper class was badly hit. As most of them employed ploughmen, harvesters, shepherds, carpenters, masons, thatchers and the other varieties of rural workers, and had to pay the higher wages, they were hard put to it to make their estates pay, for the price of agricultural produce had not risen. Parliament, which consisted almost entirely of the landowner class, decided to intervene. It was believed possible to fix wages and decision was taken to fix them at the rate obtaining before the plague. An ordinance, which became known as the Statute of Labourers, was passed into law on 18 June 1349. It ran: 'Because lately a great part of the people, and especially of servants and labourers, has died during the pestilence, and some, perceiving the pressing need of the lords, refuse to serve unless they receive excessive wages, we . . . have ordained that every man . . . shall receive only such wages as were accustomed to be offered . . . in the average five or six years preceding.'[1] Persons refusing to work were to be arrested and detained in prison till they consented to do so for the wages proscribed. So strongly did parliament feel that wages must be fixed at the previous rate, that landowners were penalized who offered the higher wages.

It was impossible, however, to enforce such an ordinance when labour was so short that many employers had either 'to give labourers what they asked or lose their crops'.[2] Nevertheless, parliament, in a series of ordinances continued its efforts to compel labour to work for less than the market rate. There is a petition dated 1351, two years after the Statute of Labourers, in which the commons pray that 'because since the pestilence the labourers will not work for the wages ordained by the King and Council, nor do they pay any heed to fines . . . but do worse and worse from day to day, may it please the King that the penalty of corporal punishment be imposed on them as well as fines.'[3]

Though these measures were ineffective in pegging wages, the efforts to make them effective by enforcing penalties put the people out of temper. They held that their rights had been denied them, for they were sufficiently advanced to conceive that every Englishman had the right to sell his labour as he could. But since it was not admitted that the working man was entitled to better wages, he had to run the gauntlet of the statute to obtain them. The chronicler Knighton declares that the peasantry now became 'arrogant, hostile and greedy'. But though the landowners, including the church, viewed them in this light, they managed to improve their standard of living. Their success was only partial, since villeinage remained. But such as it was, it gave them confidence. They had had a taste of power. More self-assured, they became more

[1] Foedera III, 1, 198 (Latin; trans. from *Illustration of Chaucer's England*, p. 152).

[2] Knighton's *Chronicon* under date 1348.

[3] Rolls of Parliament, ii, 225 of 1351 (French).

restive. When other grievances and dissatisfactions were added later, their mood grew more dangerous, their ideas more revolutionary. The Black Death was not a cause of the peasant revolt of 1381, but it set in motion forces which prepared the way for it.

Poitiers

The Black Death upset the labour market, but it did not cause Edward III to give up his ambitions in France. He and the nobility remained as eager as before to continue the conflict. The money to do so was available. There was no sign that parliament intended to withhold supplies. The adventure remained feasible. English military superiority was untouched. The army did not depend on size but on efficiency and the longbow. When ten thousand men sufficed, the reduction of the population by a third was no great matter. France's population had also been reduced, probably in the same proportion. The lure of plunder and fresh territory was even greater than before. The sack of France would make up the losses which the Black Death had caused. That was the look of things.

Nevertheless, there was a pause. The pestilence ran its course in 1348 and 1349. The truce with France which was to terminate in September 1348 was renewed. In 1351 it was still in force and peace negotiations were begun. If Edward could get all he wanted without renewed fighting, so much the better. But he pitched his claims so high that he can hardly have expected them to be accepted. In 1353 he informed Pope Innocent VI, who was acting as arbiter, that 'if his adversary (the King of France, now John II, for Philip of Valois had died in 1350) would restore to him the Duchy of Guienne, as freely as any of his ancestors had held it, the Duchy of Normandy, and the County of Ponthieu, with the lands which he has conquered from his said foe in France, Brittany, and elsewhere, and also the obedience of Flanders, whereof he is seized, all to hold freely, without homage or other service; then he would willingly resign the said crown, to bring the war to an end.'[1] He asked, in fact, that about half France be ceded to England in return for his relinquishing his claim to the whole. This was talking very big. True, he had regained in his ancestral duchy of Guienne (Aquitaine) much of what the French had taken from him; he had secured a hold on Brittany by backing the de Montfort party against de Blois who favoured France; in Normandy some of its magnates had come to his side; he had raided as far as Paris, defeated the French army at Crécy, and taken Calais. But there had been nothing decisive. France had been humiliated and damaged. But she was not reduced so far that she must accept such hard terms.

In August 1354 the Pope presided at a meeting between the plenipotentiaries of England and France in Avignon. Edward's conditions for peace were discussed, but the 'French replied that though they would gladly have peace, the King could not permit that all the rights belonging to the crown of France in Aquitaine and the aforesaid counties should be alienated, from that kingdom whose integrity they had sworn to preserve. Nevertheless, they would agree that the King of England should hold Aquitaine as his ancestors had, always provided that the sovereinty of the French crown was assured.'[2]

Edward could now claim that his overtures had been rejected. He made ready to renew the war. The problem of how to reduce the French fortified towns and castles had not been solved, but he had reason to hope that if his army marched about France ravaging and looting, as was within its power, the French would be so harassed that eventually they would agree to anything in order to be rid of so intolerable a scourge. Thus, to torment them until they ceded the wide territories demanded would be the first step. Greatly strengthened and enriched, he would then be well placed to take the further step of securing the French crown. As it happened, he succeeded in the first part of his programme, and was the founder of an overseas dominion. But neither he nor his lieutenants had the executive ability and financial resources to manage and retain what had been won, and England's first empire was soon lost. The adventure while it lasted, however, greatly

[1] Rolls of Parliament, ii, 252 (French).

[2] *The Chronicle of Geoffrey le Baker* (Latin), p. 124 of the E. M. Thompson edition, 1889.

stimulated the nation and woke the lower classes to a new sense of their importance in the world. Its ultimate failure so disgusted them that, out of temper as they already were for domestic reasons, they rose against the upper classes.

In the autumn of the next year, 1355, Edward assembled an army in Calais and made a sortie, but on hearing that the Scots, again prompted by the French king, had crossed the Border, he returned to England. The same autumn he sent his son Edward, the Black Prince, to Aquitaine, with 3,500 men. The Prince was now twenty-five. He was given the powers not only of commander-in-chief but also of viceroy of Aquitaine. His instructions were to rally the Gascon lords, for long the vassals of the English crown, and, reinforced by their contingents, make a deep raid into southern France. Count Jean d'Armagnac[1] was King John's lieutenant in that part. He was to be brought to battle and defeated.

The Prince left Bordeaux, his capital in Aquitaine, at the end of the first week of October with 5,000 men. His leading commanders were William de Montagu, Earl of Salisbury, Robert Ufford, Earl of Suffolk, John de Vere, Earl of Oxford, and Sir John Chandos, all of whom had fought at Crécy. Among the Gascon lords was Jean de Grailly, Captal de Buch, destined afterwards to rival Chandos as the most famous knight of the period. Altogether, the Black Prince had a very distinguished staff. There could hardly have been found together elsewhere so formidable a company of men of war. Themselves clad in the latest models of plate armour, their retinues of knights, esquires and retainers similarly accoutred, mounted on barded horses, supported by mounted archers, they were professional soldiers it were suicide to attack if they had time to dismount and take up a defensive position with the archers on their flanks.

The Prince headed south-east in the direction of Narbonne on the Mediterranean. As soon as the frontier of Aquitaine was passed, he started burning everything on his path, crops and towns in particular, putting all who resisted to the sword, taking prisoner any notables worth a ransom, and seizing what valuables he could

[1] Jean d'Armagnac was a Gascon nobleman of the first rank. He had some estates and castles in Aquitaine. Later on (1363) he came over to the English side and did homage to Edward. We shall meet him as one of the Black Prince's commanders at the battle of Nájera in 1367. In 1371 he returned to his allegiance to France.

carry, particularly from monasteries. The inhabitants fled when they could, abandoning their possessions. It was a terrifying visitation, particularly as hitherto this part of France had seen nothing of war. Armagnac dared not attack. The Prince avoided strongly fortified towns. He by-passed Toulouse, where Armagnac had shut himself up, and reached Carcassonne.

Today the visitor to Carcassonne sees the fortifications restored to a state resembling that in which the Prince saw them. The Carcassonne of the fourteenth century has been recreated with its outer and inner walls, both immensely stout and high, their bastions topped with conical roofs, a castle inside the inner wall, itself again fortified with walls, the whole standing on the top of a hill. The Prince did not attempt to assail such a stronghold and, after burning the suburbs down by the river, passed on to Narbonne, forty miles to the east. He had been marching over a month and had covered about 350 miles.

His arrival at Narbonne, where he again burned the outer town, alarmed the Pope at Avignon a hundred miles away. Could it be the young Prince's intention to continue his raid eastwards? He hastily sent messengers to urge a settlement with France, but the Prince refused to parley with them.

Intelligence was now received that Armagnac, largely reinforced, was approaching. In a letter written by Sir John Wingfield, one of the Prince's knights, to the Treasurer in London, we have: 'My lord had news that the power of France was come forth from Toulouse to the neighbourhood of Carcassonne, so that he wished to turn back on them unexpectedly; and he did so. On the third day, when we were to have come upon them, they had tidings of us before daybreak and withdrew, disappearing into the mountains and strong places, and went by long marches back to Toulouse.'[1]

The Prince, having failed to bring the French army to battle, decided to return home and reached Bordeaux just before Christmas 1355, 'with great pillage and many prisoners' as Froissart puts it. Summing up, Sir John Wingfield says: 'My lord rode against his enemies for eight whole weeks. . . . Since this war began against the King of France, there has never been such loss or destruction as he has suffered in this raid.' The country was a rich part of France which paid a big revenue and supplied important contingents for the army. The damage done to it, adds

[1] This letter is included in Robert of Avesbury's Chronicle *De Mirabilibus Gestis Edwardi III*.

Wingfield, had so confounded the French, that it should now be possible to extend the frontiers of Aquitaine by conducting similar raids elsewhere. His admiration for the Prince overflows; he was a great leader, energetic and proud. The way he refused the Pope's pourparlers was splendid. 'As for the answer my lord made to the messengers,' he wrote, 'you would think yourself well repaid if you knew all the manner of it.'

Immediately after Christmas the Prince sent small bodies of soldiers, commanded by the aforesaid noblemen, into French territory to rob and burn in all directions. These bands resembled brigands. Their depredations were the beginning of a long misery for France. Brigandage was to spread like a second Black Death. It grew, as will be shown, into a general anarchy, in protest against which the French peasantry, reduced to the utmost wretchedness, rose in fury. The Prince, destined soon to become the age's model of chivalry, showed by his method of waging war against the civil population what a ruthless thing chivalry could be. He will be seen in the following pages as a superb fighting general and master of the grand gesture. But his limitations as a diplomatist and a strategist will appear. He was not without endearing qualities. Though his reputation was to exceed his royal father's, he remained loyal and humbly obedient. His marriage to his cousin Joan, the Fair Maid of Kent, was a charming romance. He was capable of very warm friendships. His later disasters and long illness touch us. So, too, does the letter which he sent to Bishop Trillek of Hereford a few months after he returned from his raid to Narbonne: 'Reverend father in God . . . we earnestly entreat you that you . . . will command all your subjects, as well the religious as parsons, vicars and others of your jurisdiction, to go twice each week in procession, praying for us; and to pray daily for us in good masses by some special prayer to be appointed by you. So that by these devotions we may the better win the rights of our dear lord and our own.'[1]

In August of this year, 1356, he set out on a new raid with a somewhat larger army than the 5,000 men-at-arms and archers of the ride to Narbonne. It was aimed this time in a north-easterly direction towards the region of the Loire and the entry into metropolitan France. The object of bleeding the peasantry was the same, as was also the hope of bringing to battle the French main army.

[1] Quoted in *Illustrations of Chaucer's England* from the Bishop of Hereford's Register (French).

King Edward, moreover, had some subsidiary operations in hand in Normandy under Henry of Derby, Duke of Lancaster, who was supported by disaffected Norman lords. These operations had reached a point where Lancaster might be able to join the Prince. Edward's strategical conceptions were never very precise, but it looks as if he had planned a combined operation. The Prince and Lancaster, after junction, were intended, perhaps, to advance eastwards and oblige King John to meet them.

During August the Prince rode as far as the neighbourhood of Bourges, which is only 140 miles from Paris. He then bore westwards to the Loire 'expecting to have fallen in with our dear cousin the Duke of Lancaster, from whence we had certain tidings that he would endeavour to come to us', as he wrote afterwards to the mayor, aldermen and community of London. Though so far there had been no sign of the French army, King John was mustering it as best he could. Now at Tours on the Loire the Prince heard 'that the King had made certain resolve to fight with us'.[1]

Judging by what the Prince did on receiving this intelligence, it would seem that, though he had desired from the first a pitched battle, he did not feel well placed enough to fight the French at the moment. He had a great baggage train of loot and was 250 miles from his base. If he were to get his booty home, best to start in that direction. Accordingly, though no junction had been made with Lancaster, he took the main road south, which went (as it still goes) through Poitiers. King John, who had assembled an army three times larger than the English, decided to do what his father had done when King Edward fell back from Paris towards Crécy. He followed the Prince on a parallel road, waiting for a suitable moment to attack and meanwhile keeping out of reach.

It is a curious anomaly that, though the battle of Poitiers is a most famous fight, the details of what happened are very difficult to determine. The opening phases can be stated with a good deal of assurance, but as V. H. Galbraith is obliged to point out in a note to his edition of the *Anonimalle Chronicle* when referring to the elaborate exposition of the subject contained in Delachenal's

[1] The Prince's letter (French) to the Mayor is given in translation on p. 285 of Riley's *Memorials of London* (1868). The original is in the Letter Books of the City of London (G. Fol. LIII) a huge collection of manuscripts, on parchment, which has been carefully preserved through all the vicissitudes of history.

Histoire de Charles V: 'Delachenal's reconstruction of the tactical details of the actual battle is, like all other accounts, open to insuperable objections.' With this melancholy warning in mind one is alerted to approach the subject with care.

As already stated, the Prince left the Loire with his loot and headed south for Bordeaux, shadowed by King John. The strategy of the war demanded that the main French army should be brought to battle. Its defeat, on top of the defeat at Crécy ten years before, would suffice, it was calculated, to force King John to agree to the terms which had been offered. Otherwise the war would be a vista of raids, lasting who could tell how long. The proximity of the French army was therefore what the Prince wanted. Nevertheless, he had to be careful. He could not rush at the French. The rumour was that King John had an immense army. A figure like 60,000 was mentioned. (He had actually about 20,000, but as the Prince had only 6,000 the disparity was yet enormous.) Moreover, attack was not the winning gambit with archers. It was King John who must attack him. But when attacked, he must not be at a disadvantage. His flanks should be covered, his front protected by some obstacles which would slow up the French charge, such as the stiff slope at Crécy or as trees, bushes or the like. That was, of course, if the French were still in mind to rely on the cavalry charge, the flinging of some hundreds of tons of steel carried by men and horses at twenty miles an hour against a stationary mass of steel carried by men standing still on the ground, yet sending outwards in the form of arrows a weight which multiplied by its velocity corresponded to a charge. But supposing the French dismounted, as recent minor operations in Normandy and Brittany suggested might now be their intention, what then? Coming on in a solid mass behind their shields, and in overwhelming numbers, could they be stopped? Would the arrows penetrate? The English calculation was that the archers would be sufficiently effective against knights attacking on foot. Encumbered by their armour (alleged to have been increased in weight since Crécy), they would come slowly. There would be time to shoot many down. Those who reached the line would be tired and panting.

These questions and calculations were in the Prince's mind as he fell back from the Loire. It was not certain the French would attack. Nor possible to say where if they did. Could they be tempted to attack when he had selected a suitable position? And the plunder, the long line of waggons full of jewels, money, furs—

his movements were tied to theirs. And his food. He was running short of supplies. He could not loiter indefinitely waiting to be attacked.

It is sixty miles from the Loire to Poitiers. The Prince's waggons were slow and it took him four days to get to Châtellerault, which is twenty-one miles from Poitiers. En route at Montbazan he had been approached by Cardinal Talleyrand of Périgord, acting on instructions from the Pope, and asked to make a truce. The suspicion was that these papal approaches were bogus. The Pope, living at Avignon, was not thought to be impartial. The Cardinal might be laying some trap. He was told to go away. In the Prince's letter already cited he remarks that talk of truce was odd since 'we were there more fully certified that the King had made ready by all possible means to fight with us'.

On getting to Châtellerault the Prince waited for four days, 'to know more certainly of him (the King)' he explains. What exactly were John's intentions? Perhaps he would come and attack at Châtellerault. It seems also that there was still a hope of Lancaster coming up, though in fact the Duke had been blocked north of the Loire.

While the Prince was halting, however, King John had marched on to Chauvigny, eighteen miles south of Châtellerault. The Prince received news of this on the evening of Friday, 16 September. He also heard that the King's intention was to go on to Poitiers, fourteen miles west of Chauvigny. If he locked himself up in that stronghold, as Armagnac had in Toulouse, there would be no battle. The Prince decided to try to intercept him. 'Whereupon we resolved to hasten towards him,' he writes in his letter, 'on the road that he must take, in order to fight him.' This meant that the Prince would have to fling himself across the Chauvigny–Poitiers road before his adversary got as far as that point. He accordingly started at dawn on Saturday, 17 September, and headed for a castle and village called Chabotrie, which lay four miles east of Poitiers. No doubt, he knew of a suitable position there and, if he could arrive in time, the French army coming from Chauvigny would blunder right into him and have to attack. As we have seen, there was every sign that King John intended to attack. Driven to desperation by the Prince's cruel raids and confident that his large army would give him victory, the memory of his father's loss of as large an army at Crécy ceased to deter him.

The Prince, however, failed to reach Chabotrie in time. He

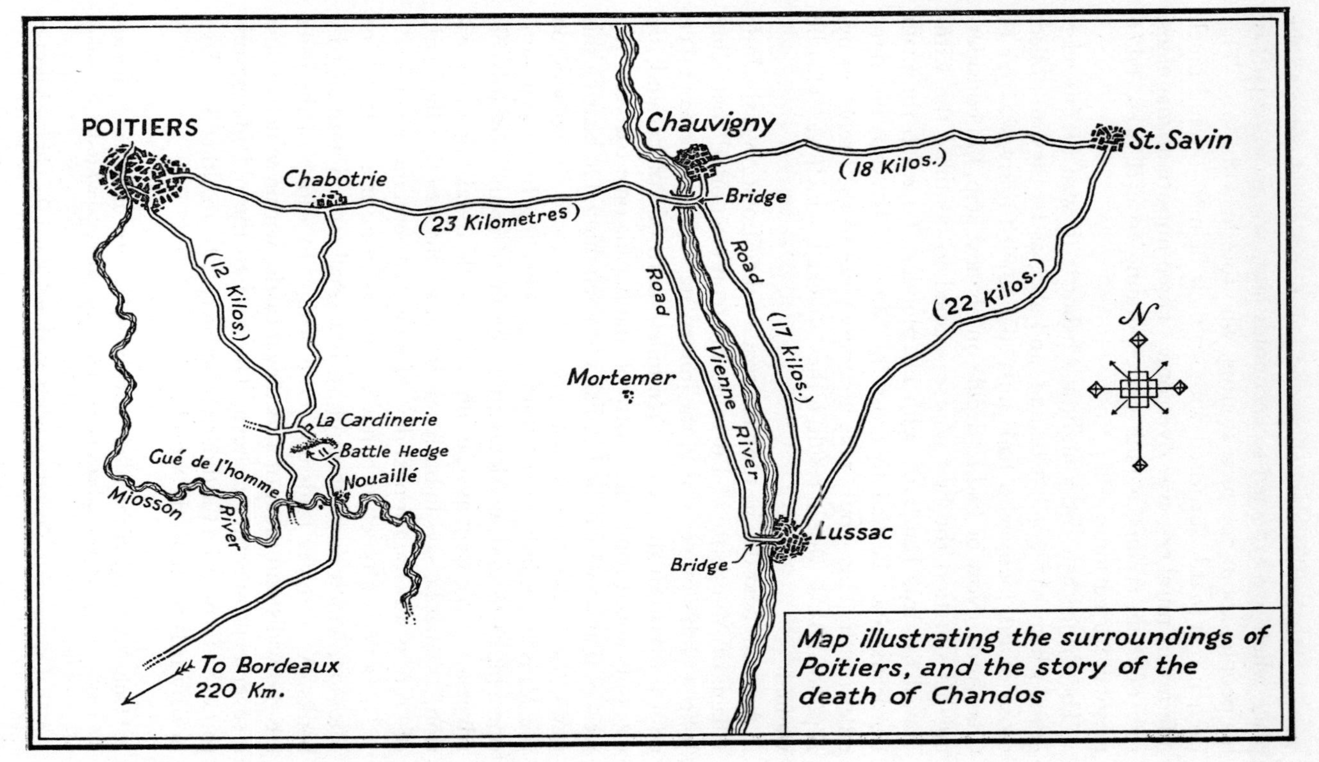

Map illustrating the surroundings of Poitiers, and the story of the death of Chandos

writes: 'His battles were all passed before we could come to the place where we expected to encounter him, saving some part of his people, about 700 men-at-arms, who fought with ours.' This French rearguard, surprised without their helmets on and much inferior in numbers, was overcome. Three important magnates, two of them counts, a rank corresponding to earl, were taken prisoner for ransom.

The Prince halted the night at Chabotrie to wait for his waggons, which had got left behind, and also, as he says, to collect those of his men, who had pursued French fugitives as far as Chauvigny. Now he had to decide on his next step. On considering his situation the best course seemed to continue the withdrawal towards Bordeaux with his plunder. To reach the main Bordeaux road he had to cross the Miosson at Nouaillé, eight miles south. This would take him very close to the French army. A pitched battle would result, if they attacked, which was what he wanted.

At dawn next day he took the road to the Miosson via the little village of Maupertuis.[1] En route his scouts reported that King John with his power was in the immediate vicinity. He had taken up a position in the fields three miles south of Poitiers and, so, was only about four miles north of Maupertuis on a road slightly west of that on which the English were marching. On hearing this news, the Prince sent his waggons of loot ahead to Nouaillé on the Miosson, a mile to the south, and wheeling his troops onto open high ground at Maupertuis, he faced round towards his adversary. 'We went as near him as we could to take up our position,' is what he says in his letter. It was in this area that the battle of Poitiers was fought next day, Monday, 19 September 1356.

Nouaillé is a quiet little nook at the bottom of a valley.[2] The Miosson, which flows through it, is a small stream with marshy banks. A causeway leads up to the bridge. In a loop of the river are the walls and moat of a medieval castle, within which is now a seventeenth-century château. The road to the old Maupertuis (now the farm of La Cardinerie) rises steeply from Nouaillé village northwards through the wood.

[1] Only one house of the village now exists, the large farm La Cardinerie. The name Maupertuis has been tacked on to Nouaillé, called today Nouaillé-Maupertuis.

[2] As it appeared to the author when he visited it and the old battlefield in 1956.

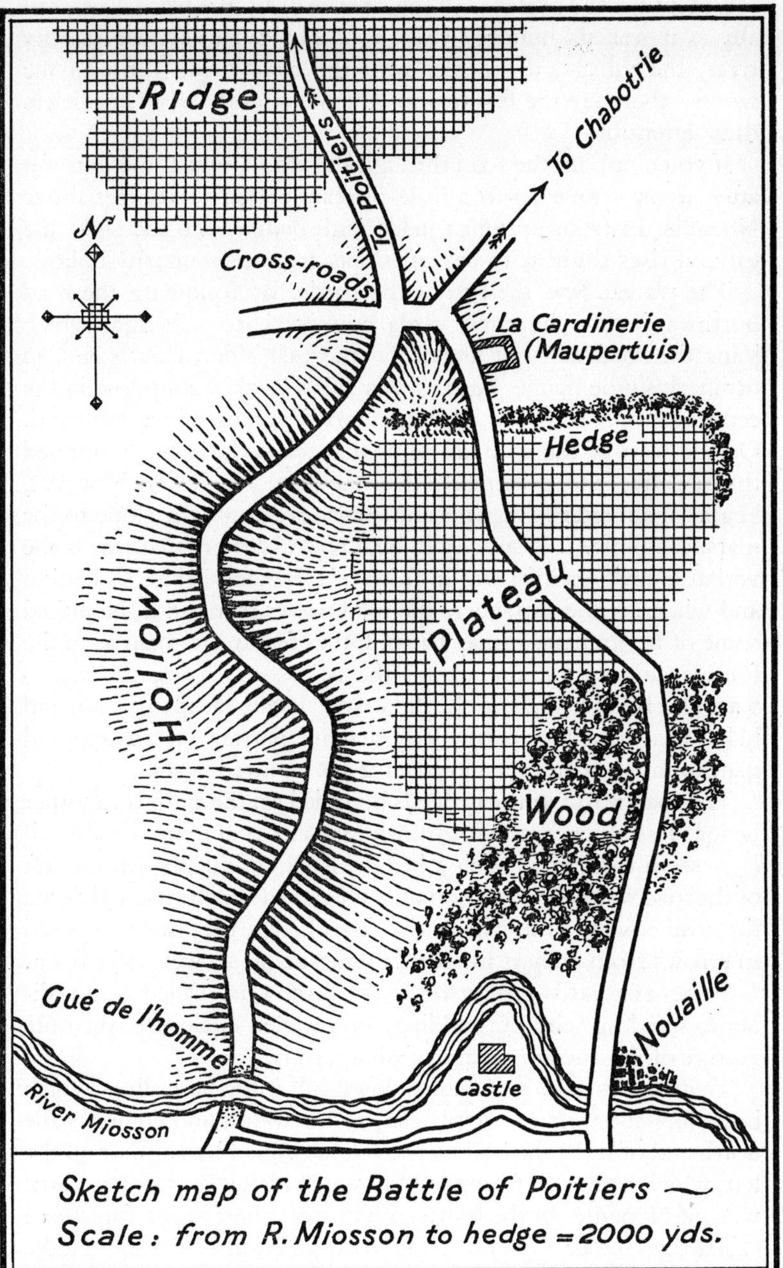

Sketch map of the Battle of Poitiers —
Scale: from R. Miosson to hedge = 2000 yds.

Except for the presence of the later château, the place is essentially as it was six hundred years ago. The causeway, the marshy river, the village, the castle, with the road rising through the wood—these are the features to which contemporary chroniclers draw attention.

If you climb up the road through the wood, you come out of it after about a mile on to a little plateau, perhaps sixty feet above Nouaillé. In front are open fields with hedges. To the right the ground rises slightly, to the left slopes towards a marshy hollow.

The plateau was the site of the battle. By following the road northwards two hundred yards you come to a hedge, which joins the road at right angles on the east side. This is not an ordinary single hedge, but is seven yards thick and hollow in the centre, composed of tall bushes, a barrier against the north wind. On the west of the road are signs that the hedge once continued there; a wire fence now marks the boundary. The hedge, however, begins again after fifty yards and continues down the slope to the marshy hollow. It is suggested by a recent writer[1] that this is the veritable hedge which was in front of the Black Prince's position and where, at the gap where the road passes through it, he placed some of his archers. It may be so. Other features remain as in the fourteenth century, the wood, the Miosson stream, the causeway, the bridge, the marsh, the castle. It is perhaps not beyond belief that a hedge, particularly a wind barrier on an exposed plateau, might continue in place for six hundred years.

The road north of the hedge is bounded on the right by another hedge, less thick but not inconsiderable. Contemporary chroniclers seem to refer to such a hedge also and add that on the left of the road was a hedge too, so that when the French attacked down the road towards the gap in the cross-hedge they were exposed to arrows from archers in each flanking-hedge as well as in front.

Some 250 yards farther on is the farmhouse called La Cardinerie, standing with outbuildings in a walled enclosure, the only vestige of the ancient village of Maupertuis.

The road now slopes gently down hill into the hollow which bounding the west of the plateau, winds round and encircles the north end of it. In the hollow the road is joined by another on the left, which comes up from the Miosson, which it crosses 600 yards west of Nouaillé. In the fourteenth century there was a ford there called the Gué de l'Homme. The road junction lies in the middle

[1] Alfred H. Burne in his *The Crécy War* (1955).

of the space which divided the English and French armies. Immediately beyond is a low hill or ridge. It was from its slopes that the French army launched its attacks.

The English position on the little plateau had no obvious natural advantages. Yet, the marshy hollow protected the left flank, the wood prevented any attack from the rear, and a wing of it extended to protect the right flank. The hedges gave cover for archers. Forward the field of view was unobstructed.

Lettenhove, in his edition of Froissart (1868), gives some interesting details of how in his day the memory of the battle survived in names used by the local people for features in the landscape. Thus, the fields on the plateau had the name of 'champ de bataille'; bits of armour were ploughed up there from time to time. A mound called 'la masse aux Anglais' was near by. At a spot called 'l'abreuvoir des Anglais' horseshoes of an archaic sort had been found. Some remains of English entrenchments used to be pointed out to visitors. Lettenhove also states that at the beginning of the eighteenth century a peasant was alleged to have found near La Cardinerie a medieval brooch containing a valuable diamond. It was believed at the time to have been King John's, lost near the spot where he was captured. Now, however, not even a notice proclaims the place, surprising in this age of tourism. But tourists have to be shown a definite object and there is nothing at the site except trees, hedges and rolling fields.

To return to the Sunday morning, 18 September. When the Prince had taken position on the plateau as near the French as he could, his army was in three divisions or battles, the vanguard under the Earl of Warwick, the centre under himself, and the rearguard under the Earl of Salisbury.[1] It is not precisely known how they were drawn up that morning, but since the Prince says: 'We were on foot and in battle array, ready to fight,' it would seem that they must have taken the positions which they afterwards occupied, Warwick on the west of the plateau, Salisbury on the east, and the Prince in the centre a little back.

While they waited to see whether King John would attack, the Cardinal of Périgord, who had appealed for a truce on 11 September at Montbazan, appeared again, 'begging right earnestly' says the Prince 'for a little sufferance, so that a parley might be

[1] Salisbury was twenty-eight, Warwick forty-three. Both were Crécy veterans.

arranged between persons selected from both sides'. The request was granted. Possibly King John had inspired the Cardinal's visit and wanted to avoid a battle? A parley might reveal his intentions. Representatives of both sides met. Discussion disclosed that the King did not intend peace, as indeed it were hard to suppose. He had followed up the Prince with a huge army and now, face to face with him, could not with any honour withdraw. But it seems that he was not quite ready to engage. His men were still coming up. The chroniclers say that the arrival of these reinforcements was visible to the English. Was the King taking advantage of the Cardinal's intervention to augment his forces? It was clear nothing was to be gained by continuing the parley, and the Prince put an end to it. 'In this wise the conflict was delayed that day,' he wrote.

There was nothing to be done but wait for King John to attack. But when would he attack? The Sunday afternoon wore on without sign of him doing so. The Prince's position was tolerably good, as we have seen. But he could not wait there indefinitely. He wanted to get his waggons of loot moving again towards Bordeaux. They were uncomfortably close to the enemy. Moreover, he was running short of provisions. The proximity of the French army since he left the Loire twelve days ago had restricted his foraging. Accordingly, he ordered Warwick, as commander of the van, to get the waggons over the Miosson at Nouaillé as the first step to a withdrawal. The herald of Sir John Chandos, who afterwards wrote a biography of the Black Prince in French verse,[1] makes the Prince say to Warwick on this occasion: 'You first shall make the passage, and shall guard our baggage. I will ride after you with all my knights. . . . The Earl of Salisbury will ride behind and lead the rearguard. . . . Thus they held converse that night.'

On receiving his orders Warwick must have taken his battle out of the line and marched to Nouaillé through the wood, a distance of about a mile. The movement is likely to have commenced after dark, so as to be invisible to the French.

In his letter the Prince has the following sentence, which puts it beyond doubt that he had decided to recommence his withdrawal towards Bordeaux: 'For lack of victuals, as well as for other reasons, it was agreed that we should set out on our march, keeping before them (the French) on their flank in such a manner

[1] *Life of the Black Prince*, ed. Pope and Lodge (1910), p. 144.

that if they desired battle or drew towards us in a spot which was not greatly to our disadvantage, we would accept it.' This sentence makes clear what the Prince intended to do the following morning. He would draw off the rest of his army from the Maupertuis plateau. If the French attacked on seeing him move, he would stand, and recall Warwick. If not, he would follow Warwick across the Miosson, with Salisbury protecting his rear and, if pursued, stand to receive any attack which might be offered.

The *Anonimalle Chronicle* records Warwick's crossing of the Miosson at Nouaillé: 'The Earl of Warwick passed by a narrow causeway over the marsh and found a town and a French castle.[1] The press of the waggons of the English host was so great and the causeway so narrow that they could not easily get over and were not across before dawn on Monday.'

While this was going on 'the battles of both sides stood all night in their places until the morrow about the hour of prime,' wrote the Prince.

To learn what happened at dawn next day, Monday 19 September, we have to turn again to the Chandos Herald who, though he was not at the battle, had subsequently in Sir John Chandos, his master, who was there, an unrivalled source of information. Early in the morning, he says, 'a great shout was raised and the Prince broke up camp. He began to ride, for that day he thought not to have battle. . . . On the other side the French called out loudly to the King that the English were fleeing and that they would speedily lose them.' After an acrimonious discussion between the two French Marshals, de Clermont and d'Audrehem, in which one accused the other of cowardice, decision was made to attack with a picked body of mounted knights. It would seem that by this time the Prince's battle, the centre, was already on its way down the road to Nouaillé and that Salisbury had wheeled the rear battle and was about to follow from a position by the gap in the cross-hedge which, as explained earlier, was well forward on the plateau near the village of Maupertuis, astride the east road to Nouaillé.

The French knights, led by the two Marshals, began to approach. The Earl, though by now beginning to move away, saw them coming, and, says the Herald, 'turned his battle towards them' and strung out his archers along the two hedges lining the road north of the gap. When within striking distance the French

[1] I.e. Nouaillé and its castle.

knights applied their spurs and charged. The Herald goes on: 'The archers that were on the two sides over towards the barded horses shot rapidly, thicker than rain falls.' And he adds: 'The Earl discomfited the Marshals and all the barded horses before the vanguard could be turned and brought across again, for it was over the river.'

These words refer to Warwick who by now was across the Miosson. On being informed, as no doubt he immediately was by galloper, of the attack on the rearguard, he left the waggons and hurried back. Says the *Anonimalle Chronicle*: 'The Earl of Warwick returned with his men and crossed the marsh after finding a good passage which had not been found before.' This passage over the marsh was not by the narrow causeway and bridge at Nouaillé, but at the ford where the western road crossed the Miosson, six hundred yards west of Nouaillé, called le Gué de l'Homme, which was easier and quicker than by the narrow causeway. He was soon galloping up the west road and took his position on the left of the plateau with his left flank on the marshy hollow and his right on Salisbury's left, a movement, which, as the distance was so short, cannot have taken long. By this time the Prince must have resumed his former position in the centre of the plateau.

This reconstruction of the opening gambits of the battle of Poitiers, resting as it does firmly on the Prince's own despatch, supported by the *Anonimalle Chronicle* and the Herald's poem, may be accepted with some confidence. It shows what a scramble occurred on the English side to get back into battle formation; and how close a thing it was that Salisbury's rearguard was not overwhelmed by the French charge. If it had been, the French main body would have swarmed over the plateau. It is difficult to imagine how the Prince, his rearguard destroyed and his vanguard separated from him by the river, could have won the battle. One is bound to say that he took a very great risk in withdrawing on the assumption that the French were unlikely to attack that day. It was well understood that English superiority depended on standing in a defensive position with flanking archers. All Sunday the Prince had so stood. As long as he stood he was safe. King John was doomed if he attacked. But the moment the Prince moved he was in jeopardy. Lack of food, anxiety about his waggons, at last caused him to move. He gambled on the French not going after him or, if they should, on his not being followed at once and so having time to take up another defensive position. But the French immediately seized the opportunity. They have been blamed for launching a cavalry charge against archers after their experience at Crécy. It has not hitherto been very clear how they could have been so imprudent, particularly as the principle demonstrated at Crécy that mounted knights could not prevail over dismounted knights supported by archers had been accepted. In deference to its general validity King John had dismounted the whole of his knights except the picked body under the two Marshals, said to have numbered five hundred. But why did he think a charge would succeed in this case? The answer is likely to be that as he had to do only with the English rearguard, and as it was moving out of position, he felt sure that in such advantageous circumstances he could overrun the archers. That he failed was partly due to Salisbury's presence of mind. The Earl, who had a long field of view, evidently saw what the French intended in sufficient time to turn his battle and post his archers. But it was the archers themselves who determined the event. Covered by the hedges they were better protected than at Crécy. They could not be ridden down and were able to take their time and shoot deliberately. They saved the rearguard and prevented what might have been a sudden disaster.

Froissart has a most vivid description of this opening charge of the Marshals, which gains by being given in Berners' translation: 'They set forthe that were apoynted to breke the ray of the archers. They entre a horsebacke into the way where the great hedges were on bothe sydes sette full of archers; assone as the men of armes entred, the archers began to shote on bothe sydes and dyd slee and hurt horses and knyghtes, so that the horses whan they felt the sharpe arowes they wolde in no wyse go forward, but drewe abacke and flang and toke on so feersly, that many of them fell on their maisters, so that for preace they coude nat ryse agayne; in so moche that the marshals batyale coude never come at the prince; certayne knyghtes and squyers that were well horsed passed through tharchers and thought to aproche to the prince, but they coude nat.'

There is a passage in Le Baker's *Chronicon* which supplements Froissart by giving additional details of the charge and which can be taken as confirming generally what has gone before. I give it in John Stow, the Elizabethan's translation: 'Clermont, thinking to come out by the gap in the hedge and so to come at the back of our vawarde[1] (i.e. Warwick) and to compasse them in, met with the earle of Salisburie who, perceiving his coming and purpose, suspected his whole intent; and so they which governed our rereward, making haste to take the gap and keepe the enemie from passing that way, sustained the first charge of the battle. . . . The archers did not slacke their dutie but, lying in safe trenches, start up above the ditche and shot over the hedge, prevailing more with their arrows then they did that fought in armes.' And in another passage Le Baker says the archers were ordered 'to shoote at the hinder parts of the horses, by means whereof the horses being gauld and wounded fell to tumbling with them that sate on their backes, or else turned backe and ran upon them that followed after, making great slaughter upon their owne masters'.

The rout of the French knights was completed by the capture of Marshal d'Audrehem and the death of Marshal Clermont. The latter, says Froissart, 'was beten downe and could not be relyved nor ransomed, but was slaim without mercy; some say that it was bicause of the wordes that he had the day before to Sir John Chandos'.[2]

The elimination by death and capture of both his Marshals was a bad start for King John. They were the only tried commanders he had. True, as Froissart says, 'there myght a been sene great nobles of fayre harnesse and rich armory of baners and penons; for there was all the flowre of France'. But no one of the military standing of his Marshals was available. His three main battles were

[1] This phrase is vague, but suggests that Le Baker mistakenly thought that Warwick had already got back from the Miosson into position on the west of the plateau and that the French cavalry, after breaking through Salisbury's battle on the east, could come on the flank and rear of Warwick's. Le Baker was a churchman who lived at Swinbrook in Oxfordshire. We do not know his sources of information.

[2] On the Sunday during the parley with the Cardinal when a truce prevailed for the moment, Chandos and Clermont rode out to reconnoitre for their sides and happened to meet in the fields between the English and French positions. By a coincidence they had both adopted the same heraldic device, says Froissart, 'a blue lady embroidered on a sunbeam on their apparel. The Lord Clermont said: "Chandos, how long have ye taken on you to bear my device?" "Nay, ye bear mine," said Chandos, "for it is as well mine as yours." "I deny that," said Clermont.' Froissart adds that they nearly came to blows and would have fought, had it not been for the truce. On parting Clermont remarked sarcastically that Englishmen, unable to invent anything new, had to copy the French. (Chandos might have retorted by pointing to the archers.)

commanded, the van by his son, the Dauphin Charles, Duke of Normandy, who was nineteen; the midward by his brother, Philip, Duke of Orleans, who was twenty-one; and the rearguard by himself.[1] Though his army was at least three times the size of the Prince's, the youth and inexperience of the commanders of the van and the midward were a serious handicap. The tactics to be employed, however, were simple and traditional. Each of his battles in turn was to advance in frontal assault in accordance with medieval practice. Yet there was the innovation. The battles would advance dismounted. King John seems to have been satisfied that Crécy had been lost because the knights were mounted and that to dismount them would give better results. The failure of the Marshals' charge will further have confirmed his opinion that a man, on a horse almost certain to be shot under him, was clearly in a more precarious position than a man on his own feet. His men at-arms would have to plod slowly up the slope, a solid mass which, though thinned by the arrows, would nevertheless arrive to engage hand to hand in sufficient numbers to overpower forces so much smaller.

The confused and conflicting accounts in the chronicles make it impossible, as we have already been warned, to reconstruct the tactical details of the battle. The broad outline, however, is fully established and can be shortly stated. After the rout of the cavalry, the Dauphin advanced with the van against Salisbury and Warwick. All the chroniclers speak highly of the Prince's bearing. They give in full his address to the archers, though it is not clear how he could have found time to deliver it before the French charge. They speak of him encouraging the faint-hearted, rebuking cowards, entering the press himself and striking many blows. When the Dauphin's battle was engaged by Salisbury and Warwick, he remained in touch, sending advice or help as it was required, by such knights of his retinue as Chandos, James Audeley of Stratton-Audeley, Oxon, and Bartholomew Burghersh, son of the Lord Chamberlain.

It is disappointing that we do not know how the archers fared against the attack of the Dauphin's dismounted men-at-arms. But at least it is certain that they failed to stop them before they reached

[1] Besides the Dauphin, King John brought his other three sons to the battle, Louis, aged seventeen, who was Duke of Anjou, John aged sixteen, Duke of Berry, and his youngest son Philip, who was only fourteen, all of whom were in full armour and were expected to fight.

the English men-at-arms. The French, however, did not prevail, either because they lost heavily to the archers before they came up or for the reason that they were tired after walking in their armour for over a mile on a warm summer day. Nevertheless, a medieval slogging match, which all the chroniclers declare to have been very ferocious, continued for some time before the Dauphin's battle drew off. It seems that it could not be rallied and is not mentioned again as taking part in the battle.

When the men of the Duke of Orleans' battle, the midward, which was following, saw the rout of the Dauphin's, they thought the day lost, and fled without striking a blow in a north-easterly direction towards Chauvigny.[1]

The accounts suggest that there was now a pause. Le Baker seems to refer to it when he writes: 'Our men carried those which were wounded to their campe and laid them under bushes and hedges out of the way, other, having spent their weapons, took the speares and swordes from them whom they had overcome; and the archers, lacking arrowes, made hast to drawe them from poore wretches that were but halfe dead; there was not one of them al, but either he was wounded or quite wearied with great labour except 400 men'[2] in reserve about the Prince's standard.

The interval was brought to an end by the sudden appearance of a fresh mass of men-at-arms coming over the crest of the low hill north of the depression, the spot from which all the attacks had emanated. As the Herald puts it: 'It was the King of France who drew nigh, bringing up a great power.' It is stated that he had more men in this one battle than the Prince in his three. And they were fresh while the English were tired. The King was throwing in his reserves and resolutely leading them himself in a desperate effort to retrieve his fortunes.

At this apparition of the French rearward and the prospect of having, as it were, to fight a second battle when they had begun to hope that the struggle was over, the English were much taken aback. Even the Prince, according to the Herald, 'was some deal abashed', and prayed aloud for divine succour. But he kept his head. He had expected that the King's battle would appear in

[1] According to Froissart it was at this stage that the King's sons, the Dauphin Charles, Louis and John, left the field on the advice of their guardians, who had been ordered to see to their safety. The youngest, Philip, was with the King, whose battle had not yet appeared.

[2] Stow's translation in his *Annals* (1580).

due course and had a plan ready. It would seem that Jean de Grailly, Captal de Buch, the most distinguished of the Gascon noblemen fighting for him, had suggested the possibility of a flank attack. The moment had come to adopt the suggestion. He was sent with a small mounted force of men and archers, probably his own retinue, to make a circuit east and north and, taking advantage of ground which would conceal his movements, come in on the left flank and rear of the King's battle. To synchronize with this manoeuvre the Prince decided to advance from the plateau into the hollow in front and charge the King as he came down the hill on the opposite side.

It is the mark of a fighting general of the first rank to know intuitively the right moment for such a stroke and to have the drive to force it through. The Prince was such a general and he had the drive. Says Le Baker: 'The Prince ordered his standard bearer, Sir Walter Woodland, to move towards the banners of the enemy and himself with a few fresh men went to meet the King.' Meanwhile the Captal de Buch was making his way round the flank unobserved and suddenly burst on the French rear, 'beating downe and killing without pitte, and the archers also shot so thicke, wounding the backes and sides of the Frenchmen in suche sorte, that the fourme of the battaile was quite spoyled, neither could they put themselves in order and array any more.'

The Prince on his side pressed the attack. The French nerve broke. The rout began. Many surrendered. Some fled back up the Poitiers road and were pursued. 'The chase endured to the gates of Poitiers,' says Froissart. 'Ther were many slayne and beaten downe, horse and man, for they of Poyters closed their gates and wolde suffre none to entre; wherfore in the strete before the gate was horrible murdre. . . . The Frenchemen yelded themselfe as farre of as they might know an Englysshman; ther were dyvers Englysshe archers that had iiii, v or vi prisoners.'

The grand finale was the capture of the King himself with his little son Philip. It was usual at this period in France to give heads of state a familiar designation. King John was known as the Good, because he was brave and generous, agreeable to meet, fond of sport and pageantry; but, as one can see from his portrait in the Louvre, he had the heavy face of a stupid man with a big obstinate jowl. It was the sixth year of his reign and he was thirty-seven. He was notorious for taking bad advice and trusting favourites of no reputation. So confident was he that the number and valour of his knights would assure him victory that he ordered no quarter to be given and hoisted the Oriflamme.[1] Little is known of his conduct of the battle so far except that he remained very far back with the rearguard, which was out of sight of the English on the far side of the hill. Only when he advanced with it over the crest and was attacked by the Prince in front and the Captal de Buch in the rear did he become involved in the mêlée. 'He had an axe in his hands and defended himself valiantly in the press', says Froissart. His son, Philip, only fourteen, was close by and very courageous. The story went afterwards that he warded off blows aimed at his father.[2] The Counts of Tancarville and Eu, and Pierre, Duke of Bourbon, were among the magnates in the royal retinue.[3] As the rear battle began to open and break, great efforts were made by both English and Gascon knights to come at the King and capture him, for he represented a fortune in ransom money. His banner, held over him by Geoffrey de Chargni, was visible at a distance, and they made at it. De Chargni was cut down, still holding the banner, the magnates of the retinue were slain or captured, and the King, easy to recognize for he wore the crown and was covered with jewels, was yelled at: 'Surrender, surrender, or you are a dead man.' But so many knights were shouting, each that he should surrender to him, that the King did not know what to do. At this moment there happened to come up a French knight called Denis de Morbecke, who had fled from France, because he had committed a murder, and been taken into employ by King Edward. He saw his chance and, says Froissart, 'pushed through the press, for he was tall and strong of body and limb, and, drawing the King's attention by speaking in good French, said: "My lord, my lord, surrender to me." The King, in such straits and so hard pressed that it was no longer worth

[1] See Froissart, Lettenhove edn. p. 409. 'Les banieres dou roy venteloient . . . et par especial li oriflambe que messires Joffrois de Chargni portoit.' The Golden Flame was of red silk split into many points and was borne on a gilt staff. That it signified no quarter see Knighton, *Chronicon*, p. 89, vol. II in Rolls edn.: 'Dominus Galfridus Charneys bajulavit vexillum rubium quod est mortis signiferum.'

[2] Recorded by the contemporary Italian chronicler Giovanni Villani in his *Istoria Fiorentini*.

[3] Tancarville was son of the Tancarville whom Edward III took prisoner at Caen before Crécy. It was Eu's predecessor as Count who likewise was taken at Caen. The present two Counts were captured at Poitiers and taken for ransom to England. The Duke of Bourbon was King John's uncle by marriage. He was killed.

while trying to defend himself, turned his face to the knight and asked: "To whom shall I surrender? To whom? Where is my cousin, the Prince of Wales. If I might see him, I would speak to him." "My Lord," replied Denis de Morbecke, "he is not here. But surrender to me and I will bring you to him." "Who are you?" said the King.' De Morbecke explained who he was and the King surrendered to him and gave him his right gauntlet. Froissart goes on: 'The knight took it with great joy. There was such a great press and hubbub about the King, for everyone was yelling: "I took him, I took him," that the King could not move nor his young son, my lord Philip.'

The capture was made, as is supposed, in the hollow south of the hill near the junction of the east and west roads to the Miosson. The Prince had moved on with the tide of battle and was now on the north side of the hill. The French rearguard was broken. The pursuit had begun. A quiet descended on the hillside. Chandos, who was beside him, begged him to rest. 'The battle is over, the victory is yours. There is not a French banner or pennon in sight. Take some refreshment. You are tired and hot.' He agreed and so that his lords might know where he was, he had his banner hoisted above a bush and trumpets sounded. He took off his helmet. His body servants hastened to pitch a little red tent and poured him out a cup of wine. Warwick and Robert Ufford, Earl of Suffolk, came up shortly. The Prince, who had been wondering about King John, asked them for news of him. 'He is either dead or taken,' they said, 'for he has not left the battle-field.' The Prince immediately said to Warwick and Lord Cobham, who was there: 'Take your horses and find out for sure what has become of him.' Mounting at once they rode to the crest of the hill and looking down the other side saw a crowd of Gascon and English men-at-arms walking slowly up, with the King in the middle of them. They had taken him away from de Morbecke and were quarrelling so violently over him, that he was in danger of getting hurt. The sight made the two lords gallop down. 'What's this, what's this?' they demanded, and ordered the men-at-arms to keep back. Then dismounting, they made the King a low reverence and conducted him to the Prince.

Froissart's description of the capture, of which the above is a rendering from his text, is one of his most vivid passages. No French king had ever been captured in battle by the English before, nor was ever to be again. The event made a profound impression in England, as did the sequel, the supper to which the Prince invited his fallen adversary, another of Froissart's famous pieces, which has often been retold, but like all good stories stands retelling. Moreover, when properly interpreted, it falls into place with the Prince's whole attitude to his victory, and throws light on why he did not make more use of it, as will be suggested later on.

Here is the supper party as rendered by Berners: 'The same day of the batayle at night the prince made a supper in his lodgynge to the Frenche kyng and to the moost parte of the great lordes that were prisoners. The prince made the kynge and his son (and certain of his lords) to syt all at one borde. . . . The prince served before the king as humbly as he coude, and wolde nat syt at the kynges borde for any desyre that the kynge coude make; but he sayd he was not suffycient to syt at the table with so great a prince as the kyng was. But than he sayd to the kyng, Sir, for Goddessake make non yvell nor hevy chere, though God this day dyde nat consent to folowe your wyle: for sir, surely the kynge my father shall bere you as moche honour and amyte as he may do, and shall acorde with you so reasonably that ye shall ever be frendes toguyder after; and sir, methynke ye ought to rejoyse, though the journey be nat as ye wolde have had it, for this day ye have wonne the hygh renome of prowes and have past this day in valyantnesse all other of your partie; sir, I say natte this to mocke you, for all on our partie . . . ar playnly acorded . . . to gyve you the price and chapelette.'

That the Prince did not maintain throughout the whole of supper such a level of exquisite politeness is suggested by a curious passage in the contemporary *Chronique des Quatre Valois*. The Prince is made to ask King John: 'Fair cousin, if you had taken me as, thank God, I have taken you, what would you have done with me?' To which question the King made no reply. He knew the Prince was referring to the Oriflamme, sign that no quarter was to be given.

But it would be as erroneous to think that Froissart's description of the Prince's wonderful manners is a fiction, as to suppose that the Prince was indifferent to the grand gesture. His civilities to King John accorded with the knightly ideal of the day, which, as is well established, he always sought to follow. The more splendid his triumph, the more correct was it for him to show a splendid courtesy. And it came natural to him to do so. He was not the sort of man to be inflated by triumph. Indeed, it was the other way. He did not realize the full implication of his present achievement, nor the extent of the power which was suddenly his. Humbled rather than puffed up by his marvellous success, he was more concerned to prove himself a perfect knight than to consider how he might exploit his victory in order to deal prostrated France her death blow.

Froissart's solemn verdict on the day will serve to sum up the Prince's achievement: 'Thus was this great battle fought which took place on the fields of Maupertuis at two leagues from Poitiers on the nineteenth day of September in the year of grace of our Lord 1356. It began at about dawn and finished at noon. But it was vespers before everyone had returned from the pursuit. And there was killed the flower of the chivalry of France, for which cause the realm of France was much enfeebled and great misery and tribulation ensued.'

It is in keeping with the Prince's character that there is not the smallest trace of self-glorification in his despatch. He does not seek to impress the mayor and corporation of London to whom he is writing. Indeed, when the battle itself is described, he passes it over so shortly that we are deprived, to history's permanent loss, of what would have been the most valuable testimony. He modestly leaves it to his messenger to give the glowing picture. All he says is this: 'The battle was joined two days before the Feast of St. Matthew; and, praised be God, the enemy was discomfited, and the king and his son taken prisoner, great plenty of other great men being captured and slain, as our dear bachelor Sir Nigel Loring our chamberlain, the bearer of this, who has full knowledge of what happened, will be able more amply to explain to you, than we may write it. To whom you shall give full faith and credence. May Our Lord have you in his keeping. Given under our secret seal at Bordeaux, the 22nd day of October.'

He might have been so much more emphatic, for, having destroyed the French army, France was at his mercy. The French fighting nobility, as far as King John had been able to assemble them, had been either killed or captured except those who had fled. At this moment of utmost confusion, the Dauphin, who was only nineteen, had to head the government. With no army, little money, and further weakened by disorder in Paris, he could not have warded off another blow, had one been delivered immediately. But it did not occur to the Prince to deliver another blow.

The Berne Chronicle, called the *Chronographia*, puts in a sentence what the Prince might have done and what would have happened if he had: 'There is no doubt that it would have been France's last day if the Prince had advanced on Paris soon after his victory.'[1]

No one of importance was killed on the English side. The Prince had his army intact. Had he marched north at once, summoned Henry Duke of Lancaster and the English force in Normandy to join him, and asked his father King Edward to come over with more troops, Paris would have fallen to their onslaught before the French could have mustered a fresh army. So great was French demoralization at the moment that the city would probably have opened its gates and Edward have got all he wanted.[2] The country was in the greatest danger. As the chronicler truly said, it looked like her last day. But the Prince was not thinking on such ruthless lines. Instead of hastening to gather strategic fruits, his mind was occupied with chivalric punctilios. King John, as his prisoner, would be taken to England and royally entertained. His ransom would be fixed and on payment of the same he would be allowed to return to France. It was not considered inconsistent that the defeated King should resume the very activities which the war was being fought to end. With views of this kind prevailing, a realistic approach by the Prince to the immediate strategical possibilities was out of the question. Such an approach belonged to a different order of ideas. The consequence was that the annihilation of the French army, and the eclipse of the French government consequent thereon, had not the decisive effect which nowadays a victory of such magnitude would certainly have. We shall see eleven years later an almost identical situation arise in Spain, when the Prince after the battle of Nájera again failed to exploit his victory.

But though he would not consider (or could not grasp) the possibilities of making Poitiers decisive, the immediate results of the battle were so exciting for the victors, high and low alike, that they may well have been disinclined for that reason alone to fight any

[1] Nec dubium est ultimam illum diem Franciae futurum fuisse, si princeps mox post victoriam urbem Parisii intendisset.

[2] True, France could not be overcome, as has been pointed out, unless her fortified towns and castles were taken, a task beyond the capacity of the English. But at this particular moment of crushing defeat and utter discouragement, a bold stroke at the capital might have been decisive before the French had time to rally. Had Paris capitulated, the fortified towns and castles would mostly have followed suit.

more. The French camp with all its contents fell into their hands. It was the custom in the fourteenth century for the nobility to campaign with a quantity of their valuables, some of which they wore in battle. The French camp was an especially rich prize because the King himself was with the army. The manner in which its contents were shared is not on record, but one has an idea what was available from the following passage in Froissart: 'Those on the Prince's side were made rich by ransoms and by the booty found in the camp, such as rich belts, vessels of gold and silver, jewels, scarlet cloaks and other fine cloths, golden rods and hats decked with pearls. Such was the plenty, that no one bothered to pick up the arms, helmets, harness and other accoutrements lying in the fields. For the King, princes, barons and knights had come lavishly provided with everything.'[1]

We have already seen how even archers had as many as six prisoners each. As the total captured exceeded what could be safely managed, a proportion of them were let go on their promise to come with ransom money to Bordeaux before Christmas. These were the smaller knights, it seems. The more valuable prisoners were taken along when the English recommenced their march to Bordeaux. Estimates of their numbers vary, but Jean de Venette, a French chronicler, who may be supposed not to have exaggerated France's loss, says there were thirteen counts, five viscounts, twenty-one barons and nineteen hundred others worth a good ransom.[2] Warwick had captured William de Melun, Archbishop of Sens, and the Captal of Buch, Jacques de Bourbon, Count of La Marche, but in general the captors were men of less note, for whom the ransom money would mean riches. Any disputes as to who had taken whom were deferred for settlement until the Prince reached Bordeaux.

There had been a long train of loot before, but now its length was much increased by the inclusion of the French waggons. It stretched for miles as the army set out for home. Says Froissart: 'They rode but small journeys because of their prisoners and the

[1] Froissart does not mention books, but there was at least one book in the camp and Salisbury acquired it, an edition of the Bible. The British Museum has it now. Inside is written in fourteenth-century French: 'This book was taken from the King of France at the battle of Poitiers, and the good Earl of Salisbury, William Montagu, bought it for 100 marks and gave it to his companion, Elizabeth the good countess.' Lettenhove ed. Froissart, vol. 5, p. 545. The book can be inspected in the Museum's Department of MSS.

[2] *The Chronicle of Jean de Venette*, ed. R. A. Newhall (1953), p. 220.

many waggons they had.' Warwick went in front to open the way, but no one opposed them or tried to rescue the King, as the Dauphin or Orleans might have done had they dared. 'All the country was so afraid that every man took refuge in the castles.' They passed the frontier into Aquitaine and at last came to Bordeaux on 2 October, thirteen days after the battle, where 'no one could describe the greatness of the citizens' welcome nor the entertainment they made for the Prince.' King John stayed with him in the Abbey of St. Andrew.

Though some knights and squires were allowed to go home 'where they were made much of', says Froissart, the Prince remained in Bordeaux till April 1357. The risk of a sea journey during the winter with such a valuable prisoner as King John, not to speak of the others and the booty, was too great to take. The six months passed pleasantly with drinking and dice. The troops, says Froissart, 'spent foolishly the gold and silver they had won'. But business was also done. The Prince paid cash to any Gascons who had captured members of the French higher nobility, for he intended to take such with him to England. Disputes were settled. The most important concerned the capture of King John. A Gascon nobleman, Bernard de Troye, claiming the honour, challenged Denis de Morbecke to single combat. The Prince, however, forbade and declared that the dispute should be argued before King Edward when they reached England. But since King John admitted that de Morbecke was his captor, the Prince privately sent him 2,000 nobles (£666 13s. 4d.) as an advance on what he might expect to get.[1]

Before John left Bordeaux for England with the Prince, he signed a truce to last two years. King Edward hoped to arrive at a settlement with him before its expiration. They would have

[1] The de Morbecke ransom case dragged on for four years and came up for final settlement when that knight was on his death-bed. Foedera III, ii, 467 has a full account of how King Edward sent clerks of the Chancery to find out whether de Morbecke was well enough to attend the royal court to hear judgment on the appeal of de Troye. The whole is a curious comment on how careful the authorities were to see justice done in the matter of ransoms. De Morbecke was a descendant of the Capetians, whose dynasty ended when Philip of Valois, father of King John, succeeded. That an heir of the Capetians should capture a reigning Valois has dramatic fitness. It is not stated what sum, if any, de Morbecke or his estate was paid. It would, of course be only a small percentage of the total ransom, which in this case was estimated by and reserved for the exchequer.

plenty of opportunity for personal discussion, for it would take King John some time to collect his ransom. Once the desired cession of territory was agreed on, a formal treaty of peace could be drawn up. Thus, instead of forcing the French when they lay, certainly for the moment, helpless after their crushing defeat, Edward relied on negotiation. He would entertain his cousin of France in a handsome manner, make a personal friend of him, as the Prince had promised at the famous supper, and gradually bring him round to the view that the crown of England had a genuine right to Aquitaine, and other French territories, and need not pay homage for them. Curiously enough, the claim to the French throne seems to have been put aside for the time being.

The Prince's entry into London took place on 24 May 1357. The citizens turned out in great numbers in their best clothes. The victory and the capture of the King had already been celebrated by services in the churches, great bonfires and wakes. The entry, however, was not a triumphal procession in the Roman style, but a progress governed by chivalry's protocol. King John rode, says Froissart, 'on a whyte courser, well aparelled, and the prince on a lytell hobbey by hym; thus he was conveyed along the cyte tyll he came to the Savoy,' the palace of the Prince's brother, John of Gaunt. The King stayed there, and also with Edward III at Windsor and the Tower. He was asked to the court functions and jousts[1] and hunted regularly with his hosts. But when

[1] John Stow in his *Annals* (published 1580) puts it well: 'In the Winter following were great and royal Justs holden in Smithfield at London, where many knightly fights of armes were done, to the great honour of the King and realme, at which were present, the Kings of Englande, France and Scotland, with many noble estates of all those kingdomes, whereof the most part of the strangers were prisoners. After this taking of King John of France, Englishmen (which before were bearded and the hayre of their heads short rounded) then used long hayre on their heads, and their beards to be shaven.' King David of Scotland had been a prisoner since his capture at the battle of Neville's Cross in October 1346. He was released in 1357 on payment of a ransom of £30,000 (Knighton's *Chronicon*, Rolls Series, p. 98).

Besides amusing himself King John made lavish gifts at the shrines of patron saints, St. Thomas à Becket at Canterbury, St. Edward the Confessor at Westminster Abbey and St. Erkonwald, the Anglo-Saxon saint buried in old St. Paul's. Of the King's visit to St. Erkonwald's shrine, Sinclair in his *Memorials of St Paul's Cathedral* gives a quotation from, I believe, Sir William Dugdale's *History of St. Paul's* as follows: 'His [King John's] offerings were those of a king, not of a prisoner. Twelve nobles (four

it came to business, he was presented with a bill amounting in English money to £500,000 as the price of his ransom,[1] a crushing figure, if we consider that an average year's revenue in England at that time only amounted to about £100,000.[2]

pounds) at the Annunciation; twenty-six nobles [£8 13s. 4d.] at the crucifix near the north door; as he approached the altar he presented four basons of gold; at the shrine of St. Erkonwald twenty-two nobles [£7 6s. 8d.].'

[1] On King John's ransom see Camden Miscellany, 3rd series, vol. 37 (1926). The ransom was 3,000,000 French gold crowns=1,500,000 English gold nobles. A noble=6 shillings and 8 pence. Hence figure of £500,000. John paid 1,000,000 gold crowns before his death. The ransom did not lapse with his death and his successor, Charles, paid 600,000 gold crowns more.

[2] *See English Historical Review*, vol. 39, 'Balance sheet for 1362–3' by T. F. Tout. Professor Tout examines the revenue accounts for that year and shows that the expenditure was £66,666 13s. 4d. There was a deficit of £26,666 13s. 4d. which had to be met from extraordinary sources such as ransoms, since the revenue for normal sources was £40,000. Tout thinks that on the average an extra £60,000 had to be found annually from one source or other, voted by Parliament or otherwise, making £100,000 as the normal amount of money required yearly to meet all expenses. But this figure should be taken only as an average. Sometimes the issues from the Exchequer were less, and sometimes considerably more.

The Jacquerie[1]

It was exhilarating for the English peasantry while the cash and plunder, which flowed into England after Poitiers, filtered down among them. They were exhilarated too by a sense of triumph, a triumph which was the common people's own, for they were the real artificers of victory. The government had not introduced the longbow, as a government nowadays introduces a new weapon. It had been taken up and made into the most formidable weapon in Europe by, as it were, a popular whim. No other nation had done this, neither the Scots nor the French. The latter, as we have seen, trusted to the crossbow, not a national invention, nor manipulated by Frenchmen, but by hired mercenaries from Italy, a weapon which, unlike the longbow, so difficult to master, anyone could quickly be taught to use. The English peasantry could feel that they had become a martial people. No longer did they depend entirely on the nobility to protect them. They could look after themselves. The peasant archer was as essential for victory as the knight. Utter subservience to the nobility was passing. A lord must now think twice before he provoked his tenants too far. The government was not as strong as formerly to impose its will on the people. The statutes of labourers fixing wages were being circumvented. Other grievances, also, would be voiced. There was, indeed, much to be thankful for when one thought of the peasantry across the Channel, helpless before their lords and the invader.

The French peasantry were dreadfully placed. Poitiers led

[1] The word is said to be derived from *jacque*, the peasant's jerkin.

straight to anarchy. Not all the Black Prince's army returned with him to England or dispersed in the Gascon principalities. Certain adventurers, English and Gascon, remained under arms and saw in France's weakness an opportunity to enrich themselves. After the Prince's departure they left Aquitaine for France proper and, joined by soldiers who had been fighting in Normandy and Brittany under Henry of Lancaster, set out to plunder systematically the French countryside, despite the truce for two years which had been signed in March 1357 by Edward and the captive John. When serving under the Prince they had become experts in how to rob the civil population. Then robbery had some connection with military operations. Now it was plain banditry. These ruffianly fellows became known as the Companions, their gangs as the Free Companies. They were very formidable, composed as they were of veteran men-at-arms and archers. Their captains were able and ruthless. The French nobility who inhabited castles in the areas where the Companions operated did not dare attack them. As will be seen, some even joined them, to get a share in the spoil. The Dauphin Charles, become Regent while his father was held in England, had not the power to suppress them. His own position was highly precarious. Etienne Marcel, leader of the Parisian merchants, and the dominating personality in the Third Estate or Commons of the French parliament, headed an opposition which held that the crown and the nobility had disgraced themselves at Poitiers and could not be trusted now to save France. He sought to gain control of the court and one day showed his power by entering the Louvre with an armed following and murdering two of the Dauphin's advisers in his very presence.

A yet more disconcerting figure was also prowling about, a young man, twenty-five years of age, treacherous and scheming, but so plausible and charming that he could persuade even those whom he had duped to believe him again. This was Carlos, King of Navarre. That a person with such a designation should be in France is confusing at first sight. The explanation is that Carlos was a member of the French royal family who had inherited the independent kingdom of Navarre in Spain and large estates in Normandy centring on Evreux, which was his headquarters at the moment. He had married in 1353 the Dauphin Charles' sister. His mother had been Jeanne, daughter of Louis X. He was therefore closer to the crown than Edward III, whose mother Isabella

1. Sir Robert Knollys as a captain of bandit mercenaries in France

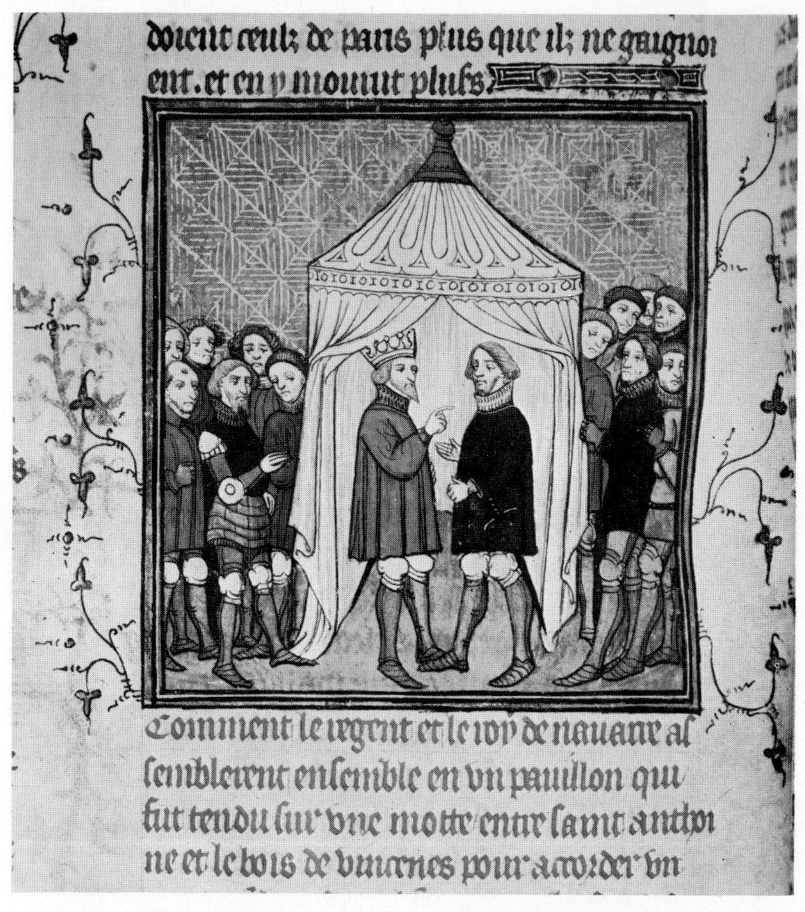

2. The Dauphin Charles conferring with Carlos, King of Navarre

was only sister of Louis X. Had there not been the rule that a woman could not transmit right to the throne, he would have been the rightful heir, not Edward. Like Edward he disregarded the rule and claimed the throne against the Valois King John. Thus there was living in France at this most troubled time a pretender, a man ready to side with anyone who might advance his ambitions. In the Parisian opposition to the Dauphin he saw his chance and came out in support of Marcel. He had already sided with Edward, calculating that, if the Valois were knocked out, the French would prefer him to Edward. Now, with King John a captive, the regent Dauphin so young, and the Valois generally so discredited, the magnates might support his claim. One can well understand how the Dauphin in such adverse circumstances was too occupied in maintaining his regency to cope with the Companions.

One of the most notable of their captains was Sir Robert Knollys, a name to note, as it was he who turned the scale at Smithfield in 1381 and saved King Richard II. Malverne, the chronicler, hardly allows that he was born a gentleman,[1] and is likely to have known for they both came from Cheshire. A professional soldier in early youth, he was twenty-six in the Crécy campaign. Knighted soon afterwards, he was one of the knights in the Combat of Thirty,[2] arranged like a joust but in deadly earnest, which greatly excited the chivalry of the time. His ability as a soldier and his flair for loot secured him after Poitiers a following of tried mercenaries. He was said to have had 500 archers. A typical soldier of fortune, he may be compared to an Italian condottiere of the period.

Now in 1357 he began as a freebooter in Normandy and the Loire valley. Other companions, English and Gascon, each had his allotted ground. Some of them operated north of Paris. Their depredations were carefully planned to bring them in a steady revenue. Having secured their base by taking a castle or a series of castles, they informed the villagers of the locality that they would have to ransom themselves from what was called 'le feu et leurs corps', that is from having their villages burnt and themselves murdered. The ransoms were fixed very high, and were paid, sometimes, by weekly instalments. Knollys is said to have

[1] 'Quasi de infimo genere', he says.

[2] See *Chronicle of Jean le Bel*, chapter 86. The combat took place on 26 March 1351 in Brittany near Morbihan (arr. Ploermel). In 1823 the supposed spot was marked by a pyramid with an inscription, which is still to be seen.

made, as his personal share, 100,000 crowns in quite a short time. The peasants who failed to pay were massacred. Froissart gives a general sketch of the brigands at work: 'On occasion, and that was often, they would select a good town two or three days journey distant. Twenty or thirty brigands would assemble and set out, by day or night, keeping to secluded tracks, and enter the place at dawn. Fire would be set to a house. The inhabitants would think that a thousand men-at-arms had come to burn the town. If they fled, so much the better. The brigands would break into the houses, smash open coffers and chests, take what they found there and then be off, laden with booty.'

Jean de Venette, the contemporary French chronicler, describes their ravages north of Paris in December 1357. 'Robbers increased to such a degree that they despoiled the inhabitants of country towns in their own houses. Charles, the king's eldest son, who was bound by right to defend the country, applied no remedy. A large proportion of the rural population, unable to stay longer in their villages, began at this time to hasten for protection to Paris. The enemy seized many castles and fortresses and captured the men who dwelt about them. Some they held for ransom; some they slaughtered miserably. Nor did they spare the monks and nuns.' He accuses French nobles of joining the marauders. 'The nobles took no thought for the mutual profit of lord and man. In no wise did they defend their country from its enemies. Rather did they trample it underfoot, robbing and pillaging the peasants' goods.'[1]

The Companions also raised a large revenue by issuing safe conduct passes, especially to merchants. Those who did not pay were waylaid and robbed. It was estimated that Knollys and two other captains, Peter Audeley (brother of the celebrated knight Sir James Audeley), and the Gascon, Bertucat d'Albret,[2] held sixty castles and had 2,000 men-at-arms in their pay. Edward III was of course aware how his subjects were breaking the truce, but he shut his eyes to what was an indirect way of bringing pressure on his prisoner, King John, to agree to his terms.

[1] *The Chronicle of Jean de Venette*. Translated by J. Birdsall, edited by R. A. Newhall, 1953, pp. 66, 67, 73.

[2] The names of other leading English captains of Free Companies were: Sir Hugh Calveley, Walter Hewet, Robert Brickett. It is somewhat surprising after what has been said that they were able to take castles. But they were probably small or were surrendered by treachery or starved out. The Companions were not in a hurry.

There were cases when a Companion, gorged with booty, would sell the castle, his centre of operations, to a newcomer, who would demand fresh ransoms and start robbing what his predecessor had left. The peasants were faced with utter destitution. They fled, they hid in caverns, they barricaded themselves in churches, they begged for mercy. But the pillage went steadily on. They grew desperate, starving, mad with rage.

Froissart has a passage which gives the point of view of the successful brigand, in this case one who had sold his practice and retired to his own estates in Gascony. He sighs for the excitements he has foregone. 'What a happy chance it used to be when, riding through the country, we came on a rich abbé or prior or a caravan of mules laden with cloth, furs, spices or silks. It was all ours to hold for ransom. Fresh chances to make money turned up every day. The villeins of Auvergne and Limousin supplied us, bringing corn to our castle, flour, baked bread, fodder and bedding for the horses, good wine, cattle, goats and fat sheep, along with hens and game. Our clothes were regal and when we went riding the whole country trembled before us. By God, it was a good life.'[1]

The French peasantry, subjected to these intolerable outrages, resolved to rise, not to fight the brigands, for they despaired of overcoming these heavily armed veterans and their archers, but to punish the nobility or such of them as could be got at in their country seats, for they held them responsible for all the ills which had overtaken France from Crécy to the present. Their rout at Poitiers when some had fled and many surrendered, and allowed their king to be captured, had covered them with ignominy. Now they supinely watched the despoliation of their people, even taking part against them on occasion. A fighting nobility, they had failed in their chief function of defending the country and protecting the inhabitants. For these delinquencies they deserved death.

The flat lands northwards from Paris to Beauvais and the coast had suffered, perhaps, more acutely than elsewhere. It was in this part that the Jacquerie broke out. That it did so was, no doubt, partly due to its proximity to Paris. Those instigating a rising were in touch with Marcel. He favoured it, for it would weaken

[1] The English rank and file did very well out of this brigandage. Henry Knighton's *Chronicon* (Rolls Series) under year 1358: 'Many who had gone out as boys and valets returned very rich. . . . There was not an Englishman so poor but soon had his fill of gold and silver, jewels and precious stuffs.'

the Dauphin, who had left the capital, which he was endeavouring to bring to heel by blocking supplies coming to it from the north by river.

The Jacquerie was a surprise, as is generally the case with popular risings. The noblesse had no inkling of what was brewing. It never occurred to them that a peasantry, hitherto docile and obedient, would take it into their heads to turn on them. That the lowest class of the community was their judge and had condemned them, would have been inconceivable, even if rumour of conspiracy had reached them.

The terror, or *les effrois* (the term used in contemporary writings), began in the last week of May 1358. The first outbreak, as in the English rising afterwards, was on a small scale, but spread instantly, for others were waiting for a lead. Jean de Venette says: 'The peasants living near Saint-Leu-d'Esséront and Clermont in the diocese of Beauvais, seeing the wrongs and oppression inflicted on them on every side and that the nobles gave them no protection but rather oppressed them as heavily as the enemy, rose and took arms against them. . . . Going forth with their arms and standards, they overran the countryside. They massacred without mercy all the nobles whom they could find, even their own lords. Not only this: they levelled the houses and fortresses of the nobles to the ground and . . . they delivered the noble ladies and their little children . . . to an atrocious death. . . . Those who had begun with a zeal for justice, as it seemed to them, . . . turned to base and execrable deeds. It is said that they subjected noble ladies to their vile lust, slew their innocent little children, as I have said, and carried off such property as they found, wherewith they clothed themselves and their peasant wives luxuriously.'[1]

The French insurgents did not march on the capital as the English were to do, nor demand to see the Regent Charles to lay their grievances before him, as the English peasants pleaded with Richard II. Nor did they seek agrarian reform or formulate revolutionary demands like the English. Their rage was directed against the nobles only. They wanted to be revenged on them, they wanted to humiliate them. They killed them indiscriminately with their families, adding torture and rape to murder, while the English did not molest women and children and limited their killings mostly to persons they specifically proscribed. The French insurgents, like the English, were not all agricultural labourers,

[1] Page 76 of *The Chronicle of Jean de Venette* as translated in op. cit.

but included village craftsmen and market stall-keepers, barrel makers, butchers, sellers of eggs, fowl and cheese; and they were joined by members of the class slightly above them, such as petty clerks and a few country priests. Yet after similarities are allowed for, there was a psychological difference between the two rebellions. The French showed a mad ferocity, a pitiless cruelty. Their mob was a truly diabolical apparition. The English, as we shall see, were bad enough, terrifying enough, fierce enough, but they had some scruples, some restraint, though the unrealized designs of some of their leaders were very bloodthirsty, as we shall see. The fourteenth-century Frenchman considered himself more advanced, more civilized, than the people north of the Channel; from Roman times he had always been a bit ahead. Yet when the peasantry of France ran amok in the Jacquerie, they suddenly became savages.

A description of the terror occurs in Froissart.[1] 'Some of the inhabitants of the country towns collected together at a place in the Beauvais district. At first there were only about a hundred of them. They declared that all the French nobles, knights and squires, shamed and betrayed the realm which would greatly profit by their destruction. . . . Without taking other advice, they gathered into a body, unarmed except for loaded clubs and knives, and went to the house of a knight who lived nearby. They broke into the house, killed the knight, his wife and his children, big and small and set fire to the building. Following this, they went to a castle, where they acted in even a worse fashion. They took the knight and tied him to a stout post, when several of them violated his wife and daughter in his sight. They then killed the lady, who was pregnant, and her daughter and other children, and tortured the knight to death. That done they burnt down the castle. They did the like in several houses and castles, their number having now increased to six thousand. Wherever they went, many of their kind joined them.'

Froissart then describes how the nobles and gentry, taken by surprise as they were and in any case unable to resist so many assailants, fled with their families to places as much as sixty miles away. Meanwhile the insurrection spread with great rapidity over the plains of Beauvais, Soissons and Laon. The insurgents were

[1] His text here derives from Jean le Bel's *Chronique* (edited by J. Viard, in 1904. See vol. II, pp. 256–60). See also Sir Thomas Gray's *Scalacronica*, translated by Sir Henry Maxwell, Edinburgh, 1907 (p. 131).

like 'mad dogs'. They prided themselves on their atrocities. 'I would not dare,' says Froissart, 'to write or speak of the dreadful and revolting things they did to women.' He cites a case, however, as being less horrible, where they killed a knight and after roasting his body on a spit, forced his wife to eat part of it and then, having violated her many times, put her to a cruel death.

Whereas at first the rebels had no leader, they soon appointed a William Câle to be Captain-General. He was also called king; it seems that he had a sort of chancellery and a seal, and had captains under him. He is said to have been a man of superior talent, who understood that the only chance the rebels had was to combine with the Parisians and also avoid further excesses, as their indiscriminate slaughter was alienating Marcel and his supporter, Don Carlos, King of Navarre. But Câle was unable to control his followers or make them see sense. They continued to rage like mad dogs. What programme he had beyond butchering nobles is not on record.

The Dauphin had left Paris about a month before the rising began. He moved with his whole court, including his wife and many ladies of the nobility, to Meaux, a town twenty miles east of the capital, where there was a large castle in an extensive enceinte. It stood in a loop of the Marne, opposite the town which was on the other bank. The Marne enclosed three sides of it and a canal the fourth on the outer side. The Regent had two reasons for going to Meaux: he thought that the court ladies would be safe there from the Parisians; and by occupying Meaux he blocked the Marne, one of the supply routes for Paris, which he planned to starve into submission. But it had a grave disadvantage. The inhabitants of Meaux town were in league with the Parisians. He thought himself strong enough, however, to keep them down.

State business obliged him to tour northwards and he was absent from Meaux when the Jacquerie broke out in May. To guard the ladies he had left only a small garrison under his uncle, the Duke of Orleans, the man who had commanded the second division at Poitiers and fled without striking a blow. Seeing their opportunity, the inhabitants of Meaux wrote urgently to Marcel asking for soldiers to assist them in an attack on the castle. They also sent messengers into the countryside and invited numbers of the insurgents into the town. The ladies, nine hundred of them, were in very grave danger. The garrison was totally inadequate to protect them. Thinking of the appalling fate which during the past fortnight had overtaken the women of rank caught by the rebels, they were terrified. From the battlements they could see across the Marne into the town, where an armed mob was assembling, uttering savage war cries and threatening a brutal vengeance.

At this critical moment, however, help arrived from a most unexpected and astonishing quarter. Two Gascon nobles, the one already very distinguished, the other one of the most curious personalities of the south, suddenly appeared on the scene with a small company of men-at-arms, and were able to cross the canal and enter the castle. The two lords were John de Grailly, Captal of Buch, and his cousin Gaston Phoebus, Count of Foix.

The Captal of Buch (a Seigneurie near Bordeaux and within the English domain) had covered himself with glory, as will be recalled, by his decisive charge on King John's flank and rear at Poitiers. Count Gaston Phoebus, however, was a vassal of King John's. He was related both to the royal house of France and of Navarre. Now twenty-seven, he had, as a boy of fifteen, been present at Crécy. He was tall, well made, had long golden hair. On account of his extraordinary good looks he had been nicknamed Phoebus. Thirty years later Froissart visited his court at Foix, by the Pyrenees, which he declared enthusiastically was all that a court of chivalry should be, though by that time Gaston Phoebus had in fact become odd and sinister, a sort of Borgia, an eccentric who supped between midnight and 2 a.m., and was subject to uncontrollable rages, as when he stabbed to death his only son. But now, coming to the rescue of the Dauphin's young wife and the other noblewomen at Meaux, he was a dashing figure.

How it happened that these two cavaliers were available at Meaux, which is four hundred miles from Buch and Foix, is as curious as anything related of them. The Captal had not gone home after Poitiers to mind his affairs. Nor had he taken advantage of the general anarchy to fill his pockets by joining the English brigand captains who were plundering France. He and Count Phoebus had had quite another idea, something nowadays we would never guess, and which reminds us that, though in the fourteenth century the Middle Ages were giving way to the Renaissance, the change of outlook was only partial. The two gallants had decided that to fill in their time they would go on a crusade, not against the pagans resident outside Europe, the Saracens, but against pagans resident within, no other than the as yet un-Christianized Prussians, who in their northern forests still worshipped Thor and Odin. When no real crusade was on, it had become a vogue for knights errant to lead a company against these savages and kill as many as possible in the name of Christ. From such a crusading expedition the Captal and the Count were returning when at Châlons-sur-Marne they heard of the Jacquerie and of the dreadful peril of the ladies at Meaux. Rescuing titled damsels in distress was the plot of all the medieval romances. The two knights must have thought themselves in luck's way to have such a chance.

On 9 June, the day after Foix and the Captal arrived, the insurgents launched their attack on the castle. There was a bridge over the Marne connecting the town with the castle, and the mob surged across it towards the castle gate. As their numbers, stated to have been 9,000, greatly exceeded the defenders, estimated at 200, the Captal and Foix, fearing that the garrison would be overrun if it remained on the defensive, conceived that their best course lay in a sortie. Their company, all tried soldiers, were well armoured. If they opened the gate and advanced on to the bridge, they could not be surrounded and, fighting face to face against mere peasants on so narrow a front, they should be able to stop them. Accordingly the gate was opened and enough of them sallied out to fill the end of the bridge.

The sequel is well described by Froissart. One catches a glimpse of the Jacques, fresh from a fortnight's butchery of the nobles, a rabble more frightening than truly formidable, for their success so far was due to surprise, overwhelming numbers and the fanaticism of their rush. 'Then the two knights and their company, sword in hand, issued out under the banners of the Count of Foix and the Duke of Orleans and the pennon of the Captal, and took their stand against the villeins, who were black little fellows[1] and poorly armed. When they beheld the compact array of the knights, composed though it was of so few, they became less furiously eager than before and the men in front began to recoil. The gentlemen stepped after them, lancing and striking them down with their swords. Those who felt the blows, or thought to receive them, fell over each other as they drew back. Then the rest of the defenders

[1] The suggestion here is that the peasants were burnt to a dark colour by exposure to the summer sun and were also very dirty. They looked small because they had no armour, and may have become thin and undernourished in the prevailing anarchy.

came out of the gate. After a while they gained the town square and went in among the rebels. They made heaps of them, killing them like beasts, and drove them in disorder out of the town. They continued killing them till they were tired, or forced them to jump into the river. In sum, they killed that day more than seven thousand and in the pursuit none would have escaped if it had been further pressed.'

The court ladies were saved. But now the victors, their blood up, began a general sack of the town. The civil inhabitants were massacred, or flung into the castle dungeons. The mayor was hung. That done the town was set on fire. Their vengeance continuing, they went out to destroy the neighbouring villages. Jean de Venette sums up: 'They went raging through the adjacent countryside . . . and slew miserably all the peasants, not only those whom they believed to have harmed them, but all they found, whether in their houses or digging in the vineyards or in the fields. The misery caused by the nobles reached such a pitch . . . that the English who had been the chief enemies of the realm before, could not have done what they did.'[1]

The main body of the Jacques, under William Câle, was not at Meaux, but at the centre of the insurrection in the Beauvais district fifty miles to the northward. Two or three days before the massacre at Meaux, Câle learned that an army led by King Carlos of Navarre was coming against him. The Jacques had believed that they could count on Carlos. Was he not in league with Marcel and the Parisians? He had professed open sympathy for the suffering people. But in fact his actions were wholly governed by his ambition to become King of France. Marcel was an embarrassment for the Regent Charles, as were the Jacques, and both had therefore their uses for him. But he could not obtain the crown unless supported by a majority of the nobles. The surest way to win their support would be for him to destroy the Jacques. On reflection, he perceived that his first impulse towards the insurgents had been a mistake. He resolved to rectify this and, by crushing them, both to win the thanks of the nobles and demonstrate that he was capable of what the Regent was incompetent.

He had come firmly to this view after receiving a deputation from the gentry of Normandy and Picardy, who now, after a fortnight of terror and outrage, were trying to assemble a force able to defeat the Jacques. Carlos had the nucleus of such a force, for he

[1] *The Chronicle of Jean de Venette*, op. cit., pp. 77, 78.

was equipped much like the captain of a Free Company. The deputation asked for his help. Their retainers would join his and under his able leadership suffice to restore order. 'You are the leading gentleman in the world,' they told him. 'If this mob of Jacques hold the field much longer and the townsmen come to their aid, gentlemen and all they stand for will cease to be.'[1]

Navarre agreed and leaving his castle at Longueville in Normandy, set out to march on William Câle, who was encamped at Clermont, near Beauvais. *En route* he increased his own retinue of 400 lances to 1,000 lances by reinforcements from the gentry and the brigands. A third of his army was composed of English Companions under a captain called Robert Sercot.

When Câle heard that the King of Navarre was coming at him with an army of experienced fighting men, he advised a withdrawal to Paris and junction with Marcel's forces there. Though it was before the rout at Meaux, he knew well enough that to defeat Carlos's army would be no light task. His followers, however, with the confidence bred of a fortnight's uninterrupted victory over the nobles, whose clothes they were wearing, at whose tables they had gorged themselves, and whose wives and daughters they had either killed or dragged along with them, refused to take their leader's prudent counsel and shouted: 'We will not withdraw an inch. We are quite strong enough to fight the gentlemen.' They numbered at the moment about 4,500, cavalry, footmen and crossbowmen. Unable to win his point, Câle chose as strong a position as he could find and drew up his men in a semblance of the military formation of the period—two battles, bowmen in front and cavalry protecting the wings. In this he had the expert advice of a Knight Hospitaller who had joined him.

What Carlos had learned of the Jacques had not prepared him for the sight of their array. His 1,000 lances probably represented considerably more than a thousand men, for a lance was a term which meant a knight and one or two followers. Whatever exactly may have been his numbers, the 4,500 Jacques gave him pause. It was evident that they were far from being intimidated by his troops. He could hear fanfares and martial music. And their banners were flying, embroidered with fleurs-de-lis, as if they represented the French nation.

Before risking an engagement he resolved to try a stratagem.

[1] For this quotation and the whole episode see *Chroniques des Quatres Premiers Valois*, ed. Siméon Luce (Paris, 1862), pp. 71–7.

He asked for an armistice and invited William Câle to a conference. The invitation was worded so cleverly and presented with such grace, that Câle thought the King of Navarre intended to treat with him as an equal and, pleased, was put off his guard. He accepted, without demanding hostages. His neglect to do so suggests, that in spite of his first inclination to ask support from Marcel, he had lost touch with reality. The peasants had elected him king. The terrible vengeance he had taken on the nobility had given him a sense of intoxicating power. It was not simplicity which prevented him asking for hostages, but conceit born of his sudden rise. The invitation confirmed his belief that he was a real king, the equal of Carlos of Navarre. Two kings were to confer. He was covered by all the punctilios of such a colloquy. He entered Navarre's camp along with his chief captains without a suspicion that he was going straight to his death.

During the parley which ensued he and his staff were seized. Carlos then immediately opened the battle. The peasant army, awaiting the return of its leader, was taken by surprise. Without him and its principal officers it was lost. Robert Sercot struck at a flank and threw it into confusion. The cavalry made a frontal charge and the rout began. As at Meaux, it was a massacre. William Câle was taken into Clermont and, after being crowned in derision with a red-hot tripod, it is said, had his head struck off. The rebellion was at an end. It had only lasted a fortnight.

A general round up of the Jacques followed. It was the nobles who now ran amok. The peasantry of the disaffected areas, whether in arms or not, were ruthlessly killed. 'One saw the nobles and gentlemen rushing on the hamlets and country villages to set them on fire and pursue through the houses, through the fields, through the vineyards and woods the poor peasants, who were miserably butchered. The memory of these bloody executions still causes the inhabitants to weep.'[1]

The chroniclers compute that twenty thousand peasants were hanged or put to the sword. These executions were not carried out according to law. No special judges were appointed to try the Jacques. In this, as we shall see, things were different in England. In August the Regent Charles was able to intervene; charters of indemnity were issued to protect those who might be accused of having committed crimes, whether nobles or peasants. But great damage had been done. By their indiscriminate vengeance,

[1] *Chronicon G. de Nangis, Continuatio* (ed. H. Géraud, Paris, 1843).

without process of law, the nobles increased the anarchy which was tearing the country to pieces. Acting on the belief that harsh treatment was what peasants best understood, the French parliament, far from compensating the dependants of those who had been illegally put to death, imposed vindictive taxes on the remainder. There followed an emigration *en masse* from the Beauvaisis into the neighbouring duchy of Burgundy and the lapse into fallow of large areas of crop land. It is a paradoxical reflection that this peasantry, treated with such cruelty and contempt, was seventy years later to save France and put her on the road to modern nationhood. From a small country village, the house of a small farmer, there came forth a little peasant maid, Jeanne d'Arc.

The English Dominion

While France was suffering in this way, King Edward and his prisoner, King John, discussed in London terms of peace. Though the two kings had become friends, personal feelings were not allowed to interfere with business. The terms parliament insisted on were very stiff, though not quite so stiff as those put forward in 1353–4 and which the French had then rejected. The main demand was for the cession of as much of south-western France as Richard Coeur de Lion had ever held as a duchy. The area, roughly as large as England, was not however, to be a duchy, but an overseas part of the realm of England, an English dominion cut out of France. The former French overlordship would cease. No homage need be paid. The King of England's sovereignty there would be absolute.

The English had never had a dominion in France, as the wide possessions there of the Norman and Angevin kings had been acquired, not by conquest, but by marriage and inheritance, and were French feudal estates. The demand now was that these feudal territories should become ceded territories. The English sought an empire in France, as they were afterwards to seek it in other parts of the globe. In return Edward would abandon his claim to the French throne. There would be peace. He would never invade France again.

King John agreed. To have refused would have exposed his

people to further suffering, perhaps ruin. The English had no legal right to Aquitaine in absolute sovereignty. Might was their only right. But, defeated and captive, he had to bow to it. A treaty ceding the territories was signed by him in London in March 1359. In May, however, the French parliament refused to ratify it. The Regent Charles and his government had grown somewhat stronger. Marcel had fortunately been murdered the previous year and the Parisians, abandoning their opposition, had invited the court back to the Louvre and withdrawn support from the King of Navarre. Charles, remarkably wise for his age, was beginning to unite the nation. Encouraged by the monarchy's increasing prestige, the magnates found the nerve to refuse ratification.

This was a severe blow for Edward. But it was his own fault. He had thrown away his chance after Poitiers of striking France a mortal blow. He had given the French three years to recover. He had erroneously believed that he could obtain his ends by negotiation. Now he would have to do what he should have done in 1356. But it would be more difficult, since the French government was no longer in such straits.

With remarkable energy he assembled at Calais that autumn a larger army than he had at Crécy or his son at Poitiers. The chronicler Le Bel alleges that he had 10,000 archers and 6,000 men-at-arms. He took command himself. With him were the Black Prince and the old crowd of veteran lords, Warwick, Northampton, Salisbury, Stafford, Sir John Chandos and the Captal de Buch. John of Gaunt, the Prince's brother, makes his first appearance in this campaign. He was nineteen years of age. Chaucer, aged eighteen, was also in the party, in the capacity of page in the royal retinue.

Edward's plan was to take Rheims, in whose cathedral the kings of France were crowned, and induce its archbishop to crown him. Then he would advance on Paris. It was a wild idea, could never have worked; and broke down at once for he failed to take Rheims. It was too strong a fortified city. Foiled in this, he marched before the spring of 1360 to Paris and appeared before the walls. Throughout the winter months the Dauphin had not attacked.

Edward found that Paris was as impossible to take as Rheims. All he could do was to ravage the neighbourhood. In April he turned south-west towards Chartres, continuing his depredations. He was disappointed. Nothing decisive had been effected. The

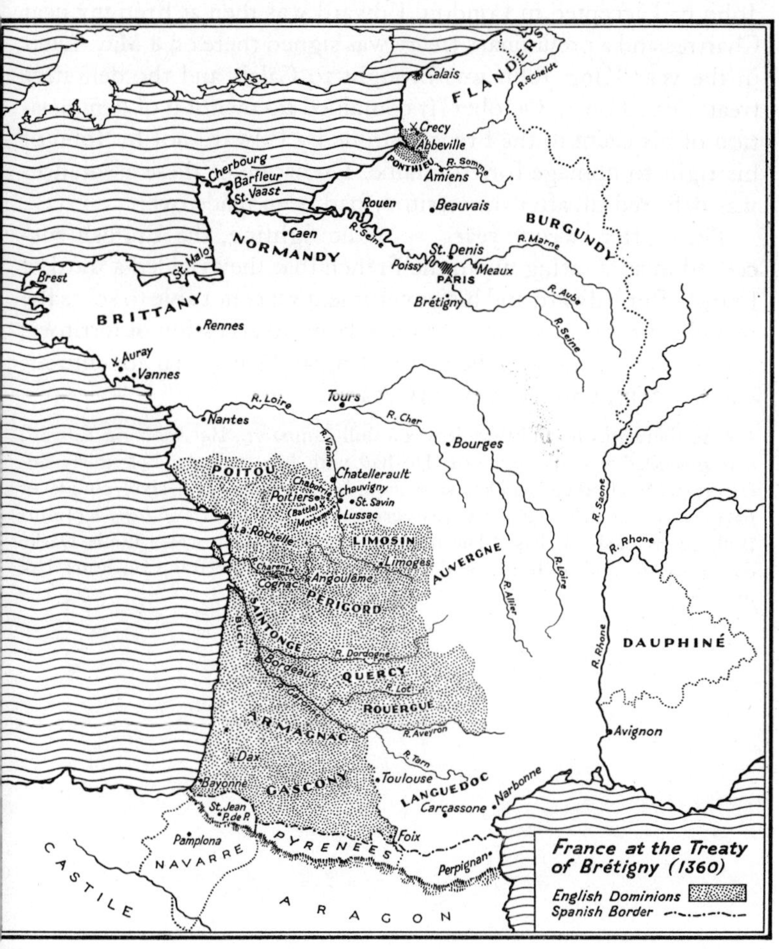

France at the Treaty of Brétigny (1360)

campaign was only another raid.[1] Then unexpectedly French nerve gave way. The long strain had proved too much. The Dauphin sent envoys offering to accept the terms which King John had accepted in London. Edward was then at Brétigny near Chartres and a preliminary treaty was signed there on 8 May. Later in the year King John was brought to Calais and the definitive treaty sealed on 24 October. It contained no mention of denunciation of his claim to the French throne by Edward nor by John of his right to homage for Aquitaine. Exchange of these assurances was deferred till after the territory had been made over.

Thus, after twenty years' sporadic fighting, the English succeeded in so wearing down the French that they yielded a third of France. But Edward and his government were not able to solve the complex problems arising out of so large an accession of territory, and the new dominion, the first of England's imperial adventures, was lost within the next twenty years.

[1] As there was no fighting, it was a dull campaign. But sporting Edward was provided with distractions. He had with him, says Le Bel, thirty falconers with all their hawks, sixty couple of hounds and sixty couple of harriers. The weather at Paris was very bad. The *Chronicle of London* (Julius Bull, ed. Kingsford) has: 'The morwe after Ester Day was a ffoule Derke day of myste, and off haylle, and so bytter colde, that syttyng on horse bak men dyed.'

3. Tomb Effigy of the Black Prince

4. Men-at-arms in combat

The Black Prince as Prince of Aquitaine

After the signature of the treaty King John was allowed to return to France on his leaving sureties, including Louis his second son, for the payment of the ransom by instalments. His stay in England had not been without its compensations. By being out of France for four years he had escaped a very trying time, of which his son had had to bear the brunt. Taking charge again now of a country still suffering the misery of disorder was hardly an agreeable prospect. The French received him back with respect and hoped for better times. He received many congratulations on his safe return, including a visit from Petrarch, who came as an envoy of the Visconti of Milan. In one of his letters written after the visit, Petrarch has this illuminating reference to the state of France and the reputation of the English: 'In my youth the Britons, whom we call Angles or English, had the reputation of being the most timid of the barbarians. Now they are the most warlike of peoples. They have overturned the ancient military glory of the French by a series of victories so numerous and unexpected that those, who were not long since inferior to the wretched Scots, have so crushed by fire and sword the whole realm that, on a recent journey, I could hardly persuade myself that it was the France that I had seen in former years.'[1]

[1] Epistolae Familiares III, Ep. 14, p. 162, edition Fracasetti, cited in translation by T. F. Tout, in his *History of England from Henry III to Edward III*, p. 402.

Petrarch was fifty-six years of age at this time. As a poet and a man-of-letters he occupied a position without parallel for such nowadays. At the age of thirty-seven he had been crowned on the Capitol at Rome as the poet laureate of all that part. Using the words of Virgil as his text—'But love of sweet Parnassus led me through hard and deserted ways'—he made a Latin oration which has sometimes been described as the opening of the Renaissance. It is good for us to see ourselves through the eyes of the trecento poet, northern barbarians hitherto innocuous who had gone on the warpath and ravaged the rich and noble realm of Gaul. But his lofty contempt (though combined with a sneaking admiration for our military science, whose longbow was a novelty which Italy had not thought of) is not so much our concern here as the fact that he represented the Renaissance, a body of disturbing ideas. Our victories and adventures overseas were the way we educated ourselves at this moment of European ferment.

Since May 1357 the Black Prince had been enjoying himself in England, hunting, breeding war horses and galloping in the lists. Soon after the Treaty of Brétigny Edward decided to make him viceroy of the ceded territories, with the title of Prince of Aquitaine. Before leaving for his capital, Bordeaux, he fell in love with Joan, daughter of his kinsman the Earl of Kent. She was thirty-two, two years older than he. Known afterwards as the Fair Maid of Kent, her career had been romantic. At the age of eleven she had married Sir Thomas Holland, then aged nineteen. Two years later, 1341, she married William de Montagu, Earl of Salisbury, during Holland's absence in Prussia. The Earl was only thirteen, her age. How this second marriage could have taken place, with Holland alive, has not been explained. It looks as if the Salisbury family exercised some undue influence or force. Joan remained married to the Earl of Salisbury for eight years.[1] In 1349 Holland appealed to the Pope to restore her to him. The Pope held the first marriage valid and restored her. By that time she was twenty-one and Holland was twenty-nine. She had two sons by him, Thomas and John, both of whom appear in this story. In 1352 her father died and she became Countess of Kent in her own right, and one of the richest heiresses in England. Her husband, Holland, died in 1360, and in October 1361 the Black Prince, the great military hero of the day, secretly married her. King Edward was not told and, when he learnt, was so annoyed that he did not attend the

[1] See *The Complete Peerage*, vol. xi, pp. 388–90.

public solemnization of the marriage at Windsor three or four months later. A papal dispensation was necessary as they were cousins within the prohibited degrees. This, then, was Joan's third spectacular love affair. She is described by Froissart as being 'en son temps la plus belle de tout la roiaulme d'Engleterre et la plus amoureuse,' and by the Chandos Herald as:

> *Une dame de grant pris,*
> *Qu bele fuist, plesante et sage.*[1]

She accompanied the Black Prince when in July 1363 he left for Aquitaine to take up his viceregal duties.[2]

We have some idea of the Prince's appearance. His recumbent effigy over his tomb in Canterbury Cathedral, one of the most exquisite medieval bronzes in existence, shows him as he must have looked at Poitiers, his basinet circled by a coronet, his plate armour covered with a surcoat embroidered with leopards and fleurs-de-lis, and wearing gauntlets with knuckle-dusters. He appears extremely elegant, a slim, strong man; but his face, despite the neat way his moustache trails over his aventail, is formidable, particularly the mouth.[3] He is very handsome. He and his wife Joan, the renowned beauty, made an arresting pair.

The court they established at Bordeaux was brilliant, and was intended to dazzle and please the lords of Aquitaine. Some of these, of course, had long been vassals of the English crown, such as the Captal de Buch, but the Treaty of Brétigny had obliged others, hitherto vassals of the French crown, to transfer their allegiance to Edward. The most important of these were Comte Jean d'Armagnac, the man who commanded the French forces in 1355 during the Black Prince's raid to Narbonne; Gaston Phoebus of Foix, the saviour of the ladies at Meaux; and the Sire d'Albret and Roger Comte de Périgord. There was also Guichard d'Angle who, unlike the others, became a permanent friend of the English and ended

[1] The Chandos Herald's life of the Black Prince, line 1587.

[2] Thomas (born 1350), the elder of her two sons by Holland, joined her and his stepfather in Aquitaine, and in 1366, aged sixteen, was captain of an English company there. Salisbury, however, her former lover, who had returned to England after Poitiers, where, as will be remembered, he commanded the rearguard, remained at home as a member of Edward III's council.

[3] The face is certainly a likeness. The Prince ordered his tomb before he died. An effigy, which was not a good likeness, would not have been accepted.

his career as Earl of Huntingdon. The Black Prince and his wife strove to win the regard of these magnates and their fellows by lavish hospitality. The Chandos Herald[1] thus describes the Prince's table: 'Since the birth of God such fair state was never kept as his, nor more honourable, for ever he had at his table more than fourscore knights, and full four times as many squires. There were held jousts and feasts in Angoulême and Bordeaux.' The author of the *Anonimalle Chronicle* puts it more bluntly: 'The Prince of Wales ran his household in such grand style and was so outrageously extravagant that no king on earth could have afforded it. To pay for it he exacted grievous ransoms and taxes on the country round about.'[2]

Though the Prince had not so easy and pleasant a manner as his father, King Edward (the *Anonimalle* declares he was 'si hauteyn et de si graunt port' that he kept suitors waiting unduly and obliged them to kneel too long when he did receive them), he had qualities to make him popular with Gascon nobles. His chief interests, besides fighting, were clothes, jewels[3] and horses. Fond of cards, he gambled heavily. His tastes were expensive, but in no way eccentric, as were those of Gaston Phoebus, an intellectual and patron of the arts, altogether very different from the Prince who, in many ways a plain man, had no interest in literature, though he could read and write. It was as a military figure that the Gascons especially admired him. His reputation as a commander of troops in the field was unrivalled in Europe.

Beyond his retinue, however, he now maintained very small forces, since peace reigned between France and England. Yet it cannot be said that the French scene was altogether peaceful. Mention has been made further back of fighting in Brittany to decide the succession to that dukedom. It had been going on all these years. Charles de Blois, the contestant sponsored by the French, was still striving to win the whole province. His rival Jean de

[1] Very little is known about Sir John Chandos's herald. He entered on his duties with Chandos in 1360. Later in life (1382) he became the Ireland King-at-Arms. Some authorities believe that he was a Breton and that his name was Guyon.

[2] The Chronicler is referring to the hearth taxes of 1364, 1365 and 1367, granted by the Aquitaine parliament, the Three Estates, but collected with difficulty as they were considered oppressive by the people.

[3] One of his rubies, still called the Black Prince's ruby, is in the imperial crown of England. See further details in an article by Peter Shaw in *History* (June 1939).

Montfort, had died in 1345, but his son of the same name carried on the contest with English support. At this time, 1363/64, the struggle entered upon its last phase and involved personalities important in this narrative. One of these was Bertrand du Guesclin, a Breton of about forty. He had made a name as far back as 1338, when at a tournament held at Rennes, to celebrate the marriage of Charles de Blois, he, though under twenty, had unseated all competitors. Thereafter he had fought on de Blois' side. He was a man so ugly as to be displeasing and could neither read nor write, but his ability was very great. Like the captains of Free Companies, of whom he was an early example, he had a band of adventurers of his own. The Breton war had many ups and downs. After Poitiers, when the Free Companies began to develop, du Guesclin came to blows with the formidable Sir Robert Knollys, was worsted, captured and ransomed. Though employed by France, at this time he was not bound to render military services like a noble, but rather was a condottiere, as, indeed, will be seen to have been all the semi-brigand captains of Free Companies.[1] In May 1364, six months after the arrival of the Prince in Aquitaine, he defeated at Cocherel a de Montfort army composed, like his own, of mercenaries belonging to the Free Companies and led by no less a person than the Captal of Buch, whom he captured. For this victory the French king made him Marshal of Normandy and Count of Longueville. As peace had been signed with France, the Black Prince was not officially concerned with the Breton campaign nor the capture therein of the most distinguished of his Gascon vassals. Nevertheless, he ransomed the Captal and sent his Constable, Sir John Chandos, in support of de Montfort. Chandos, as a reward for his services at the battle of Poitiers, had been given the magnificent castle of St. Sauveur-le-Vicomte in the Côtentin, which carried the title of Vicomte. He met du Guesclin and de Blois at Auray on 29 September 1364. As half the French force was composed of free companies, and four-fifths of the English, Auray

[1] That Knollys, Calveley, Bertucat d'Albret and the rest were veritable condottieri of the period is well illustrated by the career of Sir John Hawkwood, son of a tanner of Hedingham Sibil, Essex, who after Poitiers, instead of leading his band, called the White Company, to rob France, led them to Italy where he sold his services to warring dukes, now of Pisa, now Milan or Florence. He eventually became the most redoubtable Italian condottiere of the trecento. He married one of the Visconti of Milan. Paolo Uccello painted the posthumous portrait of him now in the Florence duomo. One of his daughters married a John Shelley, ancestor of the poet.

may be described as a condottiere's battle. Du Guesclin was defeated, captured, and later ransomed by the French king; de Blois was slain.[1]

Auray ended the war of the Breton succession. The English nominee, de Montfort, had won. But du Guesclin, though twice captured, had emerged as a military figure. Despite his somewhat chequered start, he was to become the greatest French captain of the age. The contest was to be between him and the Prince. In the end du Guesclin won. He began and continued as a leader of mercenaries, who accomplished what the French feudal army could not do. The Prince, at first the commander of an army raised in England, also tended to become a leader of mercenaries. It is a startling fact that he, Prince of Wales, heir to the English throne, model of chivalry, was also a condottiere. Not only did he grow to depend largely on men hired from the Free Companies, but like all condottieri he sold his services to other princes. As he became more of a condottiere, he became less sensitive as a statesman. His prime duty as Prince of Aquitaine was to be an administrator and diplomatist in the service of England. But like a condottiere he also sought to win for himself titles and rewards, not always strictly compatible with national policy and interests.

Before describing how this metamorphosis came about, which had such fateful results for England, we must note King John of France's death, an event of the greatest importance, for his successor, the Dauphin Charles, a much abler man, came to the throne resolved to retrieve France's misfortunes. The story of John's last days is so characteristic of the charming side of chivalry that, enjoying the exquisite sentiments we forget for a moment the plain truth of France's dreadful plight—a third of her territory gone and much of the rest overrun by the ferocious mercenaries of the Free Companies.

King John, when allowed to return to France after the ratification of the treaty of Brétigny, made his second son, Louis, as has been stated, his principal hostage for the ransom. At the end of 1363 Louis broke his parole and escaped to Guise. Since he refused to return, though told to do so by his father, the King felt that as a

[1] It is interesting to know that Charles de Blois had an extraordinary reputation for piety and was believed to have performed miracles. After his death he was declared a saint and canonized by the church. It is details of this sort which illuminate an age and prevent us from forming too narrow a

man of honour he had no option but to surrender himself again as a prisoner to Edward. His council of nobles sought to dissuade him, but he insisted on going to England. So over-punctilious did his behaviour appear that some of his lords could not believe him sincere. Jean de Venette[1] declares that they reproached him with enjoying English life so much that he was glad of an excuse to visit his friend Edward again. He landed at Dover on 3 January 1364, and next day rode to Canterbury where he offered a jewel at St. Thomas à Becket's tomb, at that time more splendid than even St. Edward the Confessor's at Westminster, and a greater place of pilgrimage. Edward was waiting to welcome him at his manor at Eltham farther up the Canterbury–London road. On his arrival there, says Froissart, John was greeted with 'great dancing and carolling'. Thence he went on to London with Edward. 'He was brought with great mynstrelsie through London to his lodgynge to Savoy. . . . And oftentymes the kynge of Englande and his children visited hym . . . and they made great feastes together, in dyvers suppers . . . and when it pleased the Frenche kyng he went to the kynges palaice of Westminster, secretly by the ryver Temes.' His presence in London made a profound impression on all classes. Such a display of chivalric behaviour was very much admired. But he fell ill very soon. By March 'he lay sore sicke at his lodgyng at the Savoy and every daye he enpayred worse and worse, the which greatly displeased the kynge of Englande.' He died on 8 April. Before his death he bequeathed his bowels to St. Paul's, his heart to Canterbury and his body to St. Denis in Paris. A sumptuous funeral was held at each of these places. At St. Paul's there were 'horses caparisoned from head to foot with the arms and lilies of France . . . and eighty great lights each twelve feet high and 4000 wax tapers.' After the second funeral at Canterbury 'the English escorted the King's body to the shores of the sea . . . and from there returned with tears, it is said.'[2]

The late Dauphin, now Charles V, immediately wrote a letter of thanks to Edward:

'Dearly beloved brother, our cousins the counts of Eu and of Tancarville,[3] and other members of the council of our dear lord

[1] *The Chronicles of Jean de Venette*, p. 116 in the edition cited.

[2] Jean de Venette, op cit., p. 120.

[3] Jean d'Artois, Comte d'Eu and Jean de Melun, Comte de Tancarville, after capture at Poitiers, remained in England till 1360. They were both in London in 1364 on business connected with the royal ransom.

and father, God rest his soul, who have been in his company in your kingdom, have made report how graciously and with what good cheer you received our dear lord and father again in your kingdom, and of the very good company with which you entertained him while he lived, and of the great diligence you showed for his health and your efforts to cure him in his illness, and of the great pomp you made for his obsequies by gathering together our dear nephews your sons and others of your blood royal, and prelates and other magnates of your kingdom, and by many other arrangements, and of the magnificent procession made for the departure of his remains from London. From these things we are made to understand clearly the great affection you bore towards our lord in his lifetime, and we thank you to the fullest extent of our ability and will always hold ourselves beholden to do anything we can for your honour and pleasure.'[1]

[1] Quoted on p. 291 of the cited edition of Jean de Venette. Charles, of course, had not the smallest intention of doing anything for Edward's honour and pleasure beyond conforming to the rules of chivalry. Edward was his mortal enemy and he intended to oust him from France if he could.

The Prince's Adventure in Spain[1]

As his father's representative in Aquitaine, the Prince had the duty of being *au fait* with Spanish affairs, no simple task since it involved a study of the interrelations of the five distinct kingdoms in the peninsula. Portugal was in its present position on the west, Aragon of about equal extent on the Mediterranean coast; the Moorish state of Granada lay near Gibraltar, Navarre on the Pyrenees; and Castile, by far the largest state, stretched down the centre from the Bay of Biscay to the Guadalquivir. The rivalries and ambitions of these states made so complicated a tangle as hardly to be unravelled, but one fact stood out clearly: both France and England needed alliance with Castile. Alliance was not desired for military reasons, for Castile's army was old-fashioned and unsuited for fighting outside Spain, but because of the Castilian fleet, which was exceptionally good. If England had it on her side, her command of the Channel and her communications with Aquitaine were assured; but should it be with France, both would be imperilled, if war broke out again, a contingency which the harshness of the terms imposed at Brétigny made not improbable.

[1] Professor P. F. Russell's *The English Intervention in Spain and Portugal in the time of Edward III and Richard II* (Oxford, 1955), is a book of capital importance for students. Resting as it does on an exhaustive examination of Spanish sources, particularly the Aragonese archives, hitherto unexplored, it throws a completely new light on many points in the Black Prince's career. I am greatly indebted to Professor Russell without whose guidance this chapter and those which follow on Spanish affairs would have been very inadequate.

The Prince was well aware of this. When he was a child in 1338 Castilian ships had joined the French fleet in the Channel and did much damage to English ports on the south coast. In 1342 Henry of Lancaster and Salisbury, the father of the Earl now with him, went on a mission to Castile to explore the possibility of a settlement and an alliance; and in 1348, two years after Crécy, his sister, Joan of the Tower, was sent to marry Don Pedro, the Castilian King, but died of plague at Bordeaux on her way there. The French had then stepped in again and Don Pedro married the French Princess, Blanche of Bourbon. The Spanish fleet reappeared in the Channel and damaged English merchant shipping. In 1350, however, it was defeated off Winchelsea.[1] Blanche of Bourbon died in 1361, allegedly murdered by her husband in order to rid himself of French interference. A breach with France was the result. To protect himself against what the French might do, Pedro turned to Edward. In 1362, while the Prince was in London, an alliance between England and Castile was solemnly concluded in St. Paul's. Edward undertook to help Pedro, if he were attacked, provided that, should necessity arise, he would range his fleet with England's. It was not, however, until September 1364, a year after the Prince's arrival in Aquitaine, that the Castilian parliament ratified the treaty. The delay is attributed to the reason that some magnates, ill disposed to Don Pedro, did not want to break with France.

But the French had ready to hand an instrument to further their Spanish ambitions in the person of Pedro's half brother, Henry of Trastamare, his father's eldest illegitimate son. This man, supported by a section of the magnates, was aiming at the throne. In 1361, at the time of Blanche of Bourbon's death, Henry was in France and took the opportunity of asking King John, just returned from his captivity in England, to help him to displace his half brother. The request found favour. To put Don Henry in Don Pedro's place would restore French influence in that region. Pedro's alliance soon afterwards with King Edward added urgency to what in principle was sound policy. When it was suggested that the Free Companies, now looting France, might be hired to set up Henry, a Spanish expedition was seen as a practical possibility. The mercenaries, combined and well led, would be a force stronger

[1] An occasion of which the Prince must have had vivid memories, for he commanded a ship in the battle and had, according to Froissart, a narrow escape from drowning when his ship foundered.

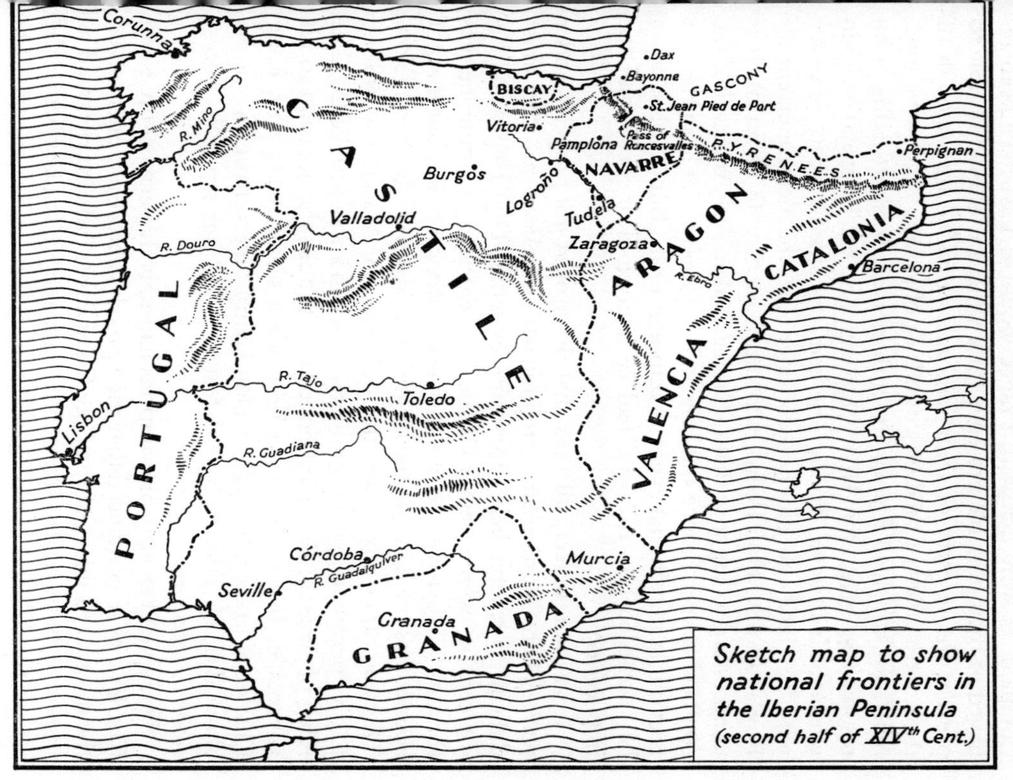

Sketch map to show national frontiers in the Iberian Peninsula (second half of XIVth Cent.)

than Pedro's medieval array. To deflect them from France to Spain and use them there to advance French interests, would in one stroke serve two purposes. Even if the expedition failed and the Companions were defeated, France would at least have been relieved of their horrible presence for a while and should be able to prevent the re-entry of their remnant, provided that enough of them were killed or died of wounds or of sickness and privations, reliefs for which all France fervently prayed. In short, King John resolved to give Don Henry his support, for he stood to gain whatever happened. Though he had concluded a treaty of peace with England, he did not consider that the dethronement of England's ally, Don Pedro, was inconsistent with its terms. It is unnecessary to suppose that he anticipated an early renewal of the conflict between France and England, or foresaw that Don Henry's fleet might play in that event an important role. But Charles, when he succeeded him in 1364, had certainly a clear idea of all the implications.

It was not, in fact, till 1365 that the project got properly under way. There were many preliminary complications, the most difficult to resolve being the route by which Don Henry and his mercenaries were to enter Castile. The entry from Aquitaine was through Navarre by the famous pass of Roncesvalles, but that, of course, was ruled out, as the English would never give permission. The only other way in was through Aragon. Aragon was willing to give permission, having suffered much in a war with Pedro. The King of Aragon, En Pere,[1] hoped also to turn the occasion to his advantage. In October 1364 he made a secret treaty with King Charles of France. Passage of Don Henry's mercenaries would be allowed if, on Don Pedro's defeat, Aragon was repaid by accessions of territory.

By September 1365 preparations had actively been begun. King Charles was so convinced that the Spanish venture not only solved the internal problem of the Free Companies, hitherto regarded as insoluble, but was also an essential strategic preliminary before the war with England could be re-opened, that he had engaged Du Guesclin, the best man he had, to muster the Companies and command them for Don Henry. Du Guesclin, well acquainted with the mercenary bands and their leaders, successfully carried out his

[1] En Pere is the Catalan for Don Pedro, and, to avoid confusion with Don Pedro of Castile, the form will be used here. Catalan, moreover, was the official language of Aragon.

instructions. During December 1365 he assembled, it is said, no less than 10,000 men at Montpellier, a formidable army of veterans in plate armour, greatly superior to Don Pedro's army, which, lacking experience of war as it had been practised since Crécy, was little better equipped than the crusadering armies of past centuries. The mercenaries were men of various nationalities, English and Gascon as well as French and Flemish, but it does not appear that English archers were included. The second in command was Marshal d'Audrehem, who had led the French mounted knights in their opening charge at Poitiers. Third in command was the English condottiere, Sir Hugh Calveley, said to have been Sir Robert Knolly's half-brother. Another English knight was Sir Matthew Gournay,[1] a veteran of fifty-six, who had fought at Sluys, Crécy, Poitiers and Auray, and was so prominent a figure of his day that he had been selected to sign as a witness the document of the Peace of Brétigny.

The Black Prince, though informed of these happenings, and, as has been explained, fully conversant with the history of Castilian relations and the necessity of keeping Pedro on his throne, was not roused to take action. He made no move to help England's threatened ally. The English captains of companies and their men were not forbidden by him to join the French expedition, whose significance seemed to be hidden from him at first. Nor did he receive guidance from his father. When Don Pedro, aware of the coming invasion, made representations in London, all Edward did was to write asking the Prince to forbid Englishmen and Gascon vassals to join du Guesclin, an order which came too late to be effective. No attempt, in short, was made to prevent Charles, king of a nation so lately defeated and forced to agree to a crippling peace treaty, from laying the strategic foundations for a French military recovery. So strong did Charles feel, that he no longer thought it necessary to handle En Pere with the discretion he had used hitherto, and flatly informed him that he would have to pay the mercenaries £50,000 or they would plunder his country.

One asks why the Prince was so supine. Was there a reason besides inability to understand the issues at stake? It has been suggested that he was so shocked by Don Pedro's alleged murder of his wife, and other allegations against his character, that he held

[1] He was the son of Thomas Gournay, one of the murderers of Edward II, and lived to be ninety-six, a great age for any period and extraordinary for a soldier in the fourteenth century.

him unworthy of support. But this seems incredible in view of the support he gave him later. If there is any reason to excuse his neutrality, it must be that he was taken unawares and was without troops or money.

Du Guesclin and his army left Montpellier in December 1365 and, marching via Toulouse and Carcassonne, crossed the Pyrenees by the low pass south of Perpignan, which now takes the main road to Barcelona. They reached Barcelona on 1 January 1366. En Pere gave a banquet in honour of the leaders. Du Guesclin and Calveley sat at the royal table. The former was created a count and the latter a baron with a life pension of 2,000 gold florins. The mercenaries, true to form, behaved like robbers. They looted at will, and though they were given the agreed £50,000, demanded more and had to be paid. Needless to say, they were not interested in the cause; they had come to make money.

The march on Burgos, capital of Castile, began. The route was up the Ebro valley to Logroño. This involved crossing the Tudela salient, a bit of Navarre south of the Ebro. We last saw King Carlos of Navarre as a Norman baron with pretensions to the French crown. King Charles had succeeded in ousting him from France, and he was back in Navarre at his capital of Pamplona. The French expedition posed for him a delicate problem. If he sided with Henry of Trastamare and his colleagues, he was afraid that his neighbour, the Black Prince, might march on him through Roncesvalles (though in fact this fear was, for the moment, illusory, as we know). If he did not favour the invaders, he ran the risk that they would ravage his kingdom or even seize it and present it to En Pere. The second danger seemed the greater, and on receiving a payment of 30,000 florins from the invaders, he opened the route through the Tudela salient, resolving, however, to change sides as often as that should be necessary in his own interests. This policy of dodging blows by deserting each side in turn he followed persistently and in history has the reputation of the greatest turncoat on record.

Du Guesclin's men-at-arms rode quickly towards their goal three hundred miles west. King Charles had thought it worthwhile to put out the canard that their objective was not Pedro but the Moors and that, as Froissart has it, they 'had enterprised by great devotion to go into the realm of Granada, to revenge the death and passion of Our Lord Jesu Christ, and to destroy the jnfidels'. But the Companions were such notorious ruffians that no one can have believed a story that turned them into pilgrims of God. 'When King Dampeter heard the tidings he did nothing but laugh,' says Froissart. But he was not laughing now. He did not expect that the attack would come via the Ebro and had disposed his forces farther south. Du Guesclin found no army to oppose him. As his mercenaries neared Burgos, Don Pedro fled south. Don Henry, proclaimed king of Castile *en route*, entered the capital on 28 March. He was crowned in the cathedral next day. Du Guesclin was made a duke.

Don Pedro in his flight reached Seville in the far south, where he had stored his personal fortune of jewels. Safe for the moment, he was in danger, if he stayed, of being handed over to Don Henry, to whom the magnates were hastening to pay homage. It was time to pack his valuables and go. Accordingly, at the end of May he crossed into Portugal, accompanied by his three daughters, Beatrice aged thirteen, Constance twelve, and Isabella eleven.[1] As the King of Portugal was embarrassed by his presence, he re-entered Castile a month later and went to the port of Coruña, whereabouts the magnates were loyal to him.

The sudden and overwhelming victory of the French cause in Castile awoke the Black Prince to a clearer view of the situation. A rumour reached En Pere of Aragon as early as May that he was mustering troops to oppose the usurper. Don Pedro learned of this favourable turn in Coruña in July and wrote asking for permission to come to Aquitaine. The Prince replied by sending Lord Poynings with an invitation and a promise of help. Pedro and his daughters took ship and arrived at Bayonne on 1 August 1366.

Froissart, despite his inaccuracies and his refusal to recognize any motives but the chivalric, has certain passages here which help to create the picture. One of Don Pedro's knights at Coruña, in urging his master to appeal to the Prince is made to say: 'The Prince of Wales, when he knows of your trouble, will I am sure have compassion. And if he will aid to set you again in your realm, there is none in all the world who can do it so well, for he is

[1] These girls were not daughters of Blanche of Bourbon, but of María de Padilla, a woman often said to have been Don Pedro's mistress, and with whom he lived during the time he was married to Blanche. But it is now thought he may have been secretly married to her before he married Blanche. The girls were not held to be illegitimate and were recognized by the Castilian parliament as heirs to the throne.

feared, redoubted and beloved by all men of war.' There is truth in this, though far from the whole truth. The Prince did not live only in a knightly dream; he had an eye to the main chance. He entertained Don Pedro as courteously as he had entertained King John, but, as in the former case, got as much out of him as he could. So when Froissart describes how the Prince went out to meet the refugee king at Bordeaux, conducted him to the Abbey of St. Andrew, where 'he was brought to a fair chamber ready apparelled for him' and how 'when he was changed he went to the princess and the ladies', we have a sketch of the outward scene, but nothing of the business projects which the Prince was turning over in his mind.

Don Pedro was the second king who had fallen to him in ten years. For Pedro was as powerless as if he had been a captive. In the case of King John it had been how much he would pay for his liberty; with Don Pedro it was how much he would pay for his crown. It went without saying that he must pay all expenses in the most liberal meaning of the term. On being reinstated, too, he would have to hand out rewards—titles, territories, estates, pensions. The Prince did not intend to contribute more than he could help. That was one of the attractions of the expedition, an adventure in itself much to his taste, for it would give him a chance of displaying again his great talents as a commander and of enhancing his fame by winning another victory as great, perhaps, as Poitiers.[1] To get praise, honour, triumph, rewards, to be held a true knight who restored a sovereign wrongfully dispossessed, to foil the French in their attempt to reassert themselves, and all at no cost to himself, surely that was the ideal emprise? What he proposed, in fact, was to sell his services to Don Pedro like a condottiere. But this did not disturb him nor seem either to contradict his conception of himself as the soul of chivalry or to clash with his responsibility to be guided solely by what would secure England's best interests.

For a Spanish expedition to be possible, it was first necessary to open the road. The only way from Aquitaine into Castile was by the pass of Roncesvalles, for no practicable road existed as at present, along the coast through St. Jean de Luz and St. Sebastian.

[1] Froissart thus describes the Prince's mood: 'In this season the Prince was in the lusty flower of his youth, and he was never weary nor full satisfied of war, since the first beginning that he bore arms, but ever intended to achieve high deeds.'

The whole of Roncesvalles was within the territory of Navarre, including its port or entry, St. Jean Pied de Port (now in France). King Carlos had taken French money and opened a way for Don Henry. But his character was known and the Prince had no doubt that, if it was made worth his while, he would do the same for the English.

On Don Carlos being sounded, he expressed willingness to discus transit through his dominions. Apart from the large sum he had received, he had got no territorial concessions from Don Henry and conceived that he had been cheated. In August he sent a delegation to Bordeaux and shortly followed himself.

The Prince's next step was to consult King Edward. The answer he received was that he should conduct the campaign as ruler of Aquitaine. The English government did not wish to sponsor an expedition which, if openly their doing, might lead to complications with France. The Prince should therefore act as if he had taken on himself the responsibility of championing Don Pedro's cause. A small force, however, of 400 men-at-arms and 800 archers, would be sent under his brother, John of Gaunt, recently become Duke of Lancaster on the decease of Henry Duke of Lancaster, the celebrated commander, whose daughter Blanche he had married.

The Prince then set to work to collect an army. The English and Gascon mercenaries with Don Henry in Castile were recalled. They obeyed the order. Don Henry either could not stop them going or thought it safer to be rid of them. They returned via Roncesvalles, robbing and murdering as they marched. Calveley and Gournay followed later with their retinues; they were owed money and had stayed to collect it. Chandos was sent to southern France where some Free Companies were operating and hired the best men who volunteered. The Prince negotiated with his Gascon vassals, particularly with the great Jean d'Armagnac. Most of them were willing to bring contingents, provided they were well paid. Gaston Phoebus of Foix, however, refused to serve in person, though promising some men, for he detested Armagnac and, moreover, liked to think of himself as a sovereign ruler with the right to be neutral, if he chose. Besides these forces there was the Prince's own retinue. Knollys and the two Feltons, Thomas and William, were also active in collecting mercenaries from other areas.

In September the Prince, Don Pedro and Don Carlos had a

series of meetings at Libourne near Bordeaux to discuss the finance of the expedition. It was then that Pedro realized what huge sums he was expected to pay and what territories he would have to cede. To provide immediate cash for advances to the mercenaries, he had to sell all his jewels, but did not get as good a price as he hoped because he flooded the market. The sum of 550,000 florins was fixed as the sum payable by him to the Prince and his Gascon lords for their help in general, a preliminary sum, for an additional bill would follow when all expenses were totalled. He also signed away large territories, the Dukedom of Biscay to the Prince and two other provinces to Carlos of Navarre. He is not stated to have expressed doubt of his ability to pay so large a sum, nor to have entered a caveat that the Castilian magnates might resist the cession of provinces to foreigners. He seems to have readily promised to do what he was asked,[1] reflecting perhaps that the more the Prince and his friends stood to gain by the venture, the more sure he was of recovering his kingdom. In the nature of things his promises had to be lavish, for a deferred payment is always larger than cash down.

The build-up of the army took longer than had been anticipated and winter set in before it could start. This involved postponement till 1367 and February was fixed for the invasion. Though this was early in the season to cross the Pyrenees, the expense of keeping the army waiting longer was prohibitive. Its number of fighting men has been estimated at 10,000, not counting the quantity of servants, grooms, clerks, armourers and pages on the pay roll. As it was, the money Pedro got for his jewels was all spent and the Prince was obliged, very contrary to his first intentions, to provide money himself, and having no cash melted down his plate.

In December King Carlos, who had returned from Aquitaine to Navarre, was bribed by Don Henry and agreed to close Roncesvalles. But the Prince managed to give him a fright and he hastened back to Bordeaux to explain that he was bluffing Henry so as to give him a false sense of security. The Prince accepted, without being deceived by, this excuse.

On 6 January 1367 the future Richard II was born at Bordeaux. Shortly afterwards the Prince left for Dax to join the army. His tender parting with his wife is described by the Herald. She is made to cry: 'Alas! what should I do . . . if I were to lose . . . him who has no peer for valiance on earth? . . . All the world says that

[1] 'He humbled himself right sweetly to the Prince,' says Froissart.

never did a man venture himself on so perilous an expedition.' The Prince comforts her. 'We shall meet again and be happy, we and all our friends. My heart tells me so.' And kisses her goodbye.[1]

In giving this scene the Herald's intention is to show the romantic side of his hero's character. To be devoted to his Fair Maid was what a true knight such as he should be. The Herald is also careful to record that the coming expedition was generally considered a dangerous adventure. It was the first time in history that an English army had ever invaded Spain, a country very remote from England, hidden behind the great barrier of the Pyrenees, little known except by reports of English shipmen, a southern land much orientalized and still the seat of a Moorish kingdom. Of the overseas adventures of the English people so far it promised to be the most extraordinary, one most likely to excite those engaged upon it, and to stir the public imagination at home. The Prince, like most of the characters of this history, including the hardest of the mercenary captains, was religious, as the word was understood at his time, and believed that God was on his side in this dramatic undertaking. The Herald puts the following words into his mouth when first discussing it with his Gascon barons. 'As you know very well, France was the most powerful Christian country, but God and right gave us the strength to conquer her. I have heard it said that the leopards and their company would spread abroad also in Spain, and if it could be in our time, we should be held the more valiant.' The phrasing where he refers to

[1] The Herald's Poem, op. cit., line 2057. The Princess says:

'Las! quoi feroie,
Dieux et Amours, si je perdoie

. . . . .

Celi qui eu monde n'a per
De vaillance, au voir recorder?

. . . . .

Car touz li mondes dit ensy
Qu'onques nuls hom ne s'enbaty
En voiage si perilleus,'

. . . . .

The Prince replies:

'Dame, encore nous reverrons
En tel point que joie en avrons,
Et nous et tout li nostre amy,
Car mes coers le me dit ensy.'
Moult doulcement, s'entracolerent
Et en baisant congie donerent.

the royal arms suggests that he is quoting a current prophecy. To be fulfilling a prophecy made the occasion gravely strange, as if he were an instrument of fate or the divine will. That he entertained these views and at the same time was taken up with rewards, personal fame and money, like a condottiere, looks at first sight a contradiction. But there are many traits hard to reconcile in the totality of the human spirit. It is true, moreover, that he could not have launched the expedition unless somebody had financed it. Neither he nor his father could afford it. Or rather, Edward did not choose to ask parliament for the money. King Charles, on the contrary, conceiving that to place Henry of Trastamare on the Castilian throne was essential in the interests of France, had found the money for his expedition, in spite of great financial difficulties. The restoration of Don Pedro was as essential in English interests, but Edward was not convinced that England should pay for it. He left it to his son to manage as best he could; and the only way the Prince could manage it was to offer his services and his mercenary army's to Don Pedro on payment. Nevertheless, the negotiations were so conducted that an expedition which rightly appertained to high strategy and international affairs, became more like a private venture. That Richard II was born at this tense and exciting moment, when his mother was worried at the prospect of the Prince's departure into unknown Spain, may have had an effect on his nervous system and helped to make him the curious person he turned out to be.

The Prince wins the Battle of Nájera

The Prince was joined by his brother, John of Gaunt, Duke of Lancaster, on 13 January 1367, when the Duke and his English contingent marched into Dax. At the end of the month the army moved down to St. Jean Pied de Port, the port or entry to the pass of Roncesvalles, a small walled town on a hill in a broad valley. It still has that appearance, for the medieval walls and gates remain. It is a picturesque little place, with the peaks of the Pyrenees standing up boldly to the southwards. The Prince's army was much too large to have been accommodated inside the walls and will have camped round about.

By the middle of February the march through the pass began. Today, as then, the road to its mouth winds up what is called the valley of Roland; one is already on the ground trodden eleven hundred years ago by Charlemagne's paladins. The first part of the pass is the defile of Val Carlos, a long stiff climb up a rocky vale, the snow peaks out of sight. The summit at 3,220 feet is 18½ miles from St. Jean Pied de Port. After a descent of 250 feet in 1½ miles the village of Roncesvalles is reached, where is a Gothic abbey and a chapel of the Holy Ghost, said to mark the spot where Roland sounded his horn and the rearguard of Charlemagne's army was cut to pieces by the Basques. This section, from Val Carlos to Roncesvalles village, a distance of eleven miles, is the most arduous part of the journey. The descent to Pamplona, twenty-seven miles on, is comparatively simple. The total distance of forty-seven miles from St. Jean Pied de Port to the Navarrese capital was too long a march for the Prince's army to have covered without a halt somewhere for the night. Today it takes about two hours in a car if the weather is good.

The Prince had no easy passage. The weather was bitterly cold, with icy winds and occasional snow. The medieval road was stony and in places very steep and narrow. The army was mounted and the horses found the going bad and slippery. The Herald, over emphatic though he is, shows how the savage loneliness affected the nerves: 'Since the just God suffered death for us on the cross there was no such painful passage, for one saw men and horses, that suffered many ills, stumble on the mountain; there was no fellowship; the father made no tarrying for the son; there was cold so great, snow and frost also, that each one was discouraged, but by the grace of God all passed in due time.'[1]

Even today in a car the passage of Roncesvalles is wild and solemn.

In his description of the march through, the Herald, though actually riding with his master, Sir John Chandos, writes as if he stood by the roadside and noted the leading figures as they passed. The Prince was not accompanied by any of the fighting Earls of Crécy and Poitiers,[2] yet there were some well-known men with him and others to be prominent later. To prevent overcrowding and blocking of the narrow road, the three divisions of the army passed at intervals of two days. The van was led by Duke John, who, being in his twenty-seventh year, was ten years younger than the Prince, his brother. He had seen active service seven years before when he accompanied his father in 1360 on the march to Rheims and Paris. Fond of his brother and emulous of his fame, he seemed a gallant enough figure as he rode by under his banner. No one could have guessed that in fourteen years' time he would be the most hated man in England. With him was Sir John Chandos, friend of royalty, already very famous, now Constable of the army and leader of the mercenaries collected from the Free Companies. As he had defeated and captured du Guesclin three years back at the battle of Auray, he no doubt felt confident of the

[1] The Herald's Poem, op. cit., line 2293 seq. in Pope and Lodge's translation.

[2] For instance, Thomas Beauchamp, Earl of Warwick, who fought at both Crécy and Poitiers, when he commanded the van, went crusading after the latter battle against the Prussians and other pagans of the north. The *Vita Ricardi* states: 'He warred against the heathens two years and brought with him the Kings' son of Lithuania and christened him in London and named him Thomas after himself.'

present issue. The two Marshals of the army, Sir Stephen Cossington and Sir Guichard d'Angle, the Gascon lord, were with him. Some younger members of the English aristocracy were conspicuous; Lord William Beauchamp, a youth of twenty, a younger son of the Earl of Warwick; Thomas Ufford, son of the Earl of Suffolk; Hugh and Ralph Hastings, kinsmen of the Earl of Pembroke; and Lord Neville of Raby. Following them was the celebrated condottiere Sir Hugh Calveley, who had already made one fortune in Spain by supporting Don Henry and hoped, by defeating him, to make a second. Other noted captains of mercenaries were Cresswell and Brickett, and the well-known Sir Matthew Gournay. The Herald also mentions the names of some knights and squires, William and Thomas Felton, Richard Taunton, a Devon gentleman, and Shakell and Hauley, later to be very well known, for, arising out of what began in Spain, Hauley was killed by officers of the law at the altar in Westminster Abbey, a sensational tale which will be related in its place.

The midward, commanded by the Prince, followed in its turn. The chief celebrities here were the two kings, Don Pedro of Castile and Don Carlos of Navarre, both men in the middle thirties. They rode with the Prince, and as the custom was wore coronets encircling their basinets. Don Pedro has come down in history with the sobriquet of the Cruel and Don Carlos of the Bad. The Prince was soon to hold a poor opinion of the first; he already had a poor opinion of the second. Among other notabilities in the midward were the Prince's stepson, Thomas Holland, the beloved Joan's son by her former husband; Hugh Stafford, son of the Earl of Stafford; the three brothers Courtenay, sons of the Earl of Devon; Lord Thomas Percy,[1] brother of Lord Henry, later Earl of Northumberland; and Simon Burley, afterwards Richard II's tutor and a leading personality at court. Lastly, not to be forgotten, was the formidable Sir Robert Knollys, after Calveley perhaps the most prominent condottiere. The Herald describes him as a man of few words, the strong silent Englishman:

S'i fu messires Roberz Knolles
Qui n'eut mie trop de paroles.[2]

[1] By an incredible turn of fate, hidden in the future thirty-four years away, Thomas Percy, then Earl of Worcester, was to be beheaded after the battle of Shrewsbury by King Henry IV of England, the son of Duke John, now leading the van.

[2] The Herald's Poem, line 2331.

The rearguard followed after another interval. It was commanded by James, titular King of Majorca, whose father had been driven from his kingdom by the King of Aragon. James had joined the expedition in the hope that he might get back his crown if the Prince won, when En Pere would, with luck, be dethroned for having facilitated Don Henry of Trastamare's invasion. As the third king in the army his name gave added cachet to the list of prominent people following the Prince. The second in command of the rearguard was the Count of Armagnac, the Prince's richest feudatory. Last of all came the Captal de Buch, in command of a detachment, no doubt sorry that his friend Gaston Phoebus had not come.

But, important as these panoplied lords and gentlemen were, the archers, the 'archers of England' as Froissart always calls them, the men from the little towns and villages, who had dealt so decisively with the French chivalry, were yet more vital to the success of the expedition. Chaucer has left us a contemporary description of one such:

This Yeoman wore a coat and hood of green.
And peacock-feathered arows, bright and keen
And neatly sheathed, hung at his belt the while
—For he could dress his gear in yeoman style,
His arrows never drooped their feathers low—
And in his hand he bore a mighty bow.
His head was like a nut, his face was brown.
He knew the whole of woodcraft up and down.
A saucy brace was on his arm to ward
It from the bow-string, and a shield and sword
Hung at one side, and at the other slipped
A jaunty dirk, spear-sharp and well-equipped.[1]

The archers in Roncesvalles were mounted for travelling. They probably were wearing steel caps and brigantines instead of coat and hood. Otherwise the description is exact enough.

The pass was traversed without appreciable loss and the army was all at Pamplona before the end of February. The mercenaries began looting food at once, though the Black Prince had promised Don Carlos that all should be paid for. 'The kynge of Naverr', says Froissart in Berners' translation, 'was sore displeased. He

[1] The Prologue, *Canterbury Tales*, translated into modern English by Nevill Coghill.

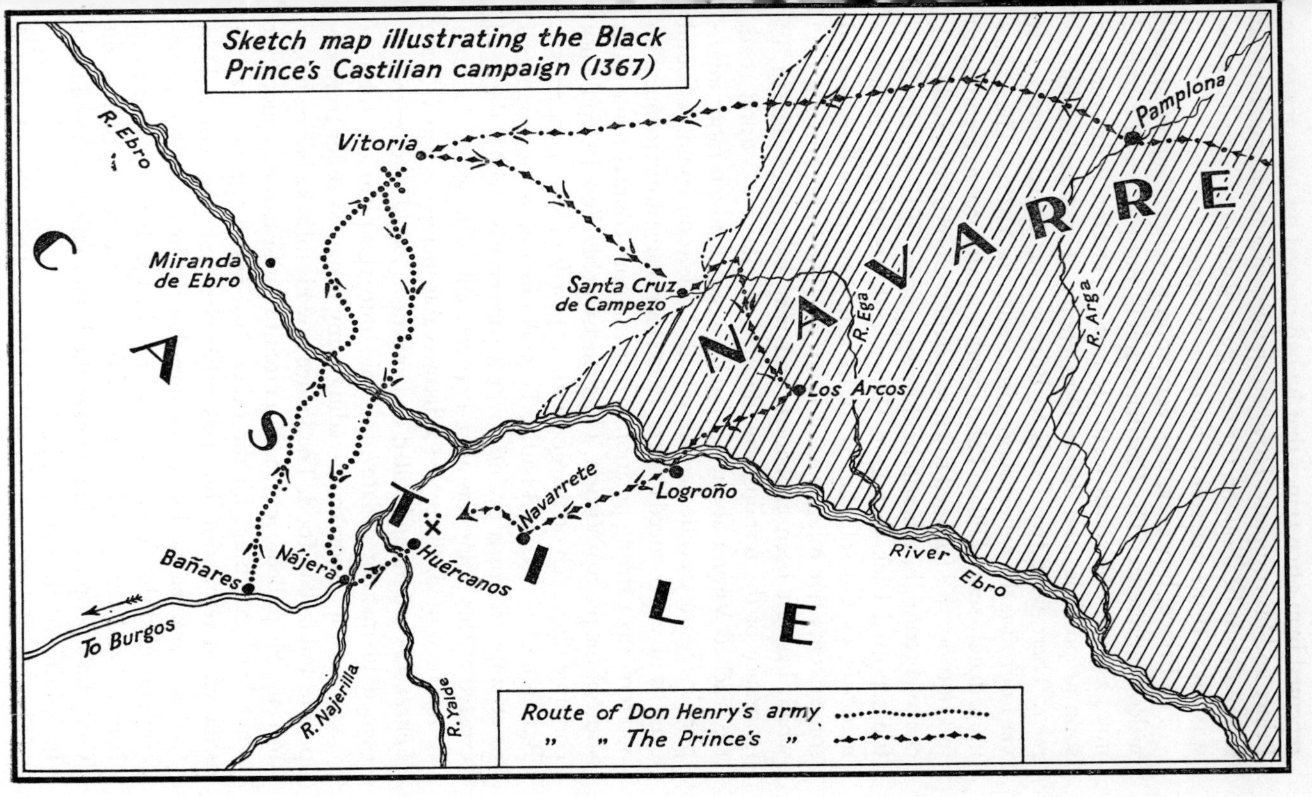
Sketch map illustrating the Black Prince's Castilian campaign (1367)
R. Ebro
Vitoria
Pamplona
NAVARRE
CASTILE
Miranda de Ebro
Santa Cruz de Campezo
R. Ega
R. Arga
Los Arcos
Logroño
Navarrete
Nájera
Huércanos
Bañares
To Burgos
River Ebro
R. Najerilla
R. Yalde
Route of Don Henry's army
" " The Prince's "

repented hym often tymes that he had opened his passages to the Prince and his company. Howbeit the season was nat than for him to say all that he thought, for he sawe well and consydered that he was nat as thane mayster of his owne countre.'

The Prince, however, was very soon to relieve him of his unwelcome presence. The Castilian capital, Burgos, was a hundred miles away to the south-west. He had to get Don Pedro there as soon as possible, and defeat Don Henry, if he attacked him *en route*. There were two roads to Burgos, one directly south-west via Logroño; the other, more circuitous, via Vitoria. The Prince immediately sent William Felton with a small force to reconnoitre to Logroño; this fortified town was over the border in Castile and, curiously enough, was still held by supporters of Don Pedro. Felton reported back that Don Henry with his army and the two marshals, du Guesclin and d'Audrehem, was on the Burgos road some twenty-five miles west of Logroño. The Prince, for a reason which has not been explained, and may have been due to his ignorance of the terrain, now decided to take the Vitoria road. He reached Vitoria about 5 March. It was a much more inhospitable region than he had supposed. Little food could be found even by his experienced looters. Don Henry came north to meet him and took up a strong position in mountainous country some miles short of the plain of Vitoria. The Prince was blocked. He could not continue his march on Burgos without first dealing with the enemy. But Don Henry refused battle. To seek him out in the mountains or attempt to brush by him over a narrow pass which the road crossed at this point was alike impracticable. Unsure of the right course he waited. There was a disagreeable incident when William Felton was caught and killed in a skirmish. Don Henry even succeeded in making a damaging raid into the plain on John of Gaunt's camp. Soon the invading army began to suffer from exposure and lack of food. The Prince saw his mistake before it was too late. He pulled back, made a circuit south-eastwards and, after some hard marching, hit the other road near Logroño. He had suffered in reputation but was otherwise none the worse. Don Carlos, however, no longer so sure that the invasion would succeed, decided that it would be safer to hedge. He went to eastern Navarre and arranged for himself to be captured by some of du Guesclin's people so that, in case the Prince failed, he would not be fighting on the losing side.

On 1 April the Prince crossed the Ebro at Logroño and camped immediately on the other side, says the Herald, 'in the orchards and under the olive trees' of the plain of Navarette. When Don Henry heard of the withdrawal from Vitoria, he immediately retraced his steps and took up a position at Nájera, some fifteen miles west of the Prince and astride the Burgos road.

From the first Don Henry had been advised by du Guesclin and d'Audrehem not to risk a pitched battle with the Prince, but to harry him and cut off his supplies. Froissart declares that d'Audrehem expressed himself to this effect: 'I submit, sir, that when you engage with the Prince in battle, you will find his fighting men clever, hardy and brave, and, rather than retreat a foot, ready to die where they stand. But if you take my advice you will discomfit them without striking a blow. Your right course is to block the roads and passages through the mountains so that no provision can reach them. Thus you will famish them, and they will be obliged to return worsted to their own country.'[1]

Henry had accepted this advice at Vitoria. He had not offered battle, had kept the passes, had famished his enemy. If the Prince had remained there, he would soon have been discomfited and obliged to return home. But he had not done so. He had slipped away and was now in a far more favourable situation. Henry had no longer a mountain pass which he might close. He was at the other end of the open Navarette plain. There was nothing between him and the Prince except the Najerilla, a small tributary of the Ebro. He had no option but to fight a battle. At least, it was that or abandoning the capital. If he did so, the magnates would probably desert him. To retreat, harassing the Prince and cutting off his foraging parties, was impracticable. For one thing, his own army would melt away if he appeared afraid to face his opponent. Besides, the Prince was too close to Burgos, only a couple of days' march. There was nothing for it but a battle. Nevertheless, the Marshals continued to warn him. Du Guesclin is reported by Froissart as saying at this stage: 'Sir, ill do you know the great power which the Prince leads. He has the best fighting men on earth. I know him so well. Therefore, sir, look carefully into the matter.'

Du Guesclin had the soundest reasons for his misgivings. The

[1] D'Audrehem was sixty-two. Writing of him two years later Froissart says: 'He was so aged and brused in armes and travayle of tyme passed, that he coude nat well helpe himselfe . . . howbeit, he wolde bere harnesse at tyme of nede.'

Prince's army was much superior. Don Henry's had a hard core of mercenaries, the residue of the Free Company men after the English had been recalled, but their number was less. These professionals apart, the rest was a mob, a large mob, no doubt, giving a total exceeding all the Prince's men, but of small value. There were the Spanish knights, a cavalry obsolete since Crécy; the semi-religious orders of Calatrava and Santiago under their Masters, the Hospitallers of St. John under their Prior, proud and brave but old fashioned, accustomed to fight Moors, but who had never met English archers. These were all heavy cavalry. Present also was a mass of light horsemen. Their mounts were the little Spanish horses called genets; their armour was poor; they carried small round shields, and javelins which they threw on getting to close quarters, tactics and equipment which were more Moorish than European. Lastly, came the thousands of spearmen and slingers, pressed country folk, ready to fight savagely if their side was winning and to flee at once if the tide turned. Except for du Guesclin's mercenaries, none of these people had the smallest chance against the Prince's armour and his arrows. Don Henry's predicament was that his cavalry and his countrified foot were useless whether he attacked or waited to be attacked. His only hope, a forlorn hope, was to remain behind the Najerilla, when perhaps his mercenaries, with the help of the river in front of them, would be able to stop the Prince. But he had not got as far as understanding his predicament. He was not convinced by what du Guesclin and d'Audrehem had told him. Like King Philip at Crécy twenty-one years earlier, he believed that his cavalry, heavy and light, could ride down the archers and so disorganize the Prince's dismounted men-at-arms that his own dismounted mercenaries could do the rest. Under this delusion on 2 April he crossed the Najerilla on to the moor on the east side, justifying this exceedingly rash act by the reflection that he could manoeuvre his cavalry there to advantage (though, in fact, the moor was certain disaster for them).

On the same day the Prince moved his army from Logroño to the village of Navarette, a distance of six miles along the Burgos road. The two hosts were now roughly nine miles apart. On learning that Don Henry had relinquished his position on the far side of the Najerilla and was drawn up in the plain, the Prince knew, as certainly as any commander can know before a battle, that he was assured of victory. The previous days there had been an exchange of letters, in the first Don Henry complaining that he had never harmed the Prince and did not deserve to be invaded; in the second the Prince answering that he was the champion of legitimacy and had come to uphold the right; in the third Don Henry accusing Don Pedro of ten murders, a rape, and of attacks on the Church. The letters, not likely to affect the issue, since battle was now certain, had propaganda value, with the Prince shown, not as a condottiere in the pay of Don Pedro, but as a knight restoring a king wrongfully driven from his kingdom, and Don Henry, though in fact illegitimate and a usurper, displayed as the defender of the good people of Castile against a tyrant and a ruffian.

The two protagonists now reviewed their armies in preparation for the morrow. Don Henry had advanced a couple of miles beyond the Najerilla. He stood astride the Burgos road with a stream, the Yalde, in front of him, an obstacle of little importance. His van consisted of du Guesclin's mercenaries with a picked body of Castilian knights. They would be dismounted when the battle began, and have supporting them such auxiliaries as crossbowmen, slingers and dart throwers. On the left wing light cavalry under Don Tello, his brother, would operate and on the right more cavalry under the Count of Denia, the son of the Aragonese Infanta, En Pere's uncle. The men-at-arms in the van are estimated by some authorities at 3,000, though the auxiliaries and cavalry made up a much larger total. Don Henry himself would be commanding the midward. It consisted of some 3,000 Castilian knights and their retinues, all of whom would remain mounted. The great mass of footmen, rustic levees, would be kept in the rear.[1]

The order and composition of the Prince's army were as in the march through Roncesvalles. On arrival at the battlefield everyone would get off his horse, which would be sent to the rear. What their exact total was is not certainly known; nor is it of great importance, for even if the Prince had had no more than three thousand picked men-at-arms from the Companies and three thousand archers from England, he could not have been defeated by an adversary who depended on cavalry. An arrow-shower of 3,000 arrows ten times repeated—30,000 arrows—was quite

[1] Froissart gives us a glimpse of Don Henry inspecting his army: 'Kynge Henry lepte on a strong mule after the usage of the countrey and rode fro batayle to batayle ryght swetely, prayeng every man that day to employ themselfe to defende and keep their honour, and so he shewed himselfe so cherefully that every man was joyfull to beholde hym.'

enough to rout all the mounted knights and genetours that Henry could muster. But the Prince had certainly far more than 3,000 men-at-arms and 3,000 archers. Conservative estimates give him 9,000 of the first and 6,000 of the second. With 6,000 archers a blizzard of 36,000 arrows could be sent driving down in *one* minute.[1] Against heavily armoured men on foot such a storm was damaging and terrifying; against cavalry and less heavily armoured men it was decisive.

The Prince's plan[2] for the morrow, 3 April, was first to reduce the nine miles which separated him from Don Henry until the two armies were face to face. He would not attack, but in accordance with experience would invite attack. If Don Henry attacked he was done for. If he did not attack—but he was bound to attack or flee, for cavalry could not be used defensively. That the armoured part of his force was all cavalry except for du Guesclin's mercenaries, the Prince must certainly have learnt from one source or another long ago. As for his rustic levees, his slingers, his javelin throwers, numerous though they were, they could be discounted.

For the Prince to be able to fight the defensive battle which he anticipated, it would not do for him to march straight down the Burgos road towards Nájera in full view of Don Henry's scouts. He had to have time to dismount his men and take up as suitable a position as the ground afforded. Either from information supplied by Felton and his knights who had reconnoitred as far as Nájera in March, or from reports of his scouts at the moment, supplemented by the use of his own eyes, the Prince was aware that a little farther on there was a hill to the right of the road. If instead of taking the road, he marched round under cover of the northern slopes of

[1] Six shots a minute is said to have been a first-class longbowman's average. Not that he continued to shoot at that pace, for he only carried about two dozen arrows. But six volleys or less sufficed to break down a charge. It is to this that the Monk of Malmesbury in his *Eulogium Historiarum* refers when he says: 'After the third or fourth, or at most the sixth, draw of the bows men knew which side would win.'

[2] The authorities for the battle of Nájera, on the Prince's side, are the Herald, who was present, and Froissart, who was not present, though he was at Bordeaux up to the time of the Prince's departure. He makes use of the Herald's account and also uses material of his own, drawn from witnesses, whose testimony he weaves into the literary narrative characteristic of him. On the Spanish side the authority is Pero López de Ayala whose Chronicle is included in *Crónicas de los reyes de Castilla*, vol. 2. Ayala was a man-of-letters and statesman, a leading personality at court. He was captured in the battle. He was thirty-five at the time.

the hill, he could approach Don Henry unobserved and, on debouching from a little valley there, would come in on his flank. While the Castilian army, disordered perhaps by the surprise, was wheeling to meet him, he could take position at leisure.

Accordingly, some time before dawn on 3 April, the advance was sounded. The army was very hungry because provisions were short, but otherwise was in good shape. The horses were mounted. Soon they left the road and bore right towards the northern part of the hill. Some 700 feet had to be climbed before they began the descent on the other side and caught sight of Don Henry's army on the moor. There it was; the rising sun shining on 'many an embroidered banner of sendal and silk,' says the Herald, who adds: 'It was on an attractive stretch of flat without a bush or tree for a good three miles.' While Don Henry was wheeling and issuing new orders, the Prince took his position. All his men dismounted and sent aside their horses under the charge of grooms. Duke John chose his ground for the van; archers were to protect his wings. The midward and the rearward formed up behind, their flanks also protected by archers. The Prince, as the Herald records, had even time to address his troops: 'Sirs, there is no other end. You know well that we are nigh overtaken by famine, and you see there our enemies who have plenty of bread and wine, salt and fresh fish. We must beat them.' That was a line which his men, mostly hardened marauders, understood very well. He also offered a prayer, as simple and direct: 'Sovereign Father, I have come here to support a rightful cause and also because I love valour and honour. Please guard me and my men.'

And he took Don Pedro by the hand exclaiming 'Today you will know whether you will ever have Castile again.' Thus the Herald, making his hero behave as a knight should.

The battle which ensued was short and exciting. What happened is much clearer than in the case of Poitiers, though the spot on the moor where the fighting took place has not been as exactly located. Nevertheless, it can be said with some assurance that Don Henry's front was in the neighbourhood of the village of Huércanos and that the ground between Huércanos and Nájera, two miles west, was fought over.

The action was opened by the advance of the Castilian van under du Guesclin. Consisting of some 3,000 dismounted mercenaries and knights, it flung itself upon the Prince's van under John of Gaunt, apparently before his archers were ready. The impact was violent and the English van had to yield a pace or two. Chandos, who was in front, had a narrow escape. He was thrown to the ground and a huge Catalan jumping on top of him tried to stab him through the vizor. But he managed to get hold of his dagger and gave his assailant a mortal wound through a joint in his harness. Though of the two vans the Castilian was the smaller, they were well matched, for the veteran mercenaries composing both were of the same quality. They remained awhile locked in a close combat. In Berners is this revealing sentence: 'Dyvers of them helde their speares in both handes, foyning and presing eche at other, and some fought with shorte swerdes and daggers.' But neither van could break its way in and split the other. The steel men struck and struck. They had the vizors of their basinets down, which gave them a curious snouted appearance.[1] The dust rose, there was a great clangour.[2] As long as a man remained on his feet, he was so well protected by his armour that he was not in great danger. But if he fell it was no fun,[3] says the Herald.

Don Henry presently ordered the light cavalry on his wings, the half Moorish genetours, to charge, envelop the Prince's van and hurl their javelins at it. The massed archers on the Prince's wings were now ready. The charging genetours were swept by their arrow-shower. Neither Henry's brother Don Tello, leading the left, nor the Count of Denia on the right could rally their shattered squadrons after the first few draws. Utterly terrified, Don Tello galloped from the field. The Count of Denia seems to have been unhorsed, for he was captured by two English squires, Robert Hauley and Richard Chamberlain.[4]

The Prince then ordered his wings, comprising both men-at-arms and archers, to close in on Don Henry's van, still locked

[1] I would like to acknowledge the valuable advice and information given me throughout the book on armour and bows by Mr. Claude Blair of the Victoria and Albert Museum.

[2] 'Et prist a lever le pourriere' (l. 3226); 'Grant fu le noise et le fumiere (l. 3271) (The Herald's Poem).

[3] 'Ce ne fut mie granz reviaux' (l. 3268 of the Poem).

[4] It has generally been thought that Hauley and John Shakell, not Hauley and Chamberlain, captured Denia. But see Edouard Perroy's article in *Mélanges d'Histoire du Moyen Age*, p. 573, entitled 'Gros profits et rançons pendant la guerre de cent ans: l'affaire du Comte de Denia.' Though Shakell was in the battle, the actual captors were Hauley and Chamberlain. But Shakell later acquired from Chamberlain the half share in the valuable ransom involved. The complicated history of this ransom is discussed on a later page.

with his own, and on the Castilian centre behind it. 'The battle began to be fierce and cruel in all parts,' says Froissart now. The Prince's wings caught the Castilian foot, slingers and others, who had followed in support of the charging genetours, and began cutting them to pieces, though some of the slingers managed to get in some shots with heavy stones, which smashed bassinets and armour plates. But the archers picked them out. Struck by a volley they broke and fled. The Prince's wings continued to close in, so that Don Henry and his mounted knights of the centre were soon encompassed. He was in great peril; the arrows beat on both his flanks, 'thicker than rain falls in winter time' says the Herald. 'Horses and men were wounded.'

'The clash increased when the Prince moved up his centre' to support his van and add weight to the envelopment of Don Henry's centre. 'Fiercer waxed the battle.' Don Henry saw his men giving way. In desperation he cried to his knights: 'Sirs, help me, for God's sake, for you have made me king and have sworn to support me loyally.' He rallied them and attempted a charge but could make no headway against the arrows. What could he do, when, as Froissart says, 'the best fighting men and the flower of the chivalry of the world were with the Prince'? It was time to be gone, but there was one blow he would strike before he departed. 'Where is that son of a whore, who calls himself King of Castile?' he cried. But he was so entangled in the press that he could not come at Don Pedro. The utmost confusion now began to prevail. The mass of rustic levies, some of whom had already suffered severely with the genetours, was wavering. They began to run as fast as they could towards the bridge over the Najerilla. Seeing the battle lost, but resolved to live to fight another day, Don Henry turned his bridle and with his retinue of knights managed to break out and fled in a southerly direction, for westwards he could see that the bridge was already choked with fugitives.[1]

The French, Breton and Norman mercenaries composing Henry's van, wholly surrounded and greatly outnumbered, felt that they

[1] The *Chronicon Angliae* of St. Albans has a vivid sentence here which no doubt preserves what was believed in England to have happened at this moment: 'On seeing the way things were turning and especially terrified by the arrows which came flying round him from all directions, the enemy leader got off the hack he was riding and mounting a swifter horse, fled at full gallop.' *Chron. Angl.*, p. 59 Rolls edn.

had done all that could be expected of them and that the moment had arrived to give themselves up, which they could safely do on condition of paying ransom. One of their captains, Adam de Villiers, called the Stutterer, had already been killed. There was no sense in continuing to resist. Du Guesclin, d'Audrehem and Don Sancho, Henry's brother, let themselves be taken, as did the rest.

While this was happening a pursuit of the foot was in progress. The Prince had ordered the King of Majorca to mount the reserve and gallop after them. No quarter need be given; they were too poor to be worth taking. As luck would have it, the Najerilla had been rising since the previous night and now its swift current was unfordable. The bridge was the only exit from the battlefield. At this bottleneck, says Froissart, 'there was a hideous shedding of blood, and many a man drowned for divers leapt into the water'. And the Herald has: 'More than two thousand were drowned. It was said that the river was red with the blood flowing from the bodies of dead men and horses. So great was the discomfiture that I think no creature ever saw the like, so help me God.' Some of the mounted knights had also fled that way, particularly, it seems, those of the Orders of Calatrava, Santiago and St. John. The pursuit swept over the bridge and the Masters of all three Orders were captured in the town of Nájera and held for ransom.

As is clear from this, anyone without money ran a very grave risk in a fourteenth-century battle. The man of means with a good suit of armour to protect him, and his coat of arms displayed to identify him, could hope to survive the mêlée and, if captured, to rejoin his side as soon as he paid his ransom, or even if he gave adequate security, such as a son as hostage. Though it was not supposed to be chivalric to fix a ransom at a figure to ruin a knight, some ransoms were fixed very high. In such cases, if the prisoner was important enough, his king paid. Otherwise he had to find the money as best he could, as by raising a loan against his estate or calling on his tenants to subscribe. Such captives had less to complain of than those of today who languish in prisoner-of-war camps. But the man of no rank was in bad case. If he fought, he was likely to be killed, since he had no armour. If he ran and was caught, he was slaughtered out of hand. There was no such thing as taking prisoners of his kind. A battle was too much of a business occasion. That a poor man was not worth capturing sealed his fate. His employers, too, were indifferent. As his pay was invariably in arrears, it was not inconvenient to them when he was killed.[1]

[1] For the whole subject see Denys Hay's "The Division of the Spoils of War in 14th Century England", *Transactions of the Royal Historical Society*, 5th series, vol. 4, p. 91. A battle was officially recognized as a great opportunity for the upper class to make money. A host of rules regulated the percentage of a ransom which a captor might keep, how much he had to pay to his immediate lord and how much to the crown. The Black Prince's share in the ransoms and also in the loot taken at a battle where he commanded was as a rule one third, though sometimes half. With such a big fortune to be made out of a victory, one can well understand that men, who from the monetary point of view were valueless, did not receive a thought from him.

After the Battle

The fighting and slaughter were over by noon. The Prince hoisted his banner on a little rise, so that the leaders might know where he was. They came in from the chase one by one, Duke John, Chandos, the Captal, Percy, Clisson, Armagnac and the King of Majorca, each planting his banner to mark his whereabouts. The last magnate to arrive was Don Pedro. The impression he created as he rode in is marvellously suggested by the words used by Berners to translate Froissart's sentence: 'Than came thyder kynge Dampeter, right sore chafed, coming from the chase on a great blacke courser, his baner beten with the armes of Castell before hym.' (It is extraordinary how huge an apparition the king becomes by force of the language. He might be one of the kings of the Apocalypse in the contemporary tapestries of the castle of Angers.) The Prince welcomed him. 'There the King would have kneeled down to thank the Prince, but the Prince would not permit it and hastened to take him by the hand. Said the King: "Dear lord, I owe you many thanks for the lovely day[1] you have given me." To which the Prince devoutly replied: "Thank God for it; his victory it is, not mine." '

All his great lords being assembled, the Prince mounted his horse and rode under his banner into Nájera. He took up his quarters in Don Henry's pavilion, which was as he had left it. His jewels and gold and silver plate were there, for he had gone campaigning with all his valuables, as was the custom, and had not in

[1] *La belle journée* in the original Froissart.

his flight halted to retrieve them. Hungry before the battle, everyone was now much hungrier. Besides plate the pavilion was well stocked with food and wine. They were soon seated before a good dinner, to which the captured Count of Denia was invited. By now the town had been sacked, a job the mercenaries were very good at.

Next day, Sunday 4 April, the matter of the prisoners was brought up. Before leaving Bordeaux Don Pedro had promised not to claim the persons or ransoms of any Castilian lords who might be taken, with the exception of Don Henry's brother, Don Sancho. He now asked that the more inveterate of his political enemies might be handed over to him to keep under lock and key, for if ransomed they would again work against him. That, of course, was the standing objection to the system of ransoms; you won a fortune but sacrificed your security. The Prince, however, refused the request, though Don Pedro had offered to buy the prisoners he wanted. But as he could not pay cash the Prince was doubtful of seeing his money. Moreover, he had the excuse that to sell the prisoners would be a breach of faith. It was understood when they surrendered that they could ransom themselves. Nevertheless, if we credit the Herald, the Prince made one exception. He handed over Gomez Carillo, one of Don Pedro's former ministers who had played him false and served Don Henry as Chamberlain. Don Pedro made an immediate example of him. The Herald's lines are condensed but grim: 'Don Pedro returned straight to where he was lodged. There Gomez Carillo was made ready, and there he was drawn, and his throat cut under his chin before all the people.'[1]

Next day the army set off on the fifty mile ride to Burgos. *En route* the Prince wrote a letter[2] to his wife, in French, invariably

[1] Ayala says that the Prince did not hand over Gomez Carillo, who was executed by Don Pedro without his knowledge. Exactly what transpired was evidently in dispute at the time. But the Herald's version seems more probable.

[2] Quoted in French, p. 171, of Galbraith's edition of the *Anonimalle Chronicle*, and in English translation on p. 308 of Newhall's edition of Jean de Venette's *Chronicle*. See also *Eng. Hist. Rev.*, XLI (1926), pp. 415 18 'A letter of the Black Prince' by A. E. Prince, which explains how the writer discovered the letter. The translation which follows here is my own. The Princess of Wales seems to have sent it just as it stood to King Edward, who had it published as a despatch from Spain. The monk who wrote the *Anonimalle Chronicle* in York evidently had direct or indirect access to it, for his description of the battle ends with a sentence from it. For the subject of French as the language of private correspondence in the fourteenth century see the article by Helen Suggett in *Transactions of the Royal Historical Society*, 4th

used by English correspondents in the fourteenth century. It begins 'Treschere and tresentier coer, bien aimez compaigne' which may be rendered 'my dearest sweetheart and much loved companion'. The translation is as follows: 'All of us here send you our warmest good wishes. As for news, on 2 April we were camped near Navarette and there heard that the Bastard of Spain was six miles away with his whole army by the river at Nájera. Early next morning we moved towards him, our scouts ahead to report on his position. They brought back news that he had drawn up his battles in a fine place and awaited us. Immediately we put ourselves in array to fight him. And by the grace of God he and his host were discomfited. Five or six thousand of his fighting men were killed. And we are so full up with his prisoners that we have not yet got all their names. But among others there were taken Don Sancho, the Bastard's brother, the Comte de Denia, Monsieur Bertrand du Guesclin, Marshal Audrehem . . . Gomez Carillo, the Master of Santiago . . . all told some two thousand gentlemen. As for the Bastard himself we do not know whether he is a prisoner or was killed or has fled. After the battle we put up for the night in his pavilion, where we were more comfortable than we had been for four or five days. We stayed there all next day. And now, Monday, the day I am writing this, we left and started off for Burgos. Thank God, we are well on our way. You will be glad to know, my darling companion, that my brother of Lancaster and all the gentlemen of our army are in good fettle, except only John Ferrers[1]—he fought well. Very dear companion, etcetera.'

In this modest way the Prince describes the most complete of his victories. At Crécy, serving under his father, the archers and men-at-arms of his division had not been required to do more than repulse the repeated and desperate charges of the French chivalry. At Poitiers, after a risky commencement he had steadied his army and in the midst of a touch and go struggle snatched victory by a brilliant counter-offensive. But now at Nájera he had fought a battle which from start to finish was beautifully co-ordinated. The masked advance, the unexpected deployment on the enemy's left, the holding of their van, the destruction of their light cavalry, the envelopment of their centre, the pursuit and slaughter of their

series, vol. 28, p. 60, entitled "The use of French in England in the late Middle Ages." The first English letter extant is one written from Florence in 1392 by the condottiere, Sir John Hawkwood.

[1] The only Englishman reported killed at the battle of Nájera.

supporting footmen, were each a step in a controlled sequence, a succession of calculated blows, the whole so finished as to appear effortless, inevitable, classic. Only one small flaw showed in what was otherwise perfection. Don Henry himself had not been killed or captured. But even if he had fled to safety, there was no reason to apprehend that he would find the means and energy to give further trouble.

The inhabitants of Burgos were careful to give Don Pedro a rousing welcome. Accommodation was found for the Prince and his army outside the city. Their object had been achieved, the restoration of England's ally. For the time being it was the Prince, however, who was the real master of the country, for he alone had an army. The Herald puts in a sentence what was clear to everybody: 'It might be truly said that in Spain the Prince had such power that all was under his sway.'[1]

[1] The Poem, lines 3622–4.

Don Pedro Defaults

Three months had now elapsed since the Prince's army left Gascony. The troops so far had received no pay. As Don Pedro was back on the throne they expected to receive their arrears at once. Soon after arrival in Burgos, the Prince asked him to fulfil the promises he had made at Bordeaux. He replied that he would be happy to do so as soon as he had collected enough money. Meanwhile, perhaps, the Prince would be good enough to give him an exact statement of expenses. By the end of the month the account was ready. Don Pedro was shown as owing the Prince £450,000 which was five times as much as the first estimate of 550,000 gold florins (about £90,000), which he had accepted and undertaken to find. When we consider that the total issues of the English Exchequer for the year 1368/9, which were larger than usual, amounted to only £144,225,[1] the demand for £450,000 is seen to be clearly outrageous. The Prince's accountants were evidently very expert. That he had the face to put such an extravagant value on his services shows that he had nothing to learn from the most grasping condottieri of the day. In presenting the bill, however, he conceded that Don Pedro might have difficulty in laying hands on so large a sum forthwith. He suggested, therefore, that he should give surety, say twenty of his most important castles. Don Pedro did not

[1] Cf. P. E. Russell's *The English Intervention in Spain and Portugal in the time of Edward III and Richard II*, pp. 66 and 110. The Exchequer's revenue and expenditure varied from year to year considerably, as the figures cited further back show.

demur at the sum, but pleaded that were he to hand over his twenty key castles, his magnates would be indignant and might rise in rebellion. The Prince agreed that this was a serious objection and asked that instead there be ceded the province of Biscay, the reward which Don Pedro had promised him. Such a cession, the other pleaded, was open to the same objection. If he were to remain King of Castile and England's useful ally, it was essential for him not to alienate his subjects. He begged the Prince to have patience. He would get his money all right.

On receiving this reply, the Prince had two courses open to him. He had the military power to seize the security he desired: he might overrun Biscay, or even take valuables by force from private persons or rich foundations. His condottieri captains were much in favour of this line. The other course was for him to trust Don Pedro to meet his obligations. This seemed the better. To use violence before giving the king a chance would be both to hurt his own reputation as a knight and enrage the Castilians, whose friendly co-operation with England was the principal reason for restoring Don Pedro. One violence would lead to another and short of subduing Castile it was not clear how he could obtain his money except with Don Pedro's help. But he would oblige him to take a most solemn oath. Pedro had no objection to another oath. He had regained his kingdom by sworn promises. His urgent need now was an extension of credit. If the extension were long enough, something favourable might turn up. One thing was certain; he could never pay £450,000. Yes, he told the Prince, he would take what oath was wanted. To make the occasion the more solemn, the cathedral was fixed for the ceremony. There on 2 May, in the presence of the Prince and his commanders, Don Pedro swore before the altar to abide by all his engagements. He also signed a paper in which he undertook to pay half the £450,000 in four months and the remainder before Easter 1368.

By insisting on the oath the Prince showed that he suspected Pedro of an intention to default. He also seems to have suspected him of being capable of foul play, for he took the precaution to enter the cathedral with a strong retinue, after securing his exit from the city by occupying a gate with men-at-arms and archers. But the manner in which the King took the oath seems to have lulled his suspicions.

Soon afterwards, Don Pedro, with the Prince's permission, departed, as he declared, to collect money. The Prince and his army also left the capital and went south to Valladolid, where food and drink were said to be more plentiful. It was understood that Don Pedro would join them there, as soon as his tax-collectors had done their work. Weeks passed without any definite news from him. He was in the far south, by Seville. There is evidence that he did press his people to pay,[1] but when no money arrived, not even a sum on account, the Prince grew increasingly uneasy. His mercenaries were always hard to control and with their arrears of pay mounting up could not be prevented from looting the countryside. The Herald says that they even took some small towns and held the inhabitants to ransom. This was both going too far or not going far enough; it was too far if the Prince was in Castile as an ally, not enough if he was master of the kingdom.

In the course of May and June disquieting news began coming in from France. Don Henry's flight from Nájera took him over the border into Aragon. En Pere was not too pleased to see so embarrassing a guest; out of fear of the Prince he had simulated neutrality at the time of the invasion, though his cousin, the Count of Denia, had taken part in the battle with an Aragonese contingent. Don Henry, afraid that he might be arrested and handed over to Pedro, soon left Aragon and took refuge in the south of France. He was a man of indefatigable energy and at once set to work hiring mercenaries with the intention, if opportunity offered, of invading Castile a second time. To embarrass the Prince and perhaps oblige him to return, he conceived the idea of raiding the outlying parts of Aquitaine. News came that he was doing this and that Sir James Audeley, of Poitiers fame, whom the Prince had left as Governor, had been obliged to take the field against him. The Princess Joan protested to the French king, that as England and France were at peace, he had no right to harbour Don Henry. King Charles went through the form of admonishing him, but, as his raids were just what the French wanted, the royal warning had not to be taken very seriously.

That Don Henry was at large, that the French would support him again if they could, and that En Pere of Aragon would certainly be asked to give him passage to Castile as before, set the

[1] P. E. Russell, op. cit., p. 113. The evidence shows that he raised money ostensibly to pay the Prince, but as there is no evidence that he paid him anything, it appears that though he imposed taxes with that object in view, he decided not to pay when it came to the point. There is therefore no argument here in favour of his bona fides.

Prince thinking hard. A new plan of action began to take shape in his mind, when June passed into July and there was still no sign of Don Pedro producing the money. He recalled that Aragon, Navarre and Portugal all aspired to extend their territories at the expense of Castile, but had never succeeded in combining for that purpose. Perhaps he might be able to contrive such a combination with himself as its leader. Castile could then be dismembered.

The project turned on his being able to detach Aragon from France. To this end he sent some of his ablest commanders to talk to En Pere, first Calveley[1] and then Chandos, Armagnac and the Captal de Buch. By the middle of August a secret draft agreement was put on paper. If Pedro did not pay his debts and surrender Biscay by April 1368, the Prince would make war on him. Aragon would join in. The Prince offered to secure Don Carlos of Navarre's concurrence, while En Pere undertook to see if he could bring in the King of Portugal. The aim of the four allies would be the complete conquest of Castile and its division among themselves. A part which would fall to the Prince would be Biscay with its ports and naval dockyards. His total share would include other territories also and, as both Don Pedro and Don Henry would be eliminated, it would be feasible for him, as ruler of the portions allotted to him, to take the title of King of Castile.[2] Further talks to develop the plan would be held in October somewhere in Gascony.

This agreement concluded, the Prince left Spain. He could not afford to stay any longer nor were his troops willing to remain

[1] Sir Hugh Calveley (also spelled Calverley) was by now a very big man. As condottiere he had picked up the Spanish titles of Count of Carrión, and Lord of Asp and Elda. He afterwards became Seneschal of Aquitaine. He retired to England with a huge fortune, some of which he used to found a college in Rome and another at Bunbury, his place of residence in Cheshire. For some time he was Governor of Brest but returned to Bunbury, where he died in 1393. His effigy in full armour is still to be seen in the chancel of Bunbury church. His wife was an Aragonese noblewoman by the name of Doña Constanza, daughter of the Sicilian magnate Bonifacio de Aragón. (P. E. Russell, op. cit., p. 189.) The country people at Bunbury believed that she was Queen of Aragon, so astonishing a figure did the old knight appear to them.

[2] See P. E. Russell, op. cit., pp. 123–5. The existence of this draft agreement between the Prince and En Pere does not seem to have been known to historians until Mr. Russell examined the Aragonese archives. Hitherto it has been thought that the Prince left Spain hopeless and bankrupt. He was certainly bankrupt but he was full of hope.

without pay. They had also suffered seriously from disease. Moreover, his presence was needed in Aquitaine on account of Don Henry's activities and the hidden machinations of the French. During his march out through Navarre to Roncesvalles, he took the opportunity to acquaint Don Carlos with the outline of the secret plan. As the promises which Don Pedro had made him had been fulfilled no more than those made to the Prince, Don Carlos liked the idea of carving up Castile and readily agreed to come in. As Froissart says, he was difficult to deal with when you wanted to get something out of him, but when he thought he could get something out of you, he was the most charming of men.

The Prince was back in Aquitaine by 29 August.

The sensational *rapprochement* with Aragon again discloses the Prince in his aspect as a condottiere. On several occasions—in his letter to Don Henry, for instance, and his prayer before the battle—he had repeated that what had brought him to Spain was to restore a rightful king, an aim which shows him as he was generally seen by Froissart and the Herald, the creators of his legend. Now he proposed to desert (more than desert, violently oppose) the cause he declared so just, because he had not been paid. There was no charge that Don Pedro was, or was likely to become, faithless in a political sense. It was not suggested that as an ally of England he was less of an asset. He was to be turned down simply because he had not met the expenses of his restoration, an enormous bill, moreover, greatly exceeding the real cost (for huge bonuses or presents must have been included) a bill which he could not have paid without pauperizing his country and endangering its tranquillity. But because he had not paid it, and for no other reason, the Prince planned to drive him out, tear up the Anglo-Castilian treaty of 1362, and also handsomely compensate himself by becoming King of Castile.

It was arguable that this last could be politically justified: for the Prince of Wales to be King of Castile was clearly better, in theory at least, than any alliance with a Castilian king. Had the Prince immediately after Nájera declared himself King of Castile, the coup, disreputable though it would have been, might have succeeded, at any rate for a time, because his army was so strong. But he was far from being a Machiavelli prince. Now, however, enraged at not being paid, he planned to do what he might have accomplished then. It took time for him, apparently, to see himself as he really was, a potential conqueror. When he did catch a glimpse of that exciting image, he liked it, particularly as it was not necessary for him to be ruthless or false, since Don Pedro had given him a satisfying excuse.

But it was a mirage that he was looking at. If his father, before setting out against France, had thought it necessary to make out a legal claim to its throne, what sort of figure would the Prince cut against Don Pedro, unquestionably the legitimate king, with three daughters, moreover, recognized as his heirs? The grandees of Castile would never accept him. True, some of them had accepted Don Henry after his *coup d'état*. But Don Henry, at least, was Castilian and the son of the late King; whereas the Prince would have no fraction of claim and be a foreigner to boot. Even if these deficiencies were conceivably overcome, there was another objection, so fatal as to render the project quite illusory. Who was going to pay for the conquest? The Prince was bankrupt. Though he was not anything like £450,000 in debt, he owed his mercenaries and his vassals very large sums. Far from being able to mount a grand offensive against Castile, poverty had just forced him to vacate the country. Was it his idea to hire himself out to Aragon, Navarre and Portugal? They would supply the finance, he conduct the fighting, and all divide the plunder? One cannot tell what his plan was.

As for what Don Pedro thought of the Prince's departure, we may be sure that his first feeling was one of relief. By the simple expedient of not paying his debts, he had got rid of the foremost soldier in Europe, who at the head of an invincible army was occupying the northern part of his dominions. But as we shall immediately perceive, he could not do without the Prince. He was not strong enough to stand alone. He should have so handled the situation as to have kept in with the one man able and willing to protect him. With Don Henry in France he was exposed to a counterstroke. He had bungled the affair and would pay the penalty with his life. So had the Prince bungled it and his mistake would cost him as dear, for in a last analysis Pedro was as necessary to him as he was to Pedro.

The Ruin of the Black Prince

The Prince was to remain in Aquitaine from August 1367 until the end of 1370. During those three years everything went wrong. Some of his misfortunes he brought on himself, but the worst one was pure mischance; he was attacked by a mortal disease. The Herald, who greatly admired him, writes with emotion: 'The malady began which thereafter lasted all his life. . . . Those who ought to have loved him turned against him. . . . When it was known that he was dangerously ill his enemies began the war again.' At his return all had been affection and pride in his victory. 'Nobly was he received at Bordeaux with crosses and processions, and all the monks came to meet him.' When he dismounted at his residence, St. Andrew's monastery, Joan was there waiting with a crowd of courtiers. Great festivities followed that evening. But after the first happiness of his homecoming he had to face the harsh realities of his situation.

As he had no money, his first act was, of necessity, the dismissal of his mercenaries with a promise to pay them their eight months' arrears when he could. On being dismissed they immediately began looting. He prevailed on them, however, to leave Aquitaine. 'The captains of the mercenary companies' says Froissart 'were all either English or Gascon', and he names in particular Robert Brickett and John Cresswell. 'As they did not want to annoy the Prince, they left the principality as soon as possible and entered France, which they called their room.' They moved across as far as Rheims and 'there wrought many evils and tribulations and were guilty of many villainous deeds'. Already preparing to strike at the Prince, King Charles became the more resolved to hurry on with his preparations, since the loosing of such marauders on France was additional proof that peace between the two countries was impossible as long as Aquitaine remained in English possession.

Besides dismissing his mercenaries without pay, the Prince was obliged to send away unrewarded his Gascon vassals who had followed him to Spain with their contingents. Armagnac, d'Albret and the rest withdrew to their castles, very dissatisfied with an adventure which had brought them no financial profit. Soon afterwards Duke John embarked for England with the contingent he had brought over. The Prince was then left without an army to face the future.

At the very moment he was divesting himself of all military power he received the news that Don Henry had set out for Spain with 3,000 mercenaries to regain what he had lost at Nájera. France was behind the venture. His entry into Spain could only be via Aragon, as on the former occasion with du Guesclin, and it was an open secret that he was going that way. When En Pere heard of the intended violation of his territory, he protested to France and directed that the passes be closed. But Don Henry crossed the Pyrenees by unfrequented tracks and was inside Aragon by the third week of September. How to hold him up was a problem. In a letter[1] addressed to the commander of his troops, En Pere shows how fully he understood the difficulty of combating the new tactics. The commander was ordered not to attack Don Henry's mercenaries when they were dismounted and had taken up a defensive position: 'That is their way of defeating their enemies,' he writes. Keep well away from them, he goes on, and they will have to remount. Then, if they wait for you, you can better attack them.

But it was one thing to know what not to do and another to be skilful enough to take such veterans at the disadvantage required to foil them. Du Guesclin was to show later that he could manage this sort of military prestidigitation. But as En Pere's man had no idea how to manipulate such effects, Don Henry marched through Aragon, just as the English had marched through France, and by the beginning of November entered Burgos. Don Pedro was 400 miles away at Seville. Don Henry had not enough men to march

[1] The relevant quotation from this interesting letter is given by Mr. P. E. Russell on p. 129 of his *English Intervention in Spain*.

there at once and fight him for the possession of the whole kingdom. Nevertheless, by his sudden stroke he had largely nullified the Prince's victory at Nájera.

There was nothing the Prince could do. He had perforce demobilized his army. It was impossible to recall the mercenaries for a new venture when their pay was in arrears for the old. Nor did he desire to rescue Don Pedro for the second time when the bill for the first was outstanding. There remained his new plan to carve up Castile in conjunction with the three other kings of the peninsula. He would continue the negotiations to that end, in the hope that they would adequately support him.

There is little sign that he had realized the gravity of his situation and the need for caution. For he chose this moment to allow du Guesclin to ransom himself. The other prisoners taken at Nájera had paid ransom or been released, like Denia, on security. It had seemed too foolish to let du Guesclin go, though not to accept a ransom was most unusual, but now the Prince was tempted to prefer cash to keeping under restraint the best general on the French side. Froissart, though he records (in Berners' rendering) that the Prince's 'vyyage into Spayne had so sore mynisshed his richesse that it was marveyle to thynke theron', records du Guesclin's release in the form of an anecdote, whose point is rather that the condottiere played successfully on the Prince's conceit of himself. The Prince happened, says the chronicler, to come across du Guesclin one day and asked him how he was. 'My lord,' replied Sir Bertrand, 'I have never been better in my life, and I have good reason, for I am honoured more than any knight in the world, inasmuch as you detain me in prison. For they say throughout France, and elsewhere too, that I am held because you dare not let me out.' 'Come now, Sir Bertrand,' remonstrated the Prince, 'do you really think that we hesitate to release you because of your military prowess? Not a bit of it, my dear sir; pay 100,000 francs and you go free.' Du Guesclin immediately closed with the offer and, helped by King Charles, paid within a month. No doubt this anecdote is partly true and the Prince was piqued because people whispered that he was afraid of du Guesclin, but it seems likely that his chief reason for allowing ransom was that he could not afford to do without the money.

Immediately on his return from Spain, the Prince had consulted his council on how to raise revenue to meet his liabilities. There was no question of asking Edward III for a grant. The King had

5. Fight on a bridge between English and French troops

6. Monument to Sir John Chandos at Lussac

made it clear from the first that the Spanish expedition was the Prince's responsibility. The council advised the reimposition of the hearth tax, which the Prince had levied on three previous occasions. A tax of tenpence for each fireplace does not seem excessive nowadays, though then it represented about two or three days' wages. The Aquitainean parliament was summoned and did not refuse the grant, as it might have, on the ground that the Spanish expedition, undertaken in the higher strategic interests of England and in accordance with the terms of the Anglo-Castilian treaty of 1362, was not a concern of the people of Aquitaine, who, moreover, had not been asked to pay for it in the first instance and now should not be expected to make good Don Pedro's default. The tax was granted and was collected in the towns without excessive difficulty. Nor did it meet elsewhere with more popular opposition than had the previous hearth taxes. But unexpected resistance was offered by certain magnates, especially d'Armagnac and d'Albret.

These lords, though they had supported the Prince with their contingents in Spain, had never been altogether anglophil at heart. They had gone to Spain, less as loyal vassals than as participants in an adventure from which they hoped to derive advantages. But they had got nothing out of Pedro, no titles, estates, not even their expenses. In this mood of disillusion the objections they had had to the Prince's rule from the start acquired fresh weight. His haughty manner seemed less bearable;[1] that his council and high officials were nearly all English seemed a graver slight. From the time he became Prince of Aquitaine his policy had been to increase his authority at their expense. Their claim to virtual independence inside their domains had been disregarded. He had interfered particularly in an attempt to centralize the administration of justice. All in all, their opinion was that they were less masters of their territories under his rule than they had been under the French King's. The hearth tax, sanctioned though it had been by a parliament consisting of three estates—lords, churchmen and burgesses—they disliked as a further trespass on their preserves. As the tax was as unpopular as are all taxes, their resistance to it gave them popular backing.

This disaffection towards the Prince coincided with King

[1] Cf. the French opinion: 'The prince was the proudest man ever born of woman.' Jean Cuvelier in his *Chronique de Bertrand du Guesclin* (ed. E. Charrière, Paris, 1839, cited p. 517 of vol. 7, Lettenhove edn. of Froissart.)

Charles' preparations to re-open the war with England. Herein the ill-disposed lords saw their opportunity. King Charles also saw in them his opportunity. If he could detach them from the Prince, it would greatly facilitate his reconquest of Aquitaine. In this he was successful. The Gascon magnates went to Paris, where they were received with an affability which contrasted with the Prince's stiffness. They poured their complaints into his ears. He was most sympathetic. D'Albret even married the Queen's sister. Charles was able to come to a secret agreement with them. As soon as he was ready to re-open the war, they would come over to his side. When they had transferred their allegiance the rest would follow suit. Large parts of Aquitaine would be regained without fighting. In this astute manner Charles succeeded in undermining the Prince's authority before beginning the reconquest.

The pourparlers with the Gascon lords took place during the first six months of 1368. King Charles' next step was to send du Guesclin to Spain to help Don Henry to finish off Don Pedro. This energetic stroke, for which he found the money and the men, contrasts strongly with the Prince's unrealistic plans to carve up Castile. It is true that he did offer to rescue Don Pedro a second time if he paid his outstanding bill, but neither he nor Edward III would face the fact that if they were to prevent the French putting in their ally, they must find money by imposing taxes in England.

Du Guesclin with a small but powerful body of mercenaries crossed into Castile via Aragon, despite En Pere's protests and attempts to stop him, and in February 1369 reached Don Henry's camp before Toledo, a city which the usurper's troops had been trying to take for some time.

Don Pedro, who had not yet fought a pitched battle with Don Henry, was at this moment marching up from Seville to the relief of Toledo with a big but old-fashioned army, containing some men-at-arms and Andalusian genetours but largely composed of Moors from Granada and Jews, who in fourteenth-century parlance were termed enemies of God and considered disreputable allies. On learning of this, Don Henry and du Guesclin went south from Toledo to attack him and on 14 March 1369 took him by surprise at Montiel, a town on the northern slopes of the Sierra Morena. There are various accounts of the battle and its sequel. A few sentences from Froissart's (in Berners' translation) will suggest the exotic colour of the encounter. Don Henry and du Guesclin's veteran mercenaries fell on Don Pedro before he could concentrate. 'There was a marveylous great and ferse batayle . . . for kyng Henry and Sir Bertram of Clesquy sought their enemyes with so coragyous and ferse wyll that none coulde endure agaynst them. Howbeit, that was nat lyghtly done, for kyng Dampeter and his company were six against one, but they were taken so sodenly that they were disconfyted. . . . The Jewes fledde and turned their backes . . . but they of Granade fought fersely with their bowes and archegays. . . . King Dampeter was a hardy knight, and fought valyantly with a great axe, and gave therwith many a great stroke. . . . And the banner of kyng Henry, his brother, mette and recountred agaynst his, eche of them cryenge their cryes.' But Don Pedro's centre began to open and the rout to commence. He was advised to withdraw into a neighbouring castle, which he did with twelve followers. Henry invested the castle. Don Pedro might have been safe, for the castle was strong; but it was not provisioned. His only course was to try to escape, no easy task, 'for they were so straitly watched day and night that a byrde coud nat come out of the castell without spyeng'. However, all perils considered he resolved to make an attempt one midnight. He issued out with his twelve followers, 'and went downe by a hye way as privelу as they coude devyce'. The night was very dark but one of du Guesclin's old comrades in arms, the Bègue de Villaines, a Gascon condottiere, was keeping close watch and heard hoof beats. 'Than the Bègue stept forthe with his dagger in his hande, and came to a man who was nere to kynge Dampeter, and sayd, What art thou? and he rushed forth with his horse fro hym, and passed by them. The Begue stept to kyng Dampeter, who was next, and sayde, What art thou? shewe me thy name or thou art but deed; and toke hym by the bridell, for he thought he shulde nat passe fro hym as the other dyde. And whan kyng Dampeter sawe suche a route of men of warre before hym, and that he coude nat scape, sayd, Sir Begue of Villayns, I am kyng Dampeter of Castell. I yelde me to you as a prisoner. . . . I shall pay to you such ransome as ye wyll desyre . . . so that I may scape from the handes of the bastarde my brother.'

De Villaines, who seems to have given Don Pedro a promise that he would be safe, took him to a house or tent near by. Nevertheless, he immediately informed Don Henry, who hastened to the scene with the Vicomte de Rochebertin. 'Assoone as king Henry was entred into the chambre, he sayde, Wher is that horeson and Jew that calleth himselfe kyng of Castell? Then kynge Dampeter, who was a ryght hardy and cruell knyght, avaunced himselfe, and sayd, Nay, thou art a hores sonne, and I am sonne to kyng Alfons.'[1]

The two kings then fought. Don Pedro caught hold of Henry and holding him down on a bench 'set his hand on his knyfe and would have slayne hym without remedy' had not the Vicomte de Rochebertin seized 'kyng Dampeter by the legge and turned him upsedowne'. Henry then plunged his dagger into him. Two of Don Pedro's followers sought to help him, but were killed. It is of interest to note that both were English, the one named Ralph Helme, generally called the Green Squire, and the other James Rolland. It seems strange employ for two English country gentlemen of the fourteenth century to be body servants of King Pedro.

'Thus ended kyng Dampeter of Castell, who somtyme reigned in great prosperyte,' concludes Froissart. Don Pedro came to a bad end because he was incompetent. He lost his throne in the first instance because he offended some of his magnates; he lost it for the second time because he did not know how to manage the Prince. Nevertheless, he had his following, the legitimists in his own country, and, later, his apologists in England, whose policy as we shall see, was founded on the fact that his was the legitimate line. Chaucer was expressing their view when in the Monk's Tale he wrote the passage beginning: 'O noble, worthy Peter, glory of Spain.'

Since Don Pedro's death put an end to the Anglo-Castilian treaty of 1362 and the advantages it was concluded to secure, it is significant of the Prince's confused thinking that he was pleased when he heard the news, reflecting that with Don Pedro out of the way, his plan to carve up Castile would be easier to realize.[2] That he should not by now have abandoned this scheme is extraordinary if we consider how rapidly his situation had been deteriorating. His health was much worse. The malady he contracted immediately after his return from Spain had been declared by the French doctors to be dropsy, says Froissart. His body swelled, his appetite failed, and he grew so weak that he could not mount his horse. Soldier and sportsman, he was becoming an invalid at the early age of thirty-eight. King Charles was kept fully informed of his

[1] For the allegation that Don Pedro was not the true son of his father King Alfonso see Jean de Venette (*Chr.*, p. 136 in Newhall edn.) who reports the rumour that he was a changeling of Jewish parentage secretly substituted for the daughter to whom Queen Maria, Alfonso's wife, had just given birth.

[2] Cf. P. E. Russell, op. cit., p. 148.

condition and felt that the moment to strike was near. A lawyer by inclination rather than a soldier, his first moves were in the sphere of law. The complaints against the Prince made by his disaffected Gascon vassals were consolidated as an appeal to the crown of France. No appeal lay since Aquitaine had been ceded to Edward III by the Treaty of Brétigny eight years before. But the treaty was open to legal objection. It had been agreed that on Edward's abandonment of his claim to the French throne, Charles would abandon his right of overlordship in Aquitaine. Formal letters to that effect were to be exchanged. They had never been exchanged. Charles was thus able to claim that he was still suzerain and that the appeal did lie. Taking his stand on this legal ground, he summoned the Prince on 25 January 1369, six weeks before Don Pedro's defeat, to answer before the parliament in Paris the charges made against him by the appellants. 'It is unnecessary to enquire,' remarks Froissart, 'whether the Prince was annoyed when he saw himself summoned in the name of his subjects to a foreign court, he who considered himself one of the grandees of the world, whom men of war everywhere obeyed.' The reply he sent back to King Charles sounded well: 'I will certainly come to Paris but with my basinet on my head and 40,000 men with me.' It did not, however, alarm King Charles, who knew it to be an empty boast. Indeed, it was what he required. It enabled him to declare the Prince a disobedient vassal and the fief of Aquitaine to be forfeit.

In April Charles sent a formal defiance to King Edward III, which amounted to a declaration of war. To make it the more insulting he had it delivered by a footman of his household. The scene is vividly described by Froissart: 'Parliament was assembled at Westminster. The King was there and his two sons, the Duke of Lancaster and the Earl of Cambridge, with the prelates, lords and knights. The footman came to the door of the chamber and told the porter he was from the King of France. "Come in with me," said the porter, impressed by the name, "and I will try to arrange for you to speak to the King." They went in together, followed a moment later by Lord Henry Percy.[1] "My lord," said the porter, "this footman here has a letter from the King of France or so he says. If it please your lordship and is correct, he may be taken forward." "Certainly," said Lord Percy. He himself went ahead, bowed to the King and his sons and the lords, and said a messenger

[1] Afterwards Earl of Northumberland, brother of Thomas Percy.

had arrived from the King of France. "Let him approach," said the King. The footman knelt and presented the letter. The King took it, opened it and had it read. It contained a plain statement that the King of France defied him. On hearing it the English lords were very surprised and looked at each other, unable to utter a word.'

The same month of April 1369 King Charles opened the war by taking possession of Abbeville, capital of Ponthieu, a small county ceded to England by the Treaty of Brétigny.

'The French king,' says Froissart, 'got him friends in all parts, or else he durst not have done what he did.' Inside Aquitaine he had the disaffected lords. Inside France he had been steadily strengthening his position.[1] The crown was appreciably stronger than in the miserable years after Poitiers. Charles' three brothers, Louis, John and Philip, last seen at Poitiers as boys in their teens, were now thirty-one, thirty and twenty-eight, Dukes of Anjou, Berry and Burgundy, important figures on whom he could rely. The nobility in general supported him in his determination to turn out the English. Something like a wind of national feeling was behind him. Negotiations in Flanders led to the marriage of his youngest brother Philip to the Duke of Flanders' daughter, an alliance that strengthened his position in the Low Countries which hitherto had leaned actively in favour of Edward. And Don Henry had signed an undertaking to let him have the Castilian fleet. The English were left with no support on the Continent beyond what mercenaries they could afford to hire. Some of the Free Companies would serve them, but others would sell their services to Charles, if they got more that way than by ravaging France. With the Gascon lords added, ready to rise in his favour when he invaded Aquitaine, his chances were better than they had ever been. What hesitations he had at the thought of the proved superiority of the English soldiery disappeared.

The Chandos Herald laments: 'All kinds of mischance arose; one after another they befell the noble Prince, who lay abed.' After the defiance at Westminster, efforts were made to strengthen Aquitaine to meet the coming attack. King Edward sent his son

[1] Cf. Lettenhove, vol. 7, p. 537. Christine de Pisan reports that Charles had all the armour in Paris put to rights; that he hired crossbowmen in Genoa, bought horses in Germany and brought armourers from Milan. On 3 April 1369 he forbade games of chance and ordered the people to practise shooting with the bow and crossbow.

reinforcements under his third surviving son, Edmund of Langley, Earl of Cambridge, and John Hastings, Earl of Pembroke, a small force, but all he could afford, of 400 men-at-arms and 400 archers. The Prince recalled from France the mercenaries who had served him in Spain. His best general, Sir John Chandos, was away in Normandy on his estate of St. Sauveur-le-Vicomte. He returned in haste. Sir Robert Knollys also hastened from his castle at Dervel in Brittany with 40 men-at-arms and some hundreds of archers. But in the course of 1369 the French, operating with small forces raised by the chief nobility of that part, gained control of Quercy and Rouergue, the two counties of Aquitaine that lay on its eastern border. Having won the lords, the castles had not to be stormed. With the castles at their disposal, they dominated the countryside. These French successes inclined other towns in Aquitaine to come over to the French side and several declared their allegiance to Charles.

While this attack was developing in the south-east, the French were also attacking Poitou in the north of Aquitaine with forces under Charles' second brother, John Duke of Berry. It was in this area that Chandos commanded and it was here, at Lussac, on 31 December 1369, that he was mortally wounded. The circumstances of his death, whose detailed description is one of Froissart's great pieces, throw light on the nature of the fighting, much of it between quite small parties.

Chandos was at Poitiers[1] with Thomas Percy, Guichard d'Angle and Louis de Harcourt, the Norman lord, and others of the nobility of Poitou, the part of Aquitaine most loyal to the Prince. On 30 December 1369 they set out with a company of 300 men-at-arms to retake the fortified town of Saint Savin, twenty-eight miles east of Poitiers, which had fallen into French hands. They reached it after dark, but failed to effect the surprise which was planned and withdrew disappointed to Chauvigny, about halfway back to Poitiers. There Chandos decided to stay the night. But Guichard d'Angle and Thomas Percy, each with his retinue, went off in different directions, in the hope that they might come on something which would compensate them for the disappointment at Saint Savin. Chandos entered a house and told them to light a good fire, for it was a cold winter night. 'Out of humour because he had failed in his purpose,' says Froissart, 'he stood in the kitchen warming himself. His men joked with him, hoping to bring him out of his

[1] For what follows see map on page 57.

melancholy.' After a while he went to sleep. Before dawn a man came into the house and told him that a French raiding party had left Saint Savin and was heading for Lussac, twelve miles south of Chauvigny. Chandos replied that he didn't care; he had no intention of going after them in the dark. But presently he changed his mind and decided to try to intercept them. His men put on their armour and they all mounted their horses.

From Chauvigny to Lussac there were two roads, one on each side of the Vienne river. When Percy had left, he crossed the Vienne at Chauvigny and, as it happened, went south towards Lussac by the western road. Chandos now took the eastern road. His information was that the raiding party intended to cross the Vienne by the bridge at Lussac and was riding towards it diagonally from Saint Savin. His aim was to get there first.

At dawn Percy, who had reached Lussac and halted, was surprised to see a French force riding on the east side of the river. He dismounted his men and hastened to occupy his end of the bridge. The French came up and also dismounted. Pages were told to take the horses a little back. The men-at-arms, a larger force than Percy's, advanced up the bridge, which was hump-backed, to force their way over.

While the French were so occupied, Chandos, who had been riding fast, came galloping up. The French knew who he was at once, for his banner was displayed. When he was within earshot he halted and shouted sarcastically at the French: 'You ride at your pleasure as if the country were all yours, but I assure it is not so. I am seneschal.' Thomas Percy neither saw nor heard anything of all this. The Vienne is a broad river and the hump-backed bridge also blocked the view.

The fight began by one of the Frenchmen rushing forward and attacking an English squire called Simkin Dodall. Hitting him on the chest, he knocked him off his horse and battered him with his sword. 'Afoot, afoot,' cried Chandos to his men; they all dismounted and formed up. Froissart then gives the following picture: 'Sir John Chandos was a big strong knight, fully accoutred, his banner before him, and his men surrounding him. Over his armour he wore a mantle which reached the ground. On it were his armorial bearings in white samite, both in front and behind. He made a very imposing figure. In this guise, sword in hand, he advanced step by step towards the enemy. Dew had fallen that morning, the ground was damp. As he went he stumbled over his long garment, slipped and fell. A squire called Jakes de Saint-Martin struck at him with his sword. The blow entered between the nose and the forehead. Sir John did not see it coming because he was blind in one eye. As mischance would have it, he had not pulled down his vizor. It was a mortal wound. He rolled over twice in agony and never spoke again.'

His knights stood round him 'like men out of their minds'. A desperate fight ensued, the English side much outnumbered. Extraordinary to relate, Thomas Percy remained at the other end of the bridge still oblivious of what was happening. The struggle ended with Sir John's men overcome and taken.

Suddenly Guichard d'Angle and his retinue galloped into view. When the French descried these fresh opponents they lost heart. They were too tired to fight a second battle. To avoid being rushed and perhaps badly hurt before they could surrender, they quickly surrendered to their prisoners. So when Guichard d'Angle's men 'came on them, their spears in their rests, crying their cries', they protested: 'Do us no hurt, we are prisoners already.' D'Angle asked Sir John's knights if that were so, and they replied it was, for that entitled them to claim the French ransoms, which otherwise would have gone to d'Angle's party.

Chandos, still unconscious, was taken out of his armour and laid on a mattress. They carried him, says Froissart, to Mortemer[1]

[1] Mortemer (now spelt Morthemer) lies eight miles north-west of Lussac. It is a small village at the foot of a hill some hundred feet high, on top of which is a Gothic castle and Romanesque church, both of which existed in Chandos' time. When I visited the church in 1956 I saw in it by the west wall what appears to be the tomb of Chandos or part of it. It consists of a heavy slab of stone, rising to a spine along the centre. There is no inscription, but on the side of the spine towards the interior of the church is carved a sword and an escutcheon. The coat of arms is not decipherable. The *Dict. Nat. Biog.* states that some lines in French were long extant under or above the tomb. The two final lines made Chandos say:

> '*Les Poictevins près Lussac me defirent:*
> *A Mortemer mon corps enterrer firent.*'

There is no trace of this now. At Lussac, where the bridge (a modern one) is called the Pont de Chandos, there is a monument to the knight. It is situated in a grove of chestnut trees a short distance from the west end of the bridge. Here a slab, similar in shape to the slab in the church of Morthemer, is supported on six stout Romanesque pillars, the whole standing on a modern plinth. By it is a stone on which is a French inscription dated 1910 which states that the monument was erected by the English in the fourteenth century to commemorate the death of Chandos at the bridge. It also states that

where he died next day, and was buried in the church. He was between forty-five and fifty. His death was a severe loss for the Prince. Another of his distinguished adjutants, Sir James Audeley, had died a few months earlier. Paris was jubilant over Sir John's death, says the Herald. It was said there: 'All will now be ours, as true as is the paternoster.'

While the Prince thus lost two of his best commanders, Charles was able to retrieve du Guesclin from Spain. Since Don Pedro's death in March 1369 the famous condottiere had continued with Don Henry. Now in July 1370 he was recalled to France and put in command of forces in the Garonne valley. He advanced into the centre of Aquitaine with the caution characteristic of him. The Prince remained too ill to take the field in person. In a very short time the county of Périgord was lost, the county of Limousin isolated from Bordeaux and its chief town, Limoges, persuaded to surrender.

During these months the Prince had another disappointment. The grandiose plan of making himself King of Castile in alliance with Aragon, Navarre and Portugal was shown to be the visionary ambition which in fact it had always been. The sovereigns of those states, aware that the Prince, hard pressed as he was in France, could give them no appreciable assistance, agreed to carve up Castile themselves. The King of Portugal had become acceptable to the legitimists and they were agreeable to his assuming the title of King of Castile. Don Henry could not expect French assistance, while France was occupied in fighting England, and to overcome him should be feasible for his three Spanish neighbours. This was not to happen; Don Henry survived; and was able to render valuable help to France with his fleet. But as things stood at the moment, the Prince had the mortification of seeing himself squeezed out of a plan, which, however illusory, had remained dear to his heart.

Du Guesclin's successes in the Garonne valley and the grave situation throughout Aquitaine in general roused King Edward to fresh efforts. In the second half of 1370 he sent over two expeditions, one under Duke John to Aquitaine, and the other

the monument was removed from its original position right on the river bank to its present site in 1910. On one side of the spined slab is inscribed a pennon and on the other a sword and escutcheon similar to those on the Morthemer slab. This escutcheon is also undecipherable. There is no inscription on the monument itself.

under Sir Robert Knollys to Calais with the object of drawing the French forces in that direction. The Prince had been more enraged by his recent loss of Limoges than by any of the reverses which had befallen him. The inhabitants of the town had, he considered, surrendered it treacherously. On the arrival of his brother, Duke John, at the end of August he resolved to retake it. Despite his increasing illness he got out of bed and was carried in a litter along with his troops. He was living at the time at Cognac on the Charente and going east from there was joined by his brother's force, marching up from Bordeaux. The combined forces invested the town. The wall was mined, a breach was made and they burst in, before du Guesclin could come up. The Prince had resolved to make an example as a warning to other towns which might desert him. He gave orders for a massacre of the inhabitants, though there was no evidence that they had pressed or even desired the garrison to surrender to the French; it was the Bishop of Limoges who was responsible. The Chandos Herald passes over the episode in silence, but Froissart, though he much admired the Prince as a great knight, was shocked by the massacre. He says: 'it was pitiable to see men, women and children kneeling before the Prince for mercy. He was so inflamed with anger that he took no heed of them. No one was heard, but all put to death, as they were met. More than 10,000 men, women and children were slain and beheaded that day.' And he adds: 'God have mercy on their souls, for indeed they were martyrs.' The Prince watched from a carriage, attended by his two brothers, Duke John of Lancaster and Edmund Earl of Cambridge.

There is nothing to show that the massacre shocked opinion in England. For instance, the monk Walsingham of St. Albans, who wrote the *Chronicon Angliae*, excuses the Prince on the ground that he had warned the inhabitants of Limoges on investing the town that if they did not surrender he would put them to the sword. Their obstinate resistance brought a just retribution. They were not massacred but punished both for resistance and for deserting to the French. If this was the view held in the monastery of St. Albans, it was no doubt the view of the church generally and of most of the laity. The Prince's brothers seem to have watched the massacre without demur. Yet neither of them were brutal men. It may well be, therefore, that Froissart's condemnation shows exceptional humanity for the period. The Prince was, after all, a captain of mercenaries who, when out of employ, were brigands. That he was no harder than he was is perhaps more surprising than his having once ordered a massacre. It seems to be a fact that his action did not abate the veneration in which he was held by high and low in England.[1]

The Prince returned to his sick bed at Cognac. The expedition to Limoges had made him worse. The situation in Aquitaine continued to deteriorate. The massacre had no effect as a deterrent. But Sir Robert Knollys' demonstration from Calais alarmed the French. They had not been able to stop him so far. By September 1370 he was near Paris. King Charles was advised to send for du Guesclin from Aquitaine and give him the command-in-chief as Constable.

On receiving the summons du Guesclin put his men into castles with orders to hold what he had won and rode the long journey from Aquitaine to Paris. He was now an international celebrity, Duke of Trastamare, Duke of Molina and had even on 29 March 1366 been crowned King of Granada.[2] Despite his unprepossessing appearance and humble birth, the French nobility were ready to serve under him. Froissart has an anecdote describing his interview with the King. On being told that he was to be Constable he said: 'I am not worthy of so high an office, being but a poor knight, though I admit that fortune has a little advanced me.' The King replied that he would take no excuses. Du Guesclin made a show of insisting: 'My birth is too low to allow me to give orders to your brothers, the Dukes of Anjou and Berry, now in command of the forces.' 'The dukes will have strict instructions to obey you and if they do not I shall be very angry,' said Charles. After this display of tact, du Guesclin accepted. The King invited him to dinner and condescended to give him a seat at his table.

Du Guesclin's immediate task was to get rid of Sir Robert Knollys, who since the death of Chandos and Audeley was, after Calveley, the leading captain of mercenaries. The Chronicles declare that he had regal wealth, a fortune founded by systematic pillage in the Loire valley when in 1357 he was head of the brigand bands. As a regular soldier he had fought at Crécy and Poitiers,

[1] Massacres have a way of happening without their perpetrators being fully aware of what they are doing. For instance in our day, General Dyer at Amritsar. He was astonished when what he did was called a massacre.

[2] For this curious fact see note on page 49 of P. E. Russell's *English Intervention in Spain and Portugal*. It is to be found in a letter written by En Pere of Aragon on 5 April 1366. The letter is quoted in R. Delachenal's *Histoire de Charles V*, vol. III, p. 281.

and he and his contingent had helped to turn the scale at Nájera, where he served in the van along with Chandos.[1] After the return to Aquitaine he held for a while the appointment of Master of the Prince's Household. He owned estates and the castle of Nerval in Brittany where he was known, as if a French nobleman, as the Sieur de Nerval. He also had a large house in London near the Tower in Seething Lane, and a manor in Norfolk.

At this time he was about fifty. The raiding party which he had led from Calais is said to have consisted of some 1,500 men-at-arms and 4,000 archers, all mounted. It may seem strange that with so small a force he was able to penetrate as far as Paris. More than one English raid had been carried as far from the time of Crécy onwards, but now, when King Charles had so much improved his situation that he could brave the Prince in Aquitaine, it is felt surprising that he could not stop Knollys. But a force of this kind, particularly when so strong in archers, could not be successfully attacked, as had been frequently demonstrated. It had to be worn down by attrition. Not till it was weary, weakened, diseased, hungry, could it be overcome. Du Guesclin was recognized as the great expert in thus wearing down an opponent.

Knollys had done a lot of damage, burning crops and villages. But as was usual in such raids, no fortified places of importance had been taken. His men were getting tired of a campaign which yielded neither glory nor ransoms. A sense of futility had begun to afflict them. Knights attached great importance to feats of arms. But the French knights had given them no opportunity to show their mettle. This sense of disillusion is shown by the following anecdote from Froissart. When Knollys' men burnt the villages in sight of the Paris garrison, no one sallied out to attack them. One English knight could stand it no longer. He must have something to boast about at home and decided to gallop alone up to the gate, strike it with his lance and return. He achieved the feat, no one took up the challenge, but on the way back through the suburbs a butcher pole-axed him.

Among Knollys' captains were some young members of the aristocracy who did not much care for him. They used to call him

[1] The *Chronicon Angliae* of St. Albans especially mentions Knollys in its short account of the battle. 'Superveniente domino Roberto Knollis, cum electa gente quae eum secuta fuerat et nostra pars augetur et animatur, et pars adversa debilitatur et terretur.' Enlivened his own side and terrified the enemy —that was the report of Knollys which reached the famous monastery.

'the old brigand'.[1] When Christmas 1370 approached and he ordered a withdrawal towards his castle in Brittany to winter there, they grumbled that he had given them no chance of distinguishing themselves. On their reaching the Loire, a certain Sir John Menstreworth, 'quick on the draw but a perverse untrustworthy fellow', prompted some of the young noblemen to refuse to go farther. The force split in two. When Knollys left for Brittany, the rest remained on the Loire. Du Guesclin at last saw his chance and, hastening to the Loire, overwhelmed at Pontvallain the forces of the malcontents on 4 December 1370. Menstreworth, who was responsible for the split, deserted to the French. He was only brought to book seven years later, when his head was stuck on London Bridge, and remained there until in 1381 its spike was taken by the Archbishop of Canterbury's head, a very curious posthumous distinction.

The Knollys raid, which fizzled out in this way, was the last military event of the Black Prince's time abroad. Next month, January 1371, he had a private sorrow; his elder son, Edward, died aged six. The Prince, now quite an invalid, had already decided to go home and had received his father's permission. With the Princess and little Richard, aged four, a very pretty child and, it was said, the image of his father, he left Bordeaux for England the same month. Before starting he summoned those lords of Aquitaine who were still faithful to him, such as Sir Guichard d'Angle and the Captal de Buch. In the farewell speech which he made them, he said he had done his best, but now must go to recover his health. He was leaving his brother, Duke John of Lancaster, in his place and asked them to serve him truly. They promised to do so and, says Froissart, did homage to the duke and kissed his mouth. The royal party embarked with five hundred men-at-arms and their complement of archers. The Prince's younger brother, Cambridge, and John Hastings, Earl of Pembroke, accompanied them. They had a good wind and arrived safely at Plymouth. The Prince, however, was too ill to travel farther and did not leave for London until after Easter. He was met outside the city by the Mayor and leading gentry on 19 April 1371 and conducted to the Savoy. Thence he was carried to Windsor to see his father, now in his sixtieth year and the

[1] 'Quem vispilionem veterem appellavit.' See *Chronicon Angliae*, p. 66 (ed. E. M. Thompson, Rolls Series) for this expression and the whole passage.

forty-fifth of his reign. From Windsor he and his family moved to Berkhamsted in Hertfordshire where he had a castle and a manor.[1] His career was at an end; he was very ill, heavily in debt and hugely disappointed.

[1] Extensive but scanty remains of the Black Prince's castle of Berkhamsted (twenty-seven miles from London) are to be seen today near the railway station. Froissart stayed here with the Prince and Princess in 1361.

The Loss of Aquitaine

The Prince's homecoming had been quiet for a national hero; for he remained a hero despite his mishandling of the Castilian problem and failure to defend Aquitaine against the French. These could not tarnish a reputation so solidly founded on the two victories of Poitiers and Nájera, the most spectacular ever won by an English commander on the continent. Moreover, the tragedy of his illness touched the heart. The *Anonimalle Chronicle* terms him 'the comfort of all England', the *Chronicon Angliae* 'the unconquerable Prince'. The mayor and aldermen of London, the richest and most influential body in England after the lords, desired to show their appreciation of his services and, recalling how he had melted down his plate to pay his soldiers at the start of the Spanish expedition, made him a present of a new service, consisting of silver porringers, salvers, handled cups, basins and ewers, salt cellars and mugs, in all 165 pieces to a total value of £688 10s. 4d., a sum comparable to £30,000 today. At about the same time they also made the Princess a gift of £333 6s. 8d. 'for which we thank you with all our heart' as she warmly wrote to them.[1]

With change and rest the Prince's health seems to have slightly improved. Though his dropsy greatly enfeebled him, he was able to get about a little and was not tied to Berkhamsted. Another manor of his was at Kennington, near the present Vauxhall bridge. He sometimes stayed there. It was convenient for the Palace of Westminster, the large moated cluster of buildings where his

[1] Riley's *Memorials of London*, pp. 351 and 362, where the relevant documents are given in full.

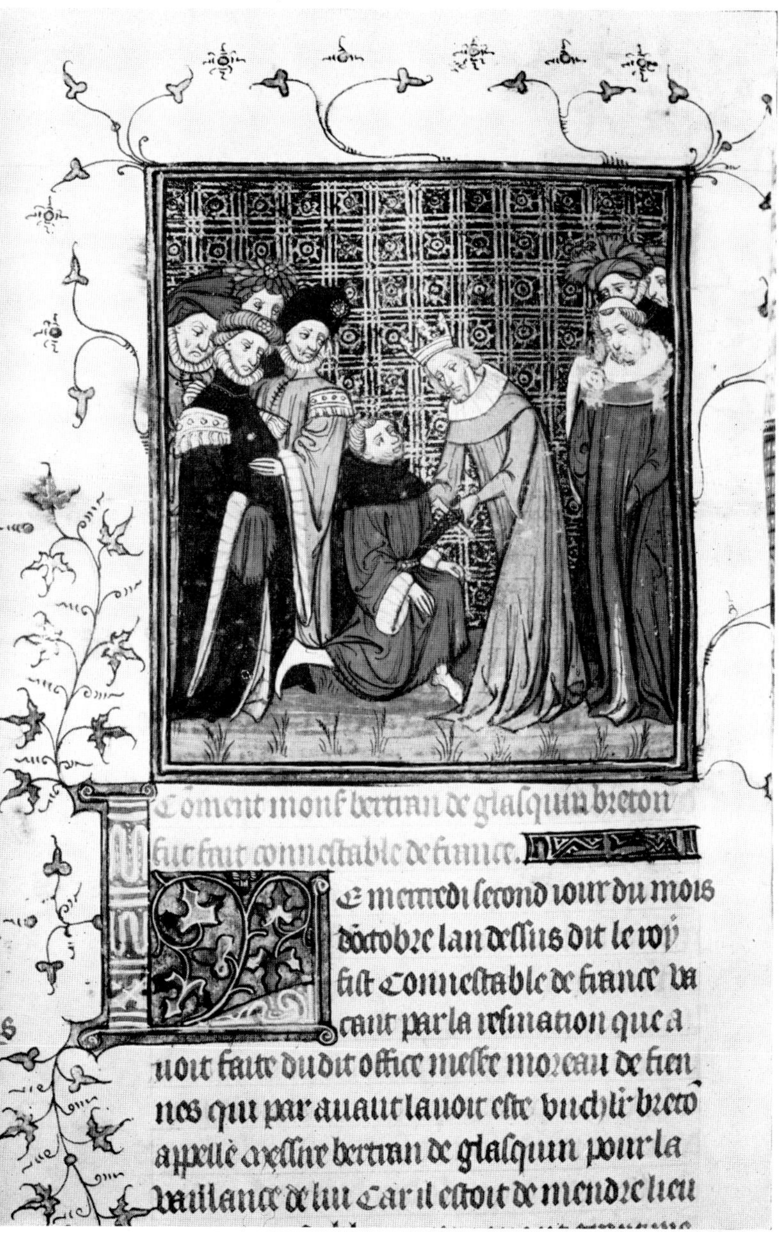

Coment mons bertran de glasquin breton
fut fait connestable de france.

Le mercredi second iour du mois
doctobre lan dessus dit le roy
fist connestable de france va
cant par la resination que a
uoit faite dudit office messe moreau de fien
nes qui par auant lauoit este
appelle a ce messire bertran de glasquin pour la
vaillance de lui car il estoit de mendre lieu

7. Charles V makes du Guesclin Constable of France

8. Sea fighting at La Rochelle

father held court, if not at Windsor or at the palace in the Tower of London. Many other manors[1] throughout the kingdom belonged to the Prince, whose rents provided him with a large income, so that in spite of his debts he was able to live in the grand style to which he and the Princess were accustomed. But it is unlikely that he took the prominent part at court functions which as heir to the throne was to have been expected. He had returned to find his father involved in a court scandal. King Edward's Flemish wife, Queen Philippa, had died two years earlier. Some time before her death he had taken up with one of her waiting-women, Alice Perrers. Her enemies declared that she was the daughter of a plasterer. But it seems her father was a Hertfordshire knight. The King was certainly very fond of her. She used her influence with him to make money, many people being ready to pay her for speaking on their behalf. The story went that she had once got on to the King's Bench in Westminster Hall and told the judges the way she wanted a verdict to go. Her power over the King was attributed to aphrodisiacs and she was said to employ a magician to bind him with spells, accusations which have been made against all royal mistresses. There is no evidence to show what attitude the Prince adopted towards her; no doubt she knew how to charm him, as a little later she was to charm his brother, Duke John. She was evidently a woman of great vitality.

Advising his father on the affairs of Aquitaine was the Prince's chief responsibility. After his departure thence a short lull supervened. The French had drawn off forces to resist Knollys. In the autumn of 1371 the great news was Duke John's marriage to Constance, Don Pedro's daughter. The three girls, Beatrice, Constance and Isabella, had been living in Gascony ever since 1366, when their father fled from Castile, or rather Constance and Isabella had, for Beatrice died in 1367. After Nájera they might have returned to Spain, but the Prince detained them as sureties for Don Pedro's debts. When he turned against Pedro and planned to make himself King of Castile, they were still detained because he did not want them to return to Spain and join the legitimist party, which would have put forward Constance as rightful Queen of Castile, as in fact she was, thereby making it more difficult for him to realize his ambition. With his departure, however, the situation

[1] The Prince also had 'a great house for the most part built of stone' (Stow's *Survey of London*) in Fish Street, near London Bridge. By Henry VIII's time it had become a hotel called the Black Bull.

changed. Duke John was a widower. His wife, Blanche, daughter of Henry, Duke of Lancaster, had died in 1369. He could do what the Prince could not do—marry Constance, and as her husband become titular King of Castile. She became an asset instead of an obstacle. It was ascertained that the legitimist party was prepared to accept this arrangement and recognize Duke John as their king. The wedding took place in September 1371. Duke John was thirty-one and Constance seventeen. By all accounts she was a pious rather dull girl with a sense of her own importance and a quiet determination to return to Castile as Queen.

Duke John's chance of succeeding where his brother, the Prince, had failed was not too bad, inasmuch as he had (what the Prince could never have had) a legal claim and the support of a party inside Castile. But as by 1371 Don Henry had greatly strengthened his position, it was an open question whether the legitimist party would be able to give much support. And the old question remained—where was the money, energy and skill coming from for an invading army strong enough to defeat Don Henry?—a very pertinent question when money, energy and skill were lacking for the defence of Aquitaine. Nevertheless, Duke John's claim to the Castilian throne continued for many years to be a major issue in English policy.

After the marriage Duke John returned to England with his bride and her sister Isabella. Guichard d'Angle was in his suite. Aquitaine was left in charge of Sir Thomas Felton, the Seneschal, a Northumbrian knight, veteran of Crécy, Poitiers, the Spanish campaign, and kinsman of the William Felton killed at Vitoria. He was not a very prominent figure, but he had to assist him, Thomas Percy and the Captal de Buch.

Duke John and his party reached London in November 1371. The Prince felt sufficiently well to join their procession as it entered the city. 'The Prince of England accompanied by several lords and knights, the Mayor of London and a great number of the commons, well dressed and nobly mounted, conducted the lady, the Duke of Lancaster's wife, through London in a great and solemn procession. In Cheapside were assembled many gentlemen with their wives and daughters to look at the beauty of the young lady. The procession passed in good order along to the Savoy.'[1]

[1] *Anonimalle Chronicle* (Galbraith's edition, p. 69). John of Gaunt began at this time to enlarge and beautify his palace, the Savoy, which had been built by his former father-in-law, Henry, Duke of Lancaster.

In January 1372 Edward's Council formally recognized Duke John as Castilian Pretender by allowing him to quarter his arms with those of Castile. In writing he was henceforth to be addressed as King of Castile and orally as Monseigneur d'Espaigne. He had his own chancery for dealing with his Spanish interests and in letters used the traditional Castilian autograph, *Nos el Rey*.

Soon afterwards Isabella was married to Duke John's brother, Edmund[1] of Langley, Earl of Cambridge, so that, in case Constance should die prematurely, he could claim the Castilian throne.

Consultations with Duke John convinced Edward that unless a great effort were made, Aquitaine would be completely lost. To get together another expeditionary force was not easy. However, what money and reinforcements could be scraped together were sent out in the early summer of 1372 under the Earl of Pembroke who, though only twenty-five, had the experience of having served before in Aquitaine. The reinforcements were not large, but they included archers and horses, and money to pay them. Guichard d'Angle, who had made a great impression in England and been created a Garter Knight, accompanied Pembroke.

King Charles of France, who had spies in England, had early news of the expedition. The moment had arrived for him to ask Don Henry to fulfil his promise of naval aid and send the Castilian fleet to intercept Pembroke before he could land at La Rochelle, the port in northern Aquitaine whither he was known to be bound. Don Henry, hitherto over busy with consolidating his position to be of use to his ally, was now able to do what was required of him. One difference between his fleet and the English was that he had proper warships with professional crews, while the English had only merchantmen. He had developed the Mediterranean galley, as used by the Venetians and the Genoese in their naval battles, into a galley capable of operating in the Atlantic. These vessels were 130 feet long with an 18 foot beam, of 200 tons, propelled by 180 oarsmen and carrying 40 crossbowmen. The oarsmen were not the criminals and slaves of later days but highly paid seamen from the Balearics. Their officers were not soldiers on sea duty, as with the English, but naval officers de carrière. As a striking force they were pre-eminent and were particularly suitable for raiding ports, since the precision with which they could arrive, manoeuvre and depart, gave them a great

[1] Edmund later became Duke of York. The Yorkist kings, Edward IV and Richard III, were great-grandsons of Isabella.

advantage over sailing-ships which tended to become immobile in enclosed waters such as estuaries, natural harbours or the like. The La Rochelle commission was exactly their line.

When Pembroke's fleet entered the approach to La Rochelle on 23 June 1372 the Castilian galleys were waiting. Their crews were able to board, burn and sink all the English ships and take prisoners who included Pembroke and Guichard d'Angle. All the money sent for soldiers' pay, said to have amounted to £20,000, fell into their hands.[1] Having effected this smashing defeat which, in effect, cut sea communications between England and Aquitaine, besides obliterating urgently needed reinforcements, some of the galleys returned to their ports in Biscay with their prisoners, leaving others on patrol. Nothing could better have vindicated King Charles' policy in supporting Don Henry than this battle, or more nakedly exposed the Prince's failure to devise a means of establishing a *modus vivendi* with Don Pedro.

The prisoners were not as well treated as they would have been by French captors. This was characteristic of Spain, as it was of the German states, where the conventions of chivalry were less binding than in France and England. Froissart looked down on the Germans for their breaches of what he considered the civilized code of Europe. 'The French do not put their prisoners in irons or the stocks, nor even in prison, as the Germans do their prisoners, so as to get a greater ransom. Cursed be they! They are a people without pity or honour.' Don Henry's treatment of the Earl of Pembroke, Guichard d'Angle and the other lords and knights he had taken was considered disgraceful. They were confined, if not in dungeons, at least under rigid lock and key in castle cells. After enduring more than a year of this, Pembroke managed to get in touch with du Guesclin, who, though now commander of the French armies, retained great influence in Spain. Du Guesclin was shocked by what he heard and rescued Pembroke and d'Angle, and also Lord Poynings, another of the seventy knights taken at La Rochelle, by the device of trading them for part of his estates in Castile. Their ransoms then became his property. D'Angle and Poynings reached England safely, but Pembroke, his health broken by his prison experience, died in Picardy on his way home.

[1] A full account of this early naval battle is given in vol. 4, p. 410, of *Histoire de Charles V* by R. Delachenal (1928). The Spanish victory was due to their galleys' superiority of manoeuvre in the tidal and sheltered approaches to La Rochelle.

His death did not absolve his heirs from having to pay du Guesclin and they shortly afterwards received a bill for 130,000 gold francs.[1]

How Sir John Harpenden, another of the captive knights, obtained his liberty is related in the *Anonimalle Chronicle*,[2] an odd tale, not found elsewhere and possibly apocryphal, which gives another example of the kind of adventure which an English knight might have at this time. One day, after the Englishmen had been in prison a long while, two lords from Ethiopia, twins by birth, arrived at Henry's court and delivered a challenge. Their mission, they said, was to prove in combat that Christ was not of the flesh and blood of the Virgin. As they were twins, however, they only counted as one man, they said, for such was the custom in their country. Was there any knight in Spain bold enough to take up their challenge? Though the odds were thus to be two to one, Henry was loath to ignore the challenge, since the visitors' allegation was so abominable a heresy. He forthwith sent invitations to the most intrepid of his knights, inviting any one of them to do battle 'in honour of God and Saint Mary', but all refused, because 'the said twins were so big and strong that no one dared fight them'. It was then suggested that the English prisoners be asked. Whereupon Sir John Harpenden volunteered, provided he were let out of prison three weeks before the fight, in order to get fit in the fresh air. This was agreed to and on the day appointed he and the two Ethiopian knights took their stations on the field. The combat was long and violent. The elder of the twins wielded a sword which was a foot broad and its length higher than his shoulders. 'But as God willed for the increase of the faith the said knight killed the elder and then the younger.' Don Henry was so delighted with the Christian victory that he gave Harpenden and all his fellow prisoners leave to depart. Not only did he remit their ransoms but presented Harpenden with four genets and a large sum of money.

Pembroke's failure to land his reinforcements at La Rochelle led immediately to grave results. Three months later (September 1372) du Guesclin took La Rochelle and the greater part of Poitou and Angoulême. The Captal de Buch[3] and Thomas Percy were both captured.

[1] P. E. Russell, op. cit., p. 194. Du Guesclin was never paid (Delachenal op. cit., p. 417). But King Charles gave him 50,000 francs in compensation.

[2] *Anonimalle Chronicle*, Galbraith edn., pp. 115 and 188.

[3] He was, says Froissart, 'put in prison under sure keeping in a tower of the

Edward made two last efforts to stem the tide of defeat. We have a picture of the old warrior King resolved to do or die. Berners translates Froissart thus: 'And whan the kyng saw howe he lost with so lytell warre the countries and landes that had cost hym so moche the wynning, he was in a great study a long space; and than he says howe that shortely he wolde go over the sea hymselfe with suche a puyssance, that he wolde abyde to gyve batayle to the hole power of France . . . and never retourne agayne into Englande, tyll he had conquered agayne as moche as he had lost.' In the autumn of 1372 he, the invalid Black Prince, and Duke John embarked in a large fleet with archers and men-at-arms, intending to land in Aquitaine, despite the Castilian fleet. Before leaving, the Prince, anxious about the succession, asked the lords to promise, if he and his father failed to return, that the child Richard should succeed to the throne. 'The prelates, lords, knights and all the comynalte loved so well the Prince for the many fayre journeys that he had acheyved . . . that they all agreed.' But the expedition came to nothing. Towards the melancholy end of the Herald's poem are the lines: 'By what I heard tell they were nine weeks at sea, nor ever could have any wind. Rather they had to turn and came back. Whereat the King and the Prince and all the bold knights were sorely cast down.' It was, however, perhaps just as well that continuous south-westerly gales prevented the English fleet of transports from making the coast of Aquitaine, for it might have been destroyed by the Castilian warships, which were waiting for it. How the Prince was able to endure nine weeks in and out of the south coast ports in cold and storm is puzzling, But we do not know exactly what was wrong with him. The diagnosis of dropsy leaves it too vague.

The year 1372 ended with a large part of Aquitaine gone and loss of command of the sea. King Charles was so sure that he, not Edward, ruled the Channel that he planned an invasion of England through Wales, in conjunction with Owen, great-grandson of the last King of Wales, who was in France and had assured him that he could guarantee a Welsh rising to coincide with a French

Temple' in Paris, where he died not long afterwards. He was too formidable an opponent to let out on ransom. And he refused to join the French, though King Charles offered him his liberty, a rich wife and high command. He and Guichard d'Angle were the most distinguished of the Gascon lords who remained faithful to the oath of allegiance which they had sworn to Edward III.

landing. Though the invasion of Wales did not come off, landings of French and Spanish troops on the south coast did great damage, as will be related. Edward had two courses open to him. It would not have been impossible to improve the English navy till it was strong enough to protect the shores of England. A naval policy of this kind, combined with a mission to Don Henry, offering to recognize him and waive Duke John's claim if the Castilian fleet were called off, might have had good results. But Edward, his advisers and parliament, could not bear to throw away the marriage, undo all Duke John's work and by recognizing the *de facto* government in Castile abandon their support of the *de jure* cause. One more military effort, a great effort, might put all right. Though for three years the French had been steadily winning back Aquitaine, their success was due to the defection of the people, clever harassing tactics, the smallness of the English forces, rather than to any defeat of the English in a pitched battle. An English army of men-at-arms and archers, standing in a good defensive position, was as invincible as ever. As such an army had utterly routed the French twice and gained Aquitaine, why should it not utterly rout them a third time and regain Aquitaine?

Edward resolved to try. As it had always been impossible to send a large army by sea to Aquitaine because the distance precluded a quick turn-round of shipping, and since now it was yet more impossible with the Castilian fleet waiting to pounce, the army would have to land at Calais and march across France. If it were attacked, it would win another Poitiers and reverse the situation in a single morning. If it were not attacked, it would set to work on arrival at Bordeaux to regain the lost dominion.

Recent researches[1] have proved, what was previously unknown, that in addition to marching to the relief of Aquitaine, the plan was to carry on over the Pyrenees, defeat Don Henry at a second Nájera and place Duke John on his throne. Duke John would be welcomed by the legitimist party. No financial crisis would arise as after Nájera, for on this occasion England would pay, though, needless to say, the cost of the expedition would not be £450,000; a figure of £60,000 would probably suffice. Our knowledge of this plan is derived from documents in the Aragonese archives; for En Pere was to come in and for his reward get the large slices of Castile which, had the Prince's proposed carve up of Castile taken place, he had been promised.

[1] C. P. Russell, op. cit., chapter X.

An English army, as large as any which had operated in France, was mustered at Calais in the middle of 1373.[1] Duke John, or as he now was called, Monseigneur d'Espaigne, was of course in command, since the expedition was to end with him on his Spanish throne. As a soldier his reputation rested on having commanded the Prince's van at Nájera. On that occasion his adjutant was Chandos. He was taking Sir Hugh Calveley with him now. But he was no second Black Prince, not even a second Edward. By a twist of fate his descendants were to rule England, Castile and Portugal, but he himself was not destined to do anything in particular.

He left Calais on 3 August and marched into France, laying waste the country as usual. Though sorely provoked, du Guesclin resisted the dangerous temptation to attack. The march continued to Paris, outside which the English army offered battle in a tantalizing way. 'But the French enemy would not issue out of the city and give battle, and so the English had to go on,' complains the author of the *Anonimalle Chronicle*. After their successful offensive in Aquitaine it was very painful for the French nobility to have to adopt such negative tactics.

Having failed to precipitate a pitched battle, the Duke continued his march via the Auvergne, and did not get to Aquitaine much before Christmas. By then his army had greatly wasted. Some of his men died of disease, some of exhaustion, for the horses failed and they had to walk. Some even died of starvation, for parts of the Auvergne were uninhabited mountains. And du Guesclin followed, harrying all the time, cutting off stragglers, ambushing small parties. The Duke reached Bordeaux in as bad trim as if he had lost a pitched battle. He was in no state to commence the recovery of the lost counties; far less was he equipped to invade Spain. The Aragonese archives, however, prove that he still negotiated with En Pere with that object. In a month or two, however, the truth dawned on En Pere that the Duke would not, could not, cross the Pyrenees and that he himself would be left in the lurch, exposed to Don Henry's retaliation. He quickly made terms with that King. The Spanish expedition was off. The Duke now ran out of money to pay his troops and had to take them back to England in April 1374. He had accomplished nothing whatever. He arrived home with a badly damaged reputation.

By the end of the year the dominion of Aquitaine had shrunk till

[1] French naval predominance in the Channel was never so complete as to prevent the English taking troops to Calais.

it consisted only of the cities of Bordeaux and Bayonne with small towns and castles in their vicinity. These areas were too strongly held for the French to take, particularly as their inhabitants were anglophil. Both sides were back where they started before Crécy. A truce was signed, but a peace treaty was impossible, because the English would not abandon their pretensions, as they did not think of themselves as defeated, but as victors who had lost ground for the moment.

The Death of the Black Prince

The reverses abroad were attributed by general opinion to the incompetence of the authorities. War had hitherto been held the King and his council's affair. Heavier taxation, however, taught the public that it was everyone's affair. In the years immediately ahead a dissatisfied commons was to make its power felt in parliament, and seek to control the crown's expenditure of public money. Discontent and criticism were not remarkable until after the death of the Black Prince, or rather until his very last days. He was so much admired that the crown and the court were sheltered by his celebrity. When he was gone, the King's growing senility, the court's corruption, the limitations of Duke John, ill-fitted to fill the role of senior statesman, and the absence of men of eminence among the nobility, became more evident.

As the Prince was not well enough to head the government under the King, that duty fell to Duke John on his return to England in the spring of 1374. The Prince, however, had one urgent concern. Fearing that he would not live to be king, he desired to make sure that his son Richard succeeded his grandfather. It has been claimed that he mistrusted his brother, certainly mistrusted by many, who credited him with designs on the crown. It was believed that he would seek to set aside the boy, Richard, on the ground that a child should not succeed in a crisis, and would claim that he himself was the right man. But there seems little evidence that he had such designs. Indeed, it is not clear how he could have taken Richard's place, short of having him murdered, and the

Duke was hardly that sort of man. His ambition was not the crown of England but the crown of Castile. At home he seems to have been content to be what he was, the leading lord in the kingdom, magnificent and influential, head of the government and with the likely prospect of ruling the country during Richard's minority. In this legitimate aim he might have succeeded, had it not been for his unpopularity, due to his lack of success as a military commander, his tactless association with disreputable figures who surrounded his father, and for certain actions of his which seemed to threaten the liberties of London, an unpopularity so great that every kind of accusation was levelled at him and found believers.

That there was any tension between the brothers is doubtful. On the contrary, the Prince now made the Duke one of the executors of his will. Nevertheless, the Prince, as his health slowly declined, remained anxious about his son. Not only did he seek more than once assurances from the nobility, but was careful to keep on good terms with the commons, so that parliament as a whole would lend Richard support.

Some time before his death, he made an elaborate will, wherein, besides a long list of his benefactions and bequests, were detailed instructions about his funeral, place of burial and the inscription to be placed on his tomb. The whole throws light on his character and way of life. As an example of his type of piety is the bequest of 'one great table of gold and silver, full of precious relics, in the middle a cross of wood of the Holy Cross' made to a college in which he was interested. Bequests to his family and friends reveal his taste in luxury, for instance the leaving to his son Richard of 'one great bed embroidered with angels, the pillows, blankets, cover and sheets thereof, and all other apparel absolutely pertaining to the said bed; item, the hangings of arras of the deeds of Saladin and also the hangings of worsted embroidered with mermen'. The instructions for his funeral are in such minute detail as to suggest that he had supervised rehearsals; and in the case of his tomb that designs had been submitted for his approval. His effigy was to be 'in relieved work of laton gilded, fully armed in the pride of battle, with our quartered arms, and our face meek and our leopard helm placed beneath the head'. The effigy, as we see it today in Canterbury Cathedral, answers to this description, though the face cannot be called meek. The inscription he chose, which is in French, and given in full in the will, accords with his Christian desire to be represented as a meek warrior. Unlike most tomb inscriptions of great men, it does not enumerate his victories and feats of arms, but, written in the first person, is a lament and a prayer for divine favour. In it he bewails the passing away of earthly splendour: 'I had great wealth and lived as a great nobleman; I had estates, houses and jewels, hangings, gold and silver, and horses, but now am poor and weak where I lie in the deep grave.'[1] He did not compose the inscription but took it from a French translation of a Latin poem called *Clericalis Disciplina*[2] then much admired. It is characteristic that he puts horses among the things he especially valued, for he was an enthusiastic sportsman and bred horses at his stud in Princes Risborough, Bucks.[3]

Both the Chandos Herald and the St. Albans *Chronicon Angliae* devote a good deal of space to describing his death on 8 June 1376 at Westminster. He had been carried down from Berkhamsted as he thought it his duty to attend the parliament which met on 28 April. On 17 May he developed what seems to have been dysentery on top of the dropsy and became violently ill. In three weeks he was dead. It was a great shock to everybody. As a national hero, he was deeply venerated. But the French chroniclers were no less laudatory. Thus Cuvellier in his *Vie de Bertrand du Guesclin* has: 'Not Alexander the Great bore himself so proudly. He was a gallant and noble prince.' And the *Chronique des Quatre Premiers Valois* records: 'He was one of the greatest knights on earth; in his time he had renown above all men.' Froissart's words 'He was the Flower of Chivalry of all the world' have already been quoted. They provide the explanation why the French chroniclers, despite the harm the Prince had done their country, despite his massacre at Limoges, could not belittle him, for he was the sum of everything that was still admired, though chivalry was on the

[1] The Black Prince's will is included in 'A collection of all the Wills . . . of the Kings and Queens of England' (J. Nichols, 1780).

[2] For the whole subject of the tomb and effigy see *English Art (1307–1461)* by Joan Evans, p. 155.

[3] See Register of the Black Prince (1346–65), preserved in the Public Record Office, publ. 1933. One of his stallions was called Tancarville, after Jean de Melun, Sire de Tancarville, who was captured by him at Caen in the year of Crécy, the father of the Tancarville already mentioned as being with King John in London. The Prince maintained in 1347 eleven war-horses or chargers. There are entries about hay and oats, 'a peck a day each'. Old memories linger on in the English countryside, and one of the hotels in Princes Risborough today is called The Black Prince.

wane. That the French chroniclers were truly echoing opinion is shown by the fact that King Charles ordered a requiem mass for the Prince to be sung in the Sainte Chapelle in Paris, which he himself attended with all the French nobility.

His deathbed was the occasion for an outburst of national grief. He had ordered the doors of his sickroom to be kept open, so that the public could bid him a last farewell. The notabilities both of the court and of London came to kneel and weep at his bedside. To the last he was anxious about his son. The Herald records that he said to the lords about his bed: 'I commend to you my son, who is very young and little, and pray you, as you have served me, to serve him.' Duke John and all those present swore to do so. The sorrow and consternation felt at his early death (for he was only forty-six) are summed up by the Monk of St. Albans in the phrase: 'English hopes died with him.'

In fact, however, hope did not die with him, for the English by no means gave up hope of regaining Aquitaine. They would win back what he had won for them, though he would not be there to lead the army. His extraordinary popularity rested ultimately on the fact that he embodied the impulse, nascent in the English character, to found dominions overseas. He had brought the impulse to light and satisfied it for a season. The English had had the nucleus of an empire in Aquitaine and from thence had entered Spain as masters. Then suddenly like a mirage the lovely prospect had vanished. Not until much later, when dominion in France was seen to be a mistaken ambition, did the national genius find its true outlet; this time in distant lands. That the Prince, at a moment when his countrymen were beginning to listen to their genius, won them a dominion, made him a national hero. His death was as grievous a sorrow to the commons as to the lords. For a moment it was as if hope was dead. But hope revived. The nation could not bear to give up its dream of dominion in Europe and though good sense demanded a settlement with France, refused to make it. In 1415 they were to think that they had found a second Black Prince in Henry V. Agincourt, however, was no more decisive than Crécy and Poitiers. The dream of dominion faded again. This time it was not a brigand become Marshal, but a peasant girl attended by angels, who turned them back. They had to wait until Columbus discovered the New World and Da Gama the sea route to India before perceiving that it was on the sea and in America and Asia that their grand adventures were to lie. Yet the essay in Aquitaine was a foreshadowing of the rest. In her time England has ruled and lost France, America, Asia. If the Black Prince was the first of the empire builders, Bertrand du Guesclin was the first of the national saviours destined to confront them.

The Commons take the Initiative

As already stated, the Prince fell seriously ill on 17 May 1376, nineteen days after the opening of parliament, the most famous parliament, as it happened, of the fourteenth century. It has sometimes been supposed that he supported the commons in the initiative they took on this occasion. He may, indeed, have given them countenance during the early days of the session, but it can hardly have amounted to much. Had they depended on him, his death on 8 June would have seriously affected them. As it was, it made no difference and they carried through their programme with unabated vigour until the end of the session on 11 July. It is true that the Prince held no brief for certain members of the royal council accused of corrupt practices,[1] whose removal was the commons' principal object, but there is no ground for supposing that their attack was in any way prompted by him. Indeed, it must have seemed to him very unpleasant, involving as it did a severe loss of face for Edward, his father, and his brother, Duke John, from neither of whom was he in any way estranged. What follows should not therefore be seen, as some have seen it, as a drama where the national hero, disgusted by the way affairs had been conducted since his retirement, inspired a national protest as the last act of his life. Whatever sympathy he or other lords may have felt, it was the commons who were the prime movers. That they were so is indicative of how deeply the public mind was disturbed.

The commons had come to Westminster resolved to purge the

[1] After the opening of parliament Lyons, one of the chief delinquents, sent him what appeared to be a barrel of fish, but was found to contain £1,000. He refused the bribe. (*Anonimalle Chronicle*, ed. Galbraith, p. 92.)

royal household of persons who were abusing their position, and to appoint a new council better able to advise the King, both very bold resolves for the commons of that date. They had no animus against the King himself. His military fame, as the victor of Crécy, remained undimmed by his son's greater fame. But members of his entourage would have to go, in particular the Chamberlain, Lord Latimer, and a rich city merchant called Richard Lyons, who was notoriously guilty of gross frauds. Alice Perrers also, who was in league with these two and was making a fortune at the public expense, would have to withdraw from court. No direct attack would be made on Duke John, though the replacement of the council of which he was head would necessarily be an indirect attack on him.

The commons had no chamber of their own, unlike the lords who met in the White Chamber, a building immediately south of Westminster Hall and on the site of the present House of Lords. The Abbot of Westminster had, however, placed at their disposal during the days when parliament met his Chapter House adjoining the Abbey on the south. The visitor to the Chapter House today can recapture something of the atmosphere of the 1376 parliament. The interior, though restored in the nineteenth century, is in general as it was in the fourteenth. The floor of tiles (the most remarkable medieval floor in London) is perfect. The frescoes of the Last Judgment and the Apocalypse, the gift of John of Northampton, a Westminster monk, which he commissioned about the time of this parliament, are still visible in part, though sculptures, said to have been numerous, have mostly disappeared. One can see the stone seats along the foot of the octagonal wall where, on cushions, it may be supposed, the members sat. Their number is estimated at 134.[1] They did not address the assembly from their seats, but walked into the centre where a lectern was placed beside the central pillar, as is expressly stated in the *Anonimalle Chronicle*, which gives a full report of the speeches. It is possible to detect today exactly where the lectern and its platform stood by the slight discolouration of the tiles at that spot. This first home of the commons was certainly more beautiful than their present House and its acoustics were better.

Before describing the 1376 session, a few explanations are required. King Edward, following the usage of his predecessors,

[1] See *Evolution of Parliament* by A. F. Pollard (1926). The shire knights predominated. Only about twenty cities were represented, each by two burgesses.

9. Duke John arriving at Calais

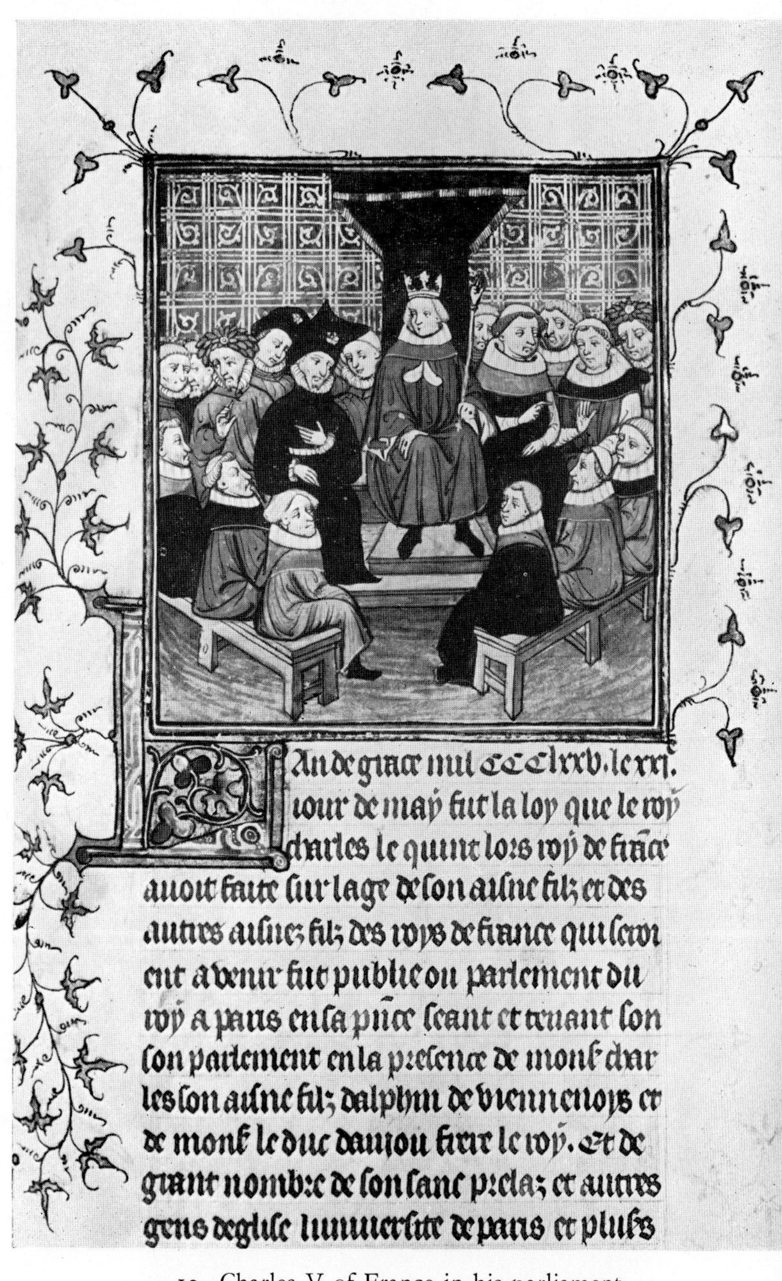

Lan de grace mil CCClxxv. le xxi.
iour de may fut la loy que le roy
charles le quint lors roy de france
auoit faite sur lage de son aisne filz et des
autres aisnez filz des roys de france qui seroi
ent a venir fut publie ou parlement du
roy a paris en sa presence seant et tenant son
son parlement en la presence de mons. char
les son aisne filz dalphin de viennois et
de mons. le duc daniou frere le roy. Et de
grant nombre de son sanc prelaz et autres
gens deglise luniuersite de paris et plus.

10. Charles V of France in his parliament

had generally appointed prelates to the chief offices of state. Churchmen on the whole were better educated than laymen and were more able to conduct the business of such departments as the chancery (the main executive secretariat) and the treasury. This had remained the practice until 1371. In that year of severe reverses in Aquitaine opinion veered and it was thought that laymen would manage better and be more subject to control than prelates, who could count on the outside support of the Pope. The young Earl of Pembroke, the same who was captured the following year by the Spaniards at La Rochelle, was put up to move a resolution in parliament[1] that in future none but laymen be Chancellor, Treasurer, Barons of the Exchequer and Clerks of the Privy Council. On this motion being carried, and the King's acceptance secured to a petition which embodied it, the Chancellor, William of Wykeham, Bishop of Winchester, resigned, as did other churchmen. Sir Robert Thorpe, a judge, became Chancellor, but was relieved the following year by Sir John Knyvett, also a lawyer. Sir Richard Scrope became Treasurer. He was a friend of Duke John's. When the Duke returned with his Spanish wife at the end of 1371, he was welcomed by the new lay officers, who were glad to have the friendship and support of so important a personage. He presided over the council, of which they were the professional members. He was at home during 1372, except for the nine weeks spent at sea with his father and brother. During 1373/4 we have seen him in France once more, leading the expedition from Calais to Bordeaux; on return he resumed his position as president of the council. During part of 1375 he was in the Low Countries sounding the French about an extension of the truce. Now in 1376 he was back in England, and, enjoying as he did his father's full confidence, was again the head of the executive. Though he had not been continuously on the spot, he was held responsible for what had been happening, and, as things went from bad to worse,

[1] It is worth noting that the word, parliament, in the *Anonimalle Chronicle*, the chief authority here, means the lay and spiritual lords. The knights and burgesses who attended at Westminister, sat separately for their deliberations. But they were not recognized yet as the second of the two Houses of Parliament. When they wanted something done they had to go to the lords and ask them to do it. They only became part of parliament when they joined the lords in the White Chamber. Nevertheless, they had gradually acquired power and influence during the fourteenth century, because experience had shown that it was impossible to impose and collect taxes without their concurrence and help.

his reputation increasingly suffered. He got the blame, not King Edward, who was considered past his work. Though not really old, for he was only sixty-four, the King had quite lost his grip. His health was not good (the decline was popularly attributed to debauchery) but it was rather in mind and character that he had fallen away. Always a jovial, pleasant man, he had become weak and indulgent. Alice Perrers and Lord Latimer formed a little court party and with the assistance of Richard Lyons, the city financier, made money by cheating the revenue, selling posts, evading the customs and other ingenious devices. Chancellor Knyvett and Treasurer Scrope, though not involved in these malpractices, had shown themselves incompetent to stop them. The churchmen who had held office before 1371 would have prevented such scandals—or so they declared; and would prevent them in future if restored to office. The commons of 1376 could therefore count on the support of the church lords in their determination to break up the court gang. They would be opposed by Duke John who, though not accused of criminal collusion with the offenders, should have shown them up, if he were an honest man, so that an attack on them would be a reflection on him, which would hurt his pride and anger him as an interference in his sphere. To balance his opposition, however, they had among the lay lords a prominent figure. The King's second son, Lionel, Duke of Clarence, born two years before Duke John, had died eight years back, leaving a daughter, Philippa, who had married Edmund Mortimer, Earl of March, now a young man of twenty-five and Marshal of England. As there was no law in England disqualifying a woman for the succession, Philippa stood next after Richard and before the Duke. March and the Duke represented therefore two great rival houses. It followed that the commons could look for support to March in what was a stroke against the Duke. Backed by him and his followers, and supported by the Church, the commons had the weight to accomplish what they did.

With these explanations in mind it is possible to make clear sense of the account given in the *Anonimalle Chronicle* of the proceedings in the 1376 parliament, the longest account extant of any medieval parliament. How the author got his information is unknown, though his latest editor, Professor Galbraith, concludes that he probably used the report (perhaps copied it) of a London eyewitness sent to his monastery of St. Mary's Abbey, York, by a correspondent in the capital.

The Commons take the Initiative

The scene at Westminster opens on 28 April in the White Chamber, the parliament house proper, where were present besides the King and his sons, the whole of the nobility including the baronets and the 134 members of the commons who attended by invitation. The Chancellor, Sir John Knyvett, made the opening speech. He pointed out the grave danger threatening the country from its enemies, the French and the Spanish, and asked parliament to make a grant to maintain the war. In conclusion he begged members to advise on any matters which in their view had been mishandled. There was no discussion that day. The King withdrew into Westminster Palace, which occupied the space between the back of the White Chamber and the river. The lords rode to London, two miles away, where some of them had residences. The commons also rode there to the inns where they were staying.

On 30 April the lords re-assembled in the White Chamber. The commons went to the Chapter House, glad to have a room of their own where 'they could discuss their business without disturbance or being bothered by other people'.[1] Their first speaker was a knight from one of the southern shires. 'He got up from his seat and crossed to the lectern in the middle of the Chapter House, where everyone could hear', and after saying a Latin grace made his speech: 'Gentlemen, you have heard how the King wants a grant of money for carrying on the war. The granting of it will be difficult as the people have been impoverished by former taxes. Moreover, what we gave in the past has been frittered away by dishonest spending. The matter requires careful looking into. It is said that certain persons have made large sums of money out of the King without his knowledge, to the great damage of the realm.'

This sufficed to introduce the main topic. The next speaker named Latimer and Lyons as having cheated the revenue by exporting wool without paying duty at Calais.[2]

[1] The *Anonimalle Chronicle*. In this connection may be read a royal proclamation issued by Edward III and preserved in the archives of the City of London: 'It is forbidden on pain of imprisonment that any child or other person shall play in any place of the Palace of Westminister, during the Parliament which is summoned thereto, at bars or at other games not befitting, and such as taking off the hoods of people or laying hands upon them; or in other way causing hindrance, whereby each person may not peaceably follow his business.' Riley's *Memorials of London*, p. 269.

[2] Since Calais had become an English possession after the Crécy campaign. it had been made the market-place for the whole English export wool crop.

A third speaker pointed out that before proceeding further with such matters of grave import it would be better to enlist some of the lords on their side. 'I propose that we ask to have assigned to us certain lords, church and lay, whom we will name. After listening to our discussion here they will help us to determine what to do.' (The assumption is that the commons had already sounded a number of lords.)

This proposal was debated. If they could get the active support of lords, who for one reason or another disliked the present régime at court, they would be greatly strengthened. One of the members, Sir Peter de la Mare, lord of the manor of Yatton in Herefordshire, was prominent in the debate. Besides being a good speaker with a grasp of affairs, he was steward to the Earl of March, Duke John's rival. The members elected him their speaker to represent their views to the lords. A message from the King on 9 May summoning them to give their assent to the tax demand made on the first day, determined them to take the opportunity to bring their business up.

Accordingly that afternoon they left the Chapter House in a body and walked across to the White Chamber, led by Sir Peter de la Mare. He was admitted, along with those close to him, but the door was shut against the others, who were told their presence was not required. It seems that Sir Peter did not notice their exclusion until he had entered the lords' chamber itself. He was annoyed and resolved to protest. The Duke was presiding. He seemed ill at ease, for no doubt some news of the commons' intentions had reached him, and demanded abruptly which of them was authorized to speak for the rest. Sir Peter made known that he was the speaker. 'Then say your say,' ordered the Duke. Sir Peter replied that he could not explain the business on hand until all the members were admitted. The Duke protested that a dozen was enough. But on Sir Peter insisting, he gave way and sent for the rest, though two hours elapsed before they could all be found and brought in. Sir Peter then addressed the lords, but instead of announcing the commons' assent to the tax demand, frankly declared that they had been debating the unsatisfactory state of public affairs and, in their deliberations to find remedies, desired the help which a delegation to them of twelve lords would provide.

The merchants of all Europe came there to buy. The exporter had to pay duty to the crown on the wool he sold there. Latimer and Lyons, however, had exported wool direct to buyers outside and so not paid customs duty.

The Duke asked for names and was given those of four bishops, including William Courtenay, Bishop of London, son of the Earl of Devon; of four earls, Edmund Mortimer, Earl of March and Marshal of England, the last name the Duke wanted to hear; Thomas Beauchamp, Earl of Warwick, a man of thirty-one, eldest son of the Warwick who commanded the van at Poitiers; William Ufford, Earl of Suffolk, son of the Earl, who fought at Crécy and Poitiers; and fourthly, Hugh, Earl of Stafford, last seen in this book with the Black Prince in Roncesvalles. Four barons were also named: Lord Henry Percy, soon to be Earl of Northumberland, brother of Thomas Percy, captured in 1372 but ransomed and now back in England; Roger Beauchamp, the Earl of Warwick's brother; Guy de Brian, a distinguished knight of the French wars, who had also acted as Admiral; and lastly Richard Stafford, the Earl of Stafford's uncle. All the eight lay lords listed by the commons had directly or indirectly been concerned with the campaigns and so were likely to be well informed on the present situation. Courtenay was a church magnate of strong character, a leader of the clerical party, which wanted to get back into power.

After demanding the help of these magnates, the commons took leave without making any reference to the tax in which their concurrence was required. The lords referred to the King, who sent word that he had no objection to the twelve lords sitting in committee with the commons.

Next day the twelve lords joined the commons in the Chapter House and after hearing the charges which it was proposed to bring against Lord Latimer, Richard Lyons, Alice Perrers and others of the court party, agreed that this should be done. In the afternoon they all went to the White Chamber and 'saluted the lords who returned their salutes. And when all was quiet the Duke asked, "who will speak?" and Sir Peter made reply.' He now felt bold enough, having the support of twelve important grandees, to say out what the commons were resolved on. 'In regard to the grant now demanded,' he said, 'we are advised that if the King's ministers had spent honestly and without extravagance the money previously granted, more money would have been unnecessary. But the King has about him certain counsellors and servants who are not loyal and have not profited the realm. They have deceived the King and taken advantage of him.'

On hearing this the Duke expressed astonishment. 'Who are

these people and in what have they taken advantage of the King?'

Sir Peter de la Mare then enlarged on the iniquities of Lord Latimer and his set in making large sums by trickery.

Lord Latimer, who was present, now interrupted to say that everything he had done was done with the knowledge and consent of the King. The Duke backed him up, declaring that he did not think the King was out of pocket. But Sir Peter courageously persisted and gave further details of Lord Latimer and Richard Lyons' corrupt practices, such as deceiving the King into agreeing to pay 50 per cent interest on a loan which they made to him. Before concluding his speech he dealt with the more delicate matter of Alice Perrers' behaviour. 'The lady,' he said, 'has yearly up to three thousand pounds from the King's coffers. The realm would greatly profit by her removal.'[1] After which he and the commons withdrew.

The Duke was very indignant at what had been said. The *Chronicon Angliae* shows him in consultation with his intimates that night. He is made to say: 'What are these low hedge-knights at? They go on as if they were kings and princes. How dare they be so monstrously conceited. Are they blind to what I can do? Well, I'll give them such a fright that they won't provoke me again.'

But one of his knights warns him to be careful. 'They have the countenance of the Prince, your brother,' said he. 'The Londoners to a man and the general public won't allow them to be touched. Take care they don't turn on you.' The Duke, rather taken aback, decides to go easy, and next day, says our chronicler, pays the commons a visit at their sitting and is so kind and gracious that they stare at him in amazement.

This anecdote has at least a basis of truth, for the Duke, as we shall see, thought it safer to let the commons have their way for the time being. The *Anonimalle* chronicler discloses the sequel. In subsequent joint sittings with the lords, the commons obliged Richard Scrope, the Treasurer, and William Walworth, a city

[1] The Rolls of Parliament give some details of the gifts she had received from the King. In 1371 the manor of Wendover, 1374 the manor of Oxeye, 1375 Bramford Speke manor. In 1372 £397 were paid for jewels for her. Later that year she was given part of the late Queen's jewels. During the pendency of the present parliament (20 May) royal accounts show that she was fitted out with new clothes for a tournament. (See under her name in *Dict. Nat. Biog.*)

magnate, to give evidence which proved Lord Latimer's and Richard Lyons' guilt. Lyons was arrested and, bail being refused, was locked up in the Tower; Latimer's property was confiscated and he was put under house arrest. At the same time Alice Perrers was turned out of the Court.[1]

For the first time in history the commons of England had taken the initiative in punishing persons round the King guilty of corruption and other misdemeanours. When this had happened before, as with the so-called Mad Parliament of Henry III in 1258 and the Lords Ordainers under Edward II in 1310, it had been the lords who intervened. It is true that on the present occasion the commons could not have achieved what they did unless they had had a section of the lords to help them.[2] Yet, it was a great triumph for the English people, or rather the classes below the aristocracy—the knights of the shire and the burgesses. The knights were country gentry, many of them military men who had fought overseas; the burgesses were the merchant capitalists of London and the country towns. They were not really the commons of England, for they did not represent in parliament any classes but their own. The great bulk of the population, the peasantry and the workers in the towns, had not elected them. Indeed, the peasantry had been dissatisfied for years with the attitude of the knights to wages and manorial duties, as had the workers in the towns to what they considered were the oppressive measures of the capitalists. Nevertheless, Sir Peter de la Mare was

[1] Two other persons, according to the *Chronicon Angliae*, were also punished. Lord Neville of Raby (last seen in Roncesvalles) lost his job in the Household for defending Lord Latimer in an abusive speech. (Latimer's daughter was Neville's wife.) Sir Richard Stury, who also had an appointment at Court, was dismissed for trying to prejudice the King against the commons. An astrologer employed by Alice Perrers was arrested. Her extraordinary influence over the King was to be explained by the power of his incantations, drugs and magical rings. He was a friar. Some members of parliament wanted to have him burnt, but he was only handed back to his own confraternity. Lynn Thorndike in his *History of Magic and Experimental Science* (vol. iii, p. 213) has: 'Hardly any class or group of men in the later middle ages were more given to astrology and even to some other occult arts and sciences than the friars.'

[2] That is to say, the Earl of March and his supporters. In estimating the achievement of the Good Parliament it has to be borne in mind that its actions, besides representing the dissatisfaction of the knights and burgesses at the government's conduct of affairs, reflected the rivalry of the houses of March and Lancaster.

widely admired for his courage in standing up to the Duke and it was said that popular songs were sung in his honour.[1] He was, after all, the nearest thing so far to a champion of the people.

But it was one thing to remove the rascals who were taking advantage of old Edward III, and another to get appointed a new council to advise him. Sir Peter and his colleagues would very shortly be returning each one to his estates in the country. Once dispersed they ceased to exist as a body. They were not organized as a permanent institution; no ministers were responsible to them. Who was going to see that the government kept to the right road? Sir Peter did not venture to suggest that he or any member of the commons should be given office and power to supervise. What he did propose, however, was to select nine lords, on whose advice the King would be bound to act. The proposal was adopted by the lords and referred to the King. He raised no objection, as no doubt was anticipated, for he had ceased to exercise the authority which was vested in him, authority which the commons would have liked to foster, had it been possible.[2] Sir Peter in consultation with the lords then made out a list of nine such counsellors.[3] Six of them were among the twelve who had been sitting with the commons, the other three were William of Wykeham, Bishop of Winchester, the former Chancellor; Richard FitzAlan, Earl of Arundel, a wealthy grandee of the highest rank, who had succeeded that year to the title at the age of thirty-two; and Simon Sudbury, Archbishop of Canterbury. Sudbury, though he was to qualify for a martyr's crown, which he did not get because his murder did not touch the nation's heart as his predecessor at Canterbury, Becket's, had done, was a secretarial type. His career so far is worth noting for it shows that a man without aristocratic connections could, if clever enough, rise to high position in the Church. Born in what was termed a respectable family in Suffolk, he took a Paris degree and became, first papal chaplain and, then, auditor in the papal palace at Avignon. In the year of Poitiers he

[1] See article under his name in the *Dict. Nat. Biog.*

[2] In modern parlance what the commons did was to turn out the ministry, for the King's council, composed of heads of the state departments and of magnates without portfolio, as we would say now, was a ministry, even though not responsible to parliament in a modern sense, but only to the King. This had never happened before at the instance of the commons.

[3] The great officers of state, Chancellor, Treasurer, etc. were additional to these, as they held their seats by virtue of their office.

was sent to England as Nuncio. For a while he held an appointment in Edward's Chancery and then returned to papal employ. An English cleric at the curia was well placed to obtain an English bishopric, for the Pope provided for those who served him well by appointing them to benefices in their countries of origin or elsewhere. It was true that in England the Statute of Provisors (1351) had declared illegal such papal appointments (an early indication that the Pope and English national feeling were difficult to reconcile) but the statute was rarely enforced. So when the Pope appointed Sudbury Bishop of London in 1361, Edward raised no objection. For fifteen years he had held the appointment and became a well-known London figure. A curious anecdote attaches to this time. It seems that in 1370 he was on his way to Canterbury where the jubilee of St. Thomas à Becket was being celebrated. One of the attractions was the plenary indulgence which the pilgrim who attended could obtain (on payment) for any sin he had committed, along with a certificate to that effect. For some reason Sudbury did not approve of the Pope raising money in this way and told a party of pilgrims whom he overtook that plenary indulgences could avail them nothing. But one of them, an irascible old knight, Sir Thomas Aldon by name, thought this a reflection on the saint, and cried: 'My Lord Bishop, why do you seek to stir up the people against St. Thomas? By my soul, your life will be ended by a foul death.'[1] On the strength of this anecdote Sudbury has been described as a man of advanced opinions. It is possible that having seen the Papal curia from within he was less credulous than rustic old Sir Thomas Aldon. A year before the 1376 Parliament met he was appointed Archbishop of Canterbury. Now selected as one of the nine councillors, he was a member of a body opposed to the Duke. As a pliant man he had accepted the nomination, though not personally one of the Duke's opponents. A strong line, however, was not to be expected of him. It is not easy to see why Sir Peter put his name forward. But as essentially a tactful man, when much tact would be required if the Council of Nine was to manage the King successfully, he may have seemed suitable.

The *Anonimalle Chronicle* suggests that, hiding his annoyance,

[1] Wharton's *Anglia Sacra*, i, 49. The story has the appearance of having been touched up to fit the fact that Sudbury did die a foul death (as we shall see). But it reflects the fact that he was not considered orthodox enough by some churchmen.

the Duke had capitulated to the commons by the middle of the session, because he had insufficient support from the lords. He is represented, for instance as having recommended the King to accept the Council of Nine, and was 'greatly thanked by the commons for his graciousness and goodwill'. He seems to have hoped that his name would be added to the list and 'was grievously put out' when it was not.[1] It was indeed a heavy blow. Between him and his father was this new council. He was excluded from the government. He had been dismissed. Though the senior Duke, the only Duke, for his younger brothers, Edmund of Langley and Thomas of Woodstock, were only Earls; though now the King's eldest surviving son, titular King of Castile, the knight who had commanded the van at Nájera, a man with vast estates, very rich, in the flower of his age (he was only thirty-six), whose palace, the Savoy, was the most splendid private residence in London; though he was all this, he had been shown the door. A galling rebuff! For those who had been put over his head he had nothing but contempt: the three prelates, Sudbury an office man of no family, William Courtenay, pushed up at thirty-two to be Bishop of London because he was the younger son of an Earl, William of Wykeham whom young Pembroke had run out of the Chancellorship because he was no good; and the lords, Stafford one of his junior captains at Nájera, March a mere youth, Arundel no more than son of a Crécy hero, Percy—well Percy was somebody—but Roger Beauchamp was only another boy and Guy de Brian, just an old soldier. And these were the people chosen to advise the King!

That the King agreed so easily to accept a new Council may be thought odd. But his acquiescence meant nothing; he was so worn out and doddering that he hardly understood what was said to him.[2] Besides the commons were tactful. A show was made of consulting him at every stage. Their sole aim, they said, was his

[1] *Anonimalle Chronicle* (Galbraith edn., p. 92). As an example of the strange kind of French used in St. Mary's Abbey, York, in the fourteenth century at the time when this chronicle was written there, I cite the sentence: 'Le duk de Loncastre nyent paie mes malement greve et anoie de ceo quil ne fuist my eslew destre une de les conseilers.' Was this like the French of Stratford-atte-Bowe (Mile End), which Chaucer laughed at the Prioress for speaking?

[2] The MS. Reg. 13 D.1 appended to the *Chronicon Angliae* has (p. 401): 'For a year or more before his death it is said that he was not stronger in mind than a boy of eight.' This is, no doubt, an exaggeration. But he was certainly not clear in the head.

protection against dishonest persons, as in fact was the case, for they were fond of him. His reign of fifty years had been the most glorious in English history. In his dotage now, he had to be looked after. The Duke had failed to protect him from crooks. It was a shame to have to hurt the old man by removing his sweetheart,[1] but she had abused her position so abominably that it was too great a risk to leave her where she was.

As we shall see, this last was the mistake, for it gave the Duke his card of re-entry.

Before the session ended the commons petitioned the King 'that it might please him . . . to cause the noble boy Richard . . . to come into Parliament so that the lords and commons of the realm might see and honour him as very heir apparent.' The request suggests a wish to show their loyalty to the King and his son, despite what they had felt obliged to do. Prince Richard, now nine years old, was introduced by Archbishop Sudbury who said that though the great Prince, his father, had passed away 'none the less the said Prince was as it were present—in leaving behind him such a fair and noble son, who was his right image and very likeness.' Richard was a pretty child, like his father perhaps in face, but more delicate and slender in body. He was accorded an affectionate welcome, for he was they said, 'the great comfort of the whole realm'.[2]

[1] The *Chronicon Angliae* is definite on this point: 'The English had tolerated her (Alice) for many years because they had great affection for the King and were afraid of offending him.' (Page 96, Rolls edn.) Though Alice Perrers was certainly loved by Edward, it is equally certain that in this very year of 1376 she was betrothed or married to a knight called William de Windsor (Rot. Parl., iii, 41b). There is no explanation of this fact, though it evidently made no difference to the King. But as the circumstances are unknown we are in the dark as to how exactly she, Edward and Windsor stood to each other. It is conceivable that the King did not know of the marriage when the commons alluded to it and that afterwards she was able to explain it away to his satisfaction. But there is the complication that the accounts show that £1,615 3s. 11d. was issued from the King's account for her to give Windsor in 1374. (See *Dict. Nat. Biog.*) The *Anonimalle Chronicle* (p. 106) adds a further complexity. On 23 April 1377, two months before his death King Edward knighted 'the son of Dame Alice Perrers'. Who was his father? The King? On this subject see 'Alice Perrers' son John' by Margaret Galway in *E.H.R.*, vol. 66 (1951), pp. 242–6. There seems no doubt that the boy knighted was Edward's son. (I am much indebted to Mr. P. S. Lewis, Fellow of All Souls, for giving me this bibliographical reference, and for other references in the course of the book.)

[2] This first public appearance of Richard is recorded in Rolls of Parliament, ii, 330.

The session ended without the grant in aid of the war being passed. Before the members dispersed the commons gave a great dinner party at Westminster to the lords. Seven earls were present, including March, Warwick and Stafford. Salisbury came, once commander of the rear at Poitiers, now Captain of the Fleet. There were bishops and barons, country knights and the leading citizens of London. The only person of eminence not present (perhaps he was not invited) was the Duke. The King, unhappy though he was at Alice's departure, sent down a present of two barrels of wine.

The Parliament of 1376 was afterwards called the Good Parliament because in breaking up the notorious court party it had done a popular thing. But on other wider needs of the moment it expressed no opinion. When one reflects that England was threatened with invasion, that the naval forces were inadequate, that no steps had been taken to strengthen the south coast defences and that the truce with France expired the following year unless by a reassessment of England's foreign relations a fresh policy was inaugurated, one perceives that the prosecution of certain swindlers and the appointment of a new council, though steps in the right direction, did not go very far. The commons made no military, naval or diplomatic proposals. They left it to the new council to devise ways and means of dealing with the crisis. The reason is not far to seek. It was not their business to advise on how the government was to conduct its affairs. And they had no idea how to do it. They did know how to protest against a scandal and insist it should end. They could name certain lords and beg the King to listen to them. But that was as far as they could go, as they lacked experience of affairs.

The Adventures and Misadventures of John of Gaunt, Duke of Lancaster

On 11 July the 1376 parliament dispersed, leaving the Council of Nine to get on with the job. The day-to-day administration was in the hands of the great officers of state. It had been agreed that the new council should not interfere in their departments. As the councillors' duties were wholly advisory, they found themselves with little active authority.[1] They could give the Chancellor or the Treasurer no orders. Nor had they any means of controlling the Duke if he professed to be acting in the King's name. And this was precisely what he proceeded to do. The King wanted Alice Perrers back more than anything. The Duke took a gamble and sent for her. The gamble came off. The three bishops on the Council of Nine, Sudbury, Archbishop of Canterbury, Wykeham, Bishop of Winchester, and Courtenay, Bishop of London, were 'like dumb dogs unable to bark' as the *Chronicon Angliae* puts it. Nor did any of the six lay lords of the Council make a protest. Alice's recall was represented as done by the King's orders, no doubt true enough inasmuch as he heartily agreed when the Duke suggested it. Under the law and custom of the constitution the King had a perfect right to get her

[1] There would appear to be a discrepancy between the Duke's annoyance at not being on the Council and the fact that the Council is now seen as not worth belonging to. The explanation may be that at first it was intended that the Council should have not only advisory duties, but a degree of administrative authority, but that the Duke, when he found himself excluded, contrived to restrict its powers. Some manoeuvre of the kind must have taken place, for we first see him smarting under a rebuff and shortly afterwards in a position actually stronger than the Council's.

back. Parliament had not the power to banish his friends against his will. The Good Parliament's action had not been illegal, for it had obtained his consent to her dismissal. He had thought it best (or been advised) to bow to the storm. Now his action in recalling her could not be questioned. It is probable, too, that there had been some revulsion of feeling. Edward was said to have suffered from shock at her departure and taken a turn for the worse. After all, the woman had not been tried. She had made money, acted scandalously, but no criminal offence was alleged against her. The bishops did not bark because they were uncertain of their ground. In the last reign the lords had expelled and eventually executed Edward II's friend Piers Gaveston, the disreputable Gascon; but he had been foolish enough to make mortal enemies of the leading grandees. Alice had offended no grandees, however. She was just a straightforward greedy mistress, whose company the old King found delightful.

After this success, which pleased Edward enormously, it was easy for his son to convince him that the rest of the late parliament's actions could be undone. 'The King now handed over everything to the Duke and permitted him to do what he wished.'[1] Armed with the royal authority, he was able to ignore the Council of Nine and restore the court party. Lord Latimer was released on bail and returned to court. Lyons was discharged from the Tower.

Had the Council of Nine been able to rally the lords, they could no doubt have exerted enough pressure to restrain the Duke. But the lords were back on their estates, enjoying the summer, hunting and shooting. By itself the Council was too feeble to resist the King's will as expressed by the Duke. Encouraged by success he continued his course. The Council's most important member, the Earl of March, was ordered in his capacity of Marshal of England to inspect the English garrisons at Calais and Bordeaux. That would get him out of the way. The order alarmed him and he resigned his appointments. The result was the same; he was off the Council. By offering Lord Henry Percy, the next most important member, the vacant Marshalship, the Duke won him over to his side.

These steps were all taken very quickly. With the Council deprived of its two chief members, the Duke now felt strong enough to get it abolished altogether. In October, four months after the end of the parliamentary session, he summoned the lords

[1] *Chronicon Angliae*, p. 102 (Rolls Series edn.).

in the King's name. Since the commons and their speaker, Peter de la Mare, were not there to prompt them, he succeeded in persuading them to dissolve the Council.

He then turned on one of its three ecclesiastical members, Bishop Wykeham, who had made himself obnoxious by testifying against Lord Latimer. Wykeham was charged before the lords with misdemeanours allegedly committed when he was Chancellor in 1372. The church lords tried to save him but a majority of the lay lords found him guilty and deprived him of his temporalities (revenues as from manors, tithes and the like) and told him to leave London.[1]

Not content with these measures, the Duke decided to give the commons a lesson and had Peter de la Mare arrested and detained in prison pending trial on various charges. The prospect was now good. He had flattened his opponents. With the King ready to endorse his wishes, he was master of England for the time being, a time, however, unlikely to be long, for the King was evidently on his last legs.

The enemies whom the Duke had made in the course of regaining his ascendancy were sure to be very troublesome once the King was dead. He had offended the church by his prosecution of Wykeham. He had gravely angered the commons by reversing their measures and imprisoning their speaker. As the commons represented not only the country gentry but also the city of London, he had alienated that powerful association of capitalists and bankers. Before all this he had been unpopular enough; his unpopularity now was much increased. In sum, his position was very precarious. The proper course for him would have been to placate church and commons. As we shall see, however, he went out of his way to provoke them further.

Now that he was head of the government his most important responsibility was to look after the safety of the realm. Indeed, he had a double responsibility, for as titular King of Castile, Don Henry was his enemy, not only because his fleet threatened England but also as rival to the Castilian throne. All his energies should be devoted to putting the country in such a posture of defence that when the truce with France ended in June of the following year King Charles would hesitate to invade. But the Duke did not measure up to these requirements.

[1] The *Anonimalle Chronicle* (p. 96 of the cited edition) gives a full account of the proceedings and how Wykeham was bullied after leaving London.

As the Good Parliament had dissolved without making a grant in aid of the war, a new parliament had to be summoned. It assembled at Westminster in January 1377. Some of the commons who had sat in the Good Parliament were re-elected, but without Peter de la Mare to lead them they were not aggressive. The mood of the commons in general was compliant and they elected the Duke's steward, Sir Thomas Hungerford, as their speaker.

The Chancellor opened the combined sitting in an alarming speech. He told the lords and commons that King Charles, having used the truce to collect men and ships, was certain to invade as soon as it expired. In the circumstances, parliament was asked to sanction a substantial grant to be used for the defence of the realm. The usual way of raising extra revenue was a tax of 1s. 4d. in the pound on moveable property in the shires, such as cows, furniture, grain, etc., and 2s. in the pound in towns, where moveables often included stocks of goods. To be taxable, moveables had to be worth a certain figure, fixed high enough to exclude from taxation the moveables of the poorer classes. The people who paid such a tax belonged, in fact, to the nobility, gentry and merchants. In the present national emergency, however, parliament thought that everyone should contribute. It was not practicable, by reducing or abolishing the valuation, to extend the tax on moveables to include all classes. But a poll tax would meet the case, and after long discussion was decided on. Such a tax had not been levied before in England, though the Black Prince's parliament in Aquitaine had imposed something like it, the hearth tax of a shilling, with unfortunate results.

The poll tax of 1377 obliged everyone of both sexes above the age of fourteen to pay 4d. There were three principal objections to it. In the first place it was not fair that the well-to-do should pay the same as the poor. It was tantamount to letting them off, as 4d. was nothing to people accustomed to paying 1s. 4d. or 2s. in the pound on moveables. Secondly, the classes who would be paying the bulk of the tax were not represented in a commons composed only of knights and merchants. The tax looked as if shifted by the upper on to the lower class, which, with no constitutional means of voicing their views, might well seek to make them known by violence. The third objection was that a poll tax had not been levied before. This fact had great weight in the villages. To say that the tax was not customary was to condemn it.

In any society these are grave objections to a tax. In fourteenth

Photo: Howgrave-Graham

11. Funeral Effigy of Edward III, Westminster Abbey

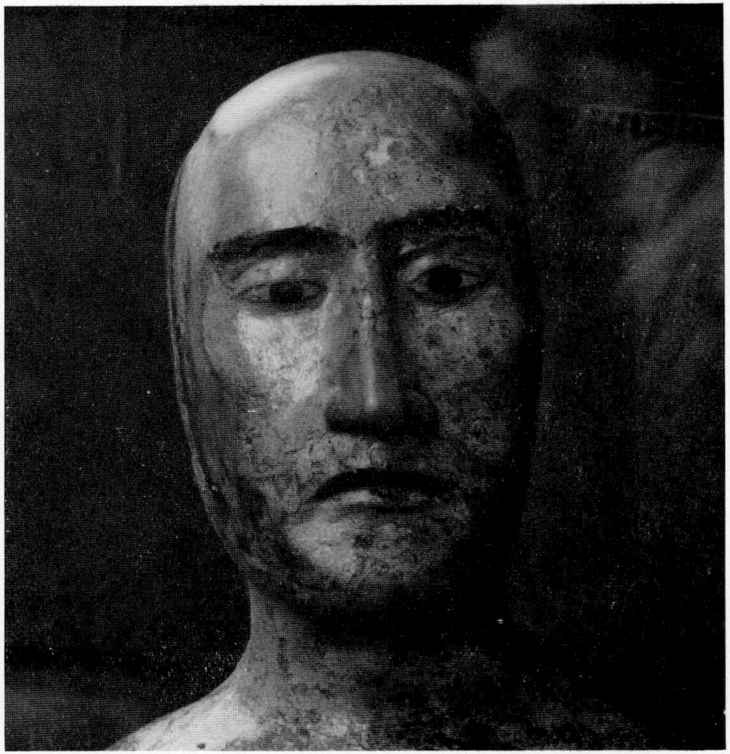

Photos: Howgrave-Graham

12. Death Mask of Edward III, museum of Westminster Abbey

century England they were particularly grave, because the English mob was under little control, as there was no standing police force. Many of the village people had been to the wars and profited by them. They were not an oppressed class, rustics labouring in silence and fear. They had shown themselves very active in asserting their right to higher wages after the Black Death. Pride in their archery, the great victories, a wild life for some with the condottieri captains, had made them formidable. They were not the kind of people it was safe to annoy, particularly when affairs were going badly. But the Duke's parliament, the commons headed by his steward, took the risky line of imposing a tax on them open to the objections enumerated above.

In the course of the session the commons paid a visit to the manor of Kennington where Prince Richard resided with his mother, the Princess. The boy heir to the throne, and likely soon to succeed, had taken the fancy of the people. The commons seem to have wished to demonstrate how fond of him they were. The visit took place on 25 January 1377, nineteen days after his tenth birthday. To amuse him it was organized as a masked procession. The annalist, John Stow, of Queen Elizabeth's time, made a translation of the section in the *Anonimalle Chronicle* where the masquerade is described, and I give part of it, though his language, unlike Berners' rendering of Froissart made some seventy years earlier, gives the scene an Elizabethan colour. 'The commons of London made great sporte and solemnity for ye yong prince. . . . In ye night were 130 men disguizedly aparailled and well mounted on horsebacke to goe mumming to ye said prince, riding from Newgate through Cheape, whear many people see them, with great noyse of minstrelsye.' The mummers are described, esquires and knights in red cloaks wearing masks, followed by comic effigies of an emperor, a pope, cardinals and legates with black masks like devils. The Duke with his younger brother, Cambridge, and with Warwick and other grandees accompanied the procession. They crossed London bridge and took the road south of the river to Kennington manor. 'And when they were come before ye manour, they alighted on foot and entered into ye haule; and sone after ye prince and his mother and ye other lordes came out of ye chambers into ye haule, and ye said mummers saluted them, shewing a peyr of dice upon a table to play with ye prince, which dice were subtilly made, so that when ye prince shold cast he shold winne. And ye said players and mummers set before ye prince three jewels each after other, ye first a balle of gould, then a cupp of gould, then a gould ring, ye which ye said prince wonne at thre castes, as before it was appointed. . . . And then ye prince caused to bring ye wyne, and they dronke with great ioye, commanding ye minstrels to play; and ye trumpets began to sound and other instruments to pipe etc, and ye prince and ye lordes danced on ye one syde and ye mummers on ye other a great while. And then they dronck and took their leave, and so departed toward London.'

The parliamentary session ended on 23 February 1377. Three months were left before the truce with France expired, months which the Duke, now supplied with money, should devote to preparations to meet the coming blow. A few days before parliament dispersed, however, he became involved in so undignified an altercation with Bishop Courtenay, and fell so foul of the London mob, that he ceased to be an effective head of the government. The Bishop, as a member of the late Council of Nine appointed by the Good Parliament at the instance of the popular Peter de la Mare, was much liked by the Londoners. The events of the previous six months, particularly the prosecution of Bishop Wykeham, had increased the ill feeling between Courtenay and the Duke, as they had between the city and the Duke, inasmuch as Peter de la Mare was still detained in prison without trial. Far from attempting to smooth things over in view of the crisis, the Duke acted in such a way as to aggravate the quarrel. The description which follows of his behaviour and what befell him is taken from the *Chronicon Angliae* and the *Anonimalle Chronicle*. Were the former the sole authority, its account might be suspect as its tone generally is prejudiced against the Duke; but the *Anonimalle*, noted for its impartiality, fully confirms it. The Duke made an utter fool of himself. He was unpopular before; he became hated now.

His support of that remarkable man, John Wycliffe, was the origin of the trouble. In 1377 Wycliffe was about fifty-seven years of age. He had been hardly heard of outside Oxford circles until two or three years previously. There he had long been prominent, for at thirty-seven he was Master of Balliol. As an intelligence he had no equal in the university. His position, however, was due not only to his intellect but to the strength of his feelings. He was both a scholar and a reformer. His lectures were highly critical of the rich and worldly ecclesiastics of the day, bishops who were really magnates. The medieval church had always its critics and reformers. The great orders of the Friars, the Augustinians, Benedictines, originated in reforming movements. In the fourteenth century a favourite subject for sermons was to denounce clerical misdemeanours; Langland's *Piers Plowman* and Chaucer's *Canterbury Tales* reflect the same tendency in general literature. Wycliffe's uniqueness, however, lay in the fact that his powerful intellect and great learning enabled him to propound a doctrine, which was not a mere reproof of abuses in the Church, but a fundamental theory of its right to exist. He declared that its only title to dominion was the righteousness of its members. Moreover, he drew the practical conclusion that the civil power had the right to take back the property it had given to the Church if it lost its dominion by unrighteousness. Though his theory was heretical, because it subordinated the Church to the State, he rooted it so solidly in the scholastic metaphysic of the period that it was extremely difficult to answer effectively. Wrapped in the obscurities of theological ratiocination its discussion had hitherto created no stir outside Oxford. But now he began preaching in London and in a manner to be comprehended by a general audience. His brilliance and learning gave him great authority.

Courtenay thought he should be stopped; the Duke, however, saw in him a means of rousing popular indignation against Courtenay, and took him under his protection. Wycliffe could not but be flattered by the attention of so celebrated a lord. With such backing his preaching would bear fruit. A scholar little used to public affairs, he lent himself to what was really a political manoeuvre.

The parliament of January 1377 had still a few days to go when Wycliffe received a summons to appear before Sudbury and Courtenay on 19 February in St. Paul's Cathedral to answer for his opinions. When the Duke was informed of this, he decided to accompany him and overawe the churchmen by his presence.

It happened that at this time he was contemplating measures to bring the city of London to heel. Governed by its mayor and aldermen under royal charters which allowed it among many other privileges the right to have its own courts and prisons, it was in his opinion too independent, particularly as it had shown itself so ill disposed to him in its support of the Good Parliament. His idea was to put the mayor under the Marshal of England, his new adherent Lord Henry Percy, who would have power to make arrests inside the city and imprison in his own gaol. As the city was at this time petitioning to extend its jurisdiction across the river to the suburb of Southwark, which was under the Marshal, the contrary proposal to restrict its jurisdiction inside the boundaries was certain to cause an uproar. Events were quickly to show how greatly the Duke miscalculated in thinking himself strong enough to browbeat the city in this way. The attempt to overawe Courtenay was a fiasco because London violently espoused his cause.

Old St. Paul's, where Wycliffe had his rendezvous with Courtenay, was the largest cathedral in England. In those days the Fleet river was a considerable stream running through what is now Ludgate Circus. There was a bridge there, and a man standing on it had Fleet Street to the west of him leading to the Duke's palace of the Savoy, and through open country to Westminster. Eastwards half way up the hill was Ludgate, a Norman port set in the wall which encircled the city, the same old Roman wall which had always been there, for fourteenth century London was the same size as Roman London. Above the wall he could see rising up the great Gothic fane. Its bulk on the top of the hill was lifted skyward by a spire no less than eight-five feet higher than Salisbury's, at the present day the highest spire in the country.[1] Passing through Ludgate he had on his right the huge Dominican monastery of the Black Friars, with the wall surrounding the cathedral court immediately ahead, a large enclosure wherein, besides the cathedral, was the Bishop of London's palace, St. Paul's Cross (used as a place for public meetings) and the graveyard. Thence the city stretched eastwards as far as the Tower, having a population which has been estimated at 34,000;[2] (few towns in England at this date had as many as 5,000). With its ninety-nine parish churches; the great stone houses of such lords as Warwick, Salisbury, Northampton and Suffolk; and of the city magnates, Walworth, Philpot and Brembre; the Halls of the

[1] The dimensions of old St. Paul's were: 600 feet long, 104 feet broad; 101 feet height of vaulting in choir; and the height of the spire 489 feet. Compare York's 486 feet length, 104 feet breadth, 99 feet vault and 203 feet tower.

[2] *British Medieval Population*, Josiah Cox Russell, 1948. Professor Oman quoting on p. 163 of his *The Great Revolt of 1381* from the poll tax accounts of 1377 shows that 23,314 London adults over fourteen paid the poll tax that year. The gap between this figure and Mr. Russell's total is filled by children and beggars.

Goldsmiths, Vintners, and Fishmongers and the Guildhall itself; the many monastic closes, Grey Friars, Austin Friars, Crutched Friars and of the Holy Trinity; and these all standing in narrow streets of timbered houses, except for the Cheap, so wide a thoroughfare that jousts were held there—such was London, a dirty, smelly but infinitely more beautiful city than it is today, for the whole, from the top of the cathedral spire down to the house of the shopkeeper, was in one style, the Gothic, a style which continued on through the clothes, governed by Paris fashions which were very fantastical at the moment, multi-coloured and extravagant, on to furniture, the cupboards carved like the façade of a church, and extending to every utensil, covered cups, spoons, knockers and even pots.

On 19 February Bishop Courtenay sat waiting for Wycliffe in the Lady Chapel of his cathedral. He was an irascible man, a great lord, afraid of nobody. With him was Archbishop Sudbury, in the chief seat no doubt, and treated with all deference, yet inevitably second, for he was much less of a personality than the bishop. The Duke set out from the Savoy with his party: Wycliffe, philosopher become heretic, don become public figure, attended by four Friars, doctors of law, to assist him; Lord Henry Percy, Marshal of England, Knight of the Garter, lord of the northern marches since 1368, a feudal baron old style; and the retinue of the two magnates. It is recorded[1] that the Duke maintained a retinue of 125 knights and 132 esquires, with their complement of grooms, pages and archers, the whole a little army of at least five hundred men. How large was Percy's retinue is not on record, nor can we guess how large a suite the two lords had with them that day. But they certainly did not walk up Ludgate Hill unaccompanied. News had gone round that they were coming and the cathedral was crowded with people, a rough mob and under little control.

The Duke and his party entered the cathedral by the west door. To reach the Lady Chapel they had to traverse the whole building. Henry Percy was in front with his Marshal's staff of office. That very morning he had arrested a citizen called John Prenting for slandering the Duke and locked him up in Newgate in anticipation of the authority within the city which it was proposed should be given him. He now intended to display his authority inside the cathedral. When the crowd pressed forward to get sight of

[1] Armitage-Smith's *John of Gaunt* and *John of Gaunt's Register*, ed. Lodge and Somerville, Camden 3rd series, vols. lvi–lvii (1937).

Wycliffe and blocked the nave, he shouted at them to give room for the Duke and threatened them with his staff. By the time the party was past Sir John Beauchamp's tomb (the knight who had carried the royal standard at Crécy) and the celebrated statue of the Virgin at its foot, he and his knights were pushing the onlookers back with violence. Bishop Courtenay, coming from the Lady Chapel to meet the Duke, was very annoyed at the sight. 'You have no authority in my church,' said he to Percy. An altercation ensued. With their tempers on edge the Duke and the Marshal reached the Lady Chapel and were shown to seats. But Wycliffe was left standing. 'You had better take a chair,' said Lord Percy to him. 'There will be a lot of questions to answer and you will be more comfortable seated.' Hearing this Courtenay objected, saying Wycliffe should stand, since he had been cited before the Archbishop and himself to answer charges of heresy. Words then passed between Percy and the Bishop. The Duke joined in hotly, saying that in his opinion Wycliffe had a better right to a seat than any of the churchmen present. The Bishop replied that he would not allow it. Was the Duke trying to maintain Wycliffe in what he had said against Holy Church? It was shocking the way he had pushed in and was interfering in a matter which did not concern him. The Duke retorted that the Bishop evidently was depending on the Earl, his father,[1] or he would hardly have dared to speak so. 'But I will make you bend,' said he, 'you and all the rest of the bishops.' The populace thronging the entrance to the Lady Chapel were indignant witnesses of the Duke's rudeness. London was behind the Bishop to a man because of his support of the Good Parliament, and was deeply prejudiced against the Duke. The quarrel waxing hotter, the Duke called on Lord Percy to exercise his authority as Marshal and arrest those who were demonstrably hostile. The Bishop said that anyone who dared to make an arrest in his cathedral would be excommunicated. At this point the Duke was heard to mutter that rather than have to put up with such insolence he would prefer to drag the Bishop out of the church by the hair. The threat roused the Londoners to fury and they began yelling that they would not have the Bishop insulted. So menacing did they look that the Duke thought it prudent to withdraw and, with Percy and Wycliffe, forced his way out of the cathedral. His intention in coming had been to upset the proceedings. In this he

[1] Bishop Courtenay was not only son of the Earl of Devon, but was directly descended through his mother from Edward I.

had succeeded. Courtenay would think twice before summoning Wycliffe again.

The affair, however, was by no means over. The Londoners went home thoroughly angry. They now heard that in parliament that morning proposals were debated to extend the Marshal's jurisdiction over the city. A meeting of citizens was called for next day, not a corporation meeting but rather a general assembly of the lower classes. They came together in much agitation. Rumours were flying about. It was said that the Mayor's office was to be done away with and the city administered directly by the government. Hatred of the Duke increased so fast that he was believed to have threatened to behead (or had even beheaded) the Bishop. The news that Lord Percy had arrested John Prenting and locked him up in Newgate, now reached the assembly. The meeting was, no doubt, conducted by responsible citizens, but the rank and file were grim and turbulent men, who got out of hand when they heard of Prenting's arrest. Snatching up arms, some rushed to Percy's house at Aldersgate to kill him if they could find him and some to Newgate to release his prisoner. Prenting was found in stocks and taken out. Percy's doors were broken in and a hunt for him began. They went from room to room, stabbing the tapestries with lances and even searching the latrines. When it was evident that he was not at home, they thought he might be dining at the Savoy with the Duke and set off there shouting like madmen.

One of the Duke's knights saw them pass and, conceiving that not only Lord Percy but also his master was in danger of being murdered by the mob, hastened to warn the Duke at the address where in fact he and Lord Percy were dining with a rich Flemish wool merchant, John of Ipres, one of those who had been encouraged to settle in London and introduce improved weaving methods. The knight knocked loudly at the door, but the porter, a man called Haviland, seemed in no hurry to open. 'If you love my lord and value his life, let me in at once,' cried the knight. The porter, alarmed, ushered him into the dining-room, where he found the Duke and Percy at table, and reported with agitation that the mob was after them. The Duke, very startled at the news, got up from his place so hastily that he banged his leg hard against the table, and was in such pain that his host, much concerned, pressed on him a cup of wine. 'No,' said the Duke, 'we must go at once.' And hurrying with Percy down to the Thames where his barge was waiting, he ordered the boatmen to row as fast as they could to Prince Richard's wharf at Kennington. Landing there, they went straight to the royal manor. The Princess received them and on hearing their story offered them asylum and promised to do what she could to mollify the Londoners.

Meanwhile the mob had rushed out of the city towards the Savoy. On the way they met a priest who was foolish enough to speak slightingly of their hero, Peter de la Mare. They turned on him savagely and beat him to death. Word had reached Bishop Courtenay, who was also at dinner, that a mob was out to murder the Duke and Percy. As the proper authorities, the mayor and aldermen, seemed to be doing nothing, he went to the rescue, angry though he was with the Duke. Common sense told him that his enemies would suspect him of having incited the mob if he did not. So leaving his dinner, he hurried down the hill and up Fleet Street. At sight of him coming along behind, the crowd stopped, delighted to see him safe, for the rumour, as they told him, was that the Duke had beheaded him. 'Your bishop as you may observe is in excellent health,' he replied. 'And now, for God's sake, go home. I will see to it that all your wrongs are put right.' They listened, calmed down and dispersed.

Incidents, however, continued to occur. Some person or persons unknown got hold of escutcheons of the Duke's arms and hung them upside down on the cathedral and Westminster Hall. Beside them they put up placards which declared the Duke to be the son of a butcher of Ghent, in infancy substituted for the true son of the late Queen. And there were minor incidents. A knight of his, Sir John Swinton, was pulled off his horse when he paraded the city wearing the Duke's badge in what seemed a provocative manner, and might have been killed had the mayor not rescued him. Others of his staff thought it prudent to hide his badges in their sleeves. The Princess, however, did not forget her promise. She sent two members of her household, Aubrey de Vere,[1] uncle of the young Earl of Oxford, and Simon Burley, who was with her late husband at the battle of Nájera, to beg the Londoners, for love of her, to make it up with the Duke. But they refused to do so unless Peter de la Mare was let out of prison and given a fair trial.

[1] The de Vere family had a manor and large estate at Kensington. The present Earls Court is where the court of the manor stood. Simon Burley was appointed Richard's tutor soon afterwards. He was probably nephew of the Walter Burley who had been the Black Prince's tutor.

These events greatly excited the English public. They demonstrate the strength and ferocity of the London mob, only to be eclipsed by the stronger and yet more ferocious mob which four years later was to swarm into London from Kent and Essex. The Duke, who was no coward, felt powerless before the threat of their violence, despite the men-at-arms of his retinue. In taking refuge with the Princess and young Richard, he rightly judged himself safer there than anywhere else, for no mob, no matter how savage, would break into the house where the great Prince had died so recently. At this time the Princess was a woman of forty-nine and getting very stout. But dressed as always in the latest and most expensive fashion, she still looked almost as beautiful as when she had captivated the Prince seventeen years before. But it was not only her looks and because she was the widow of the national hero that made her so popular. She was a warm-hearted good woman, very feminine and appealing, against whom no one had a word to say.

The more one reflects on the episode of the riot, the more extravagant it seems that the head of the government and the Marshal of England, after a disgraceful scene in the metropolitan cathedral, should have had to run for their lives and take refuge with the Fair Maid of Kent. How could the Duke live down such a thing, how hold up his head again? He had become a laughing stock. It is on record that the Londoners lampooned him mercilessly. It made the joke all the better that he claimed to be King of Castile. Well, they had known how to make the King of Castile take to his heels. No wonder he had been a failure as a military commander. And how amusing to imagine the pleasantries of the Castilian nobles, their wives and ladies-in-waiting, the supporters of his cause who had come over from Spain and were his guests at the Savoy, where—how ridiculous!—a royal etiquette was observed. What did they think now of their Monseigneur d'Espaigne after so ludicrous an escapade? On all hands the poor Duke was sneered at, jeered at, caricatured, burlesqued.

When the excitement had died down a little, Adam Stable, the mayor, and the aldermen, thought it prudent to send a conciliatory deputation to the King. Their failure to control the mob provided the government with an additional reason for putting the city under the Marshal. His Majesty was somewhat better for the moment. He had been down with Alice at his manor of Eltham in Kent to recuperate and was now near Putney, at his manor of

Sheen. The deputation was led by Alderman John Philpot, the rich and energetic head of the Grocers' Company. He assured King Edward that the cause of the riot was the threat to take away the liberties of the city. The surge of popular indignation had been uncontrollable. They had been powerless to prevent it. Edward gave them a mild answer, saying that he had no intention of curtailing their rights and advising them to come to terms with the Duke. On their way out they ran across him in the hall of the manor. Civilities were exchanged, but it was clear that he intended to insist on more than a private apology. There must be a public expression of their penitence. And some penalties would have to be imposed. How else could he clear his name? Early in March he asked his father to summon Mayor Stable and the aldermen. This time they found the King in his bedroom, propped up in a chair, hardly able to speak and more like an image than a living man. The Chamberlain addressed them. They were held responsible for the riot. It was no good their pretending they could not have stopped it. Had not Bishop Courtenay succeeded in doing so? In result Stable was replaced by a new Mayor, Nicholas Brembre. As a mark of the city's contrition it was agreed that the corporation would erect a marble pillar in the middle of Cheap with the Duke's escutcheon, properly gilded, hanging on it, and that a procession of citizens would carry a wax taper from Cheap to St. Paul's and offer it to the image of the Virgin there. This was done after Easter, but the lower classes refused to join in the procession, which thus had not the appearance of the general repentance it was intended to have, but of an official act done under pressure.

Distracted by this worrying upheaval the Duke was unable to give his mind to what was brewing across the Channel. He remained inert while King Charles put the finishing touches to his preparations. Though intelligence was received in June that a large Castilian fleet, consisting partly of galleys and partly of armed merchantmen, had joined the French fleet at Harfleur in Normandy, the Duke produced no counter plan nor was one in preparation. Even the coast defences were not repaired. No troops were posted at strategic points.

The Duke's negligence may also in part be attributed to the near approach of an event which he knew would end his power. His father, the source of all his authority, was dying. He had been well enough on 23 April to attend the celebration of St. George's day at Windsor and create new knights, including little Richard, and the Duke's son Henry, but the exertion had been too much for him and on his return to Sheen he died on 21 June, aged sixty-five. His reign of fifty years had been eventful, to say the least. Never before had the English enjoyed so stimulating a time. Suddenly to become the foremost military power was like a relevation of destiny; to have a leader like the Black Prince was an inspiration. Victories, loot, ransoms, feats of arms—they had had them all abundantly. Though ending in sad reverses, nevertheless it had been a wonderful reign. Among the crowd of remarkable figures, two names stood far above the rest, the King and his eldest son's. Now they were both gone.

Though latterly Edward had suffered in reputation because of the irregularities in his entourage, he had never lost his popularity. His death, though it had been long expected, was as great a shock when it came as the Black Prince's. If he had lost grip of affairs, he remained the figurehead. It was possible to go and see him. His mind was feeble, but he was still, it seems, capable on occasion of giving sound advice. His amiability appears to have been remarkable, though the Duke is reported to have told the deputation under John Philpot to be careful not to irritate him, as it would be bad for his health. He seems to have kept up his spirits to the end. What amused him best was to talk about hunting and shooting. Like most of his ancestors he adored the chase and had huge preserves of game. Hawking, too, had been a great pastime. The St. Albans chronicler, often a tedious prig, thought it deplorable that, as death drew near, he was still talking of hounds and hawks, when his thoughts should have turned to higher things. But others found it charming to watch the old face, the face of the man who on an unforgettable summer afternoon thirty-one years ago had looked from the windmill by Crécy village and seen the jewelled chivalry of France charge and charge again on the slope, and wilt and die under the stream of arrows. Of the King's last hours the said chronicler has a long description which reads falsely like a set piece, and is more likely to have been what the St. Albans' monastery hoped were his dying sentiments, than a true report of them. He expires with the word Jesus on his lips. Alice was by his bedside. Of course she was, says the chronicler, because she hoped in his final weakness to get more out of him, though he had already given her so much. And she stayed on too, he adds, to get his ring; slipped them from his dead fingers and made off in haste. This story has been repeated ever since by every historian. Alice Perrers has come down history as a mistress who knew not only how to make money in a big way but also by petty theft. Only the St. Albans' monk, however, tells the story of the rings. And he drags it in clumsily, after first stating that the repentant King repulsed Alice and sent her away, and that a faithful chaplain remained with him till the end. How Alice returned and stole the rings he does not explain. But it was unnecessary to do so for his monkish readers. For them she was not only an immoral woman, but, worse, one who had been involved with the Abbot in a protracted litigation over the manor of Oxeye.[1] Yet, she was evidently not disliked at court. She could not have lasted ten years as the King's intimate if the aristocracy had objected to her. It was the commons who agitated for her removal, probably because the Latimer gang had been clever enough to use her to shelter them. It is significant of her wide popularity that at a great tournament held by the King at Smithfield in 1374 she appeared as Lady of the Sun.[2]

[1] The dispute between Alice Perrers and the Abbot of St. Albans over the manor of Oxeye, Herts, is described at length in *Gesta Abbatum Monasterii Sancti Albani*, pp. 234 seq. The author of the *Gesta* was Thomas Walsingham, the same monk who wrote the *Chronicon Angliae*, and the *Historia Anglicana*, the revised form of the *Chronicon Angliae*.

[2] John Stow's *Survey of London* (Everyman edn., p. 339): 'The 48th year of Edward III, Dame Alice Perrers (the king's concubine) as Lady of the Sun, rode from the Tower of London, through Cheape, accompanied of many lords and ladies, every lady leading a lord by his horse-bridle, till they came into West Smithfield and then began a great joust, which endured seven days after.'

The Coronation of Richard II

A week after King Edward's death the French struck their first blow. In consort with the Castilian fleet they issued from Harfleur and on 29 June landed several thousand men in the estuary leading up to Rye. King Charles can hardly have hoped to do in England what the English had done in France—march through the country at will. But he calculated that his command of the Channel enabled him to land unexpectedly, now here, now there, and rob, burn, massacre, ransom, in the neighbouring countryside, only withdrawing to his ships when English forces came up. For many reasons he could not acquire a fortified bridgehead, as the English had in Calais. His earlier plan to operate from Wales had fallen through. But if he could sack the south coast ports, terrorize the village populations behind them, perhaps occupy the Isle of Wight and threaten London, he would at least have had his revenge. At best he would obtain a peace treaty advantageous to France, for, unaccustomed to the horrors of war in their own country (and his soldiers would make it as ferocious as possible) the English would be very rudely jostled.

There were no forces at Rye to oppose the French landing and the town was speedily taken and sacked. The invaders, however, did not attempt to penetrate farther, perhaps because the Prior of Battle Abbey, Hastings, was known to be hurrying towards them. They re-embarked next day, after firing Rye and ravaging the vicinity. It was a savage raid. In the words of the *Anonimalle Chronicle*: 'They killed all the men, women and children they could find, except the girls, whom they carried off to France with them.'

They did not, however, go straight back to France, but sailed along the coast westwards till they reached the little port of Rottingdean, seven miles due south of Lewes. The inhabitants, who were quite unprotected, fled. The invaders then marched inland on Lewes. The Prior of Lewes, having hastily collected what archers and footmen he could from the villages, attempted to block the road, but was defeated and captured. The French entered the town and evidently stayed there for some time, looting and burning the villages around. No government forces came up to engage them. However, they did not think it safe to advance farther. When they had taken all the loot they could, they burnt Lewes and, re-embarking, sailed away eastwards to attack other ports.

King Edward's death on 21 June partly explains the government's failure to send troops and their leaving of it to local levees to resist the invaders. For the moment, Westminster was not functioning. The Duke's quarrel with London, though damped down, still smouldered. The city's opposition, and critics and enemies elsewhere, rendered him impotent now that Edward's backing was removed. And there was nobody else to give a lead. The Princess and her advisers saw that Richard, though only ten and a half, must be crowned as soon as possible and thereafter the government entrusted to a council deriving its power from him. There could be no question of making the Duke regent. He was too widely distrusted. The belief, unfounded though it was, that he aspired to the throne, was still held, particularly in London. It was this suspicion which prompted the mayor and aldermen, as soon as they heard of Edward's death, to send a deputation under John Philpot to assure the Princess that their money and their lives were at Prince Richard's disposal.

The Princess, however, did not want to take up a stand against the Duke. She knew that he was quite loyal. To force him into what might develop into a dangerous opposition seemed to her a foolish policy. After all, he was the richest territorial magnate in the kingdom. He could make things very unpleasant. When he had taken refuge in her house from the London mob, she did what she could as peacemaker, but the Londoners had held out for the release of de la Mare, a concession which the Duke refused. She now approached him again to meet their wishes, urging him, one surmises, to end an embarrassment so harmful to a peaceful accession for his nephew. This time he consented; de la Mare was set free to the great rejoicing of the London public.

After a formal reconciliation between the Duke and the city had been publicly proclaimed in the King's presence at Westminster, when the Duke kissed each of the city's representatives, it was possible to fix an early date for the coronation with a prospect that it would not be spoilt by open enmity between lords, commons and Londoners. The day selected was 16 July. Before that, King Edward's funeral took place. On 5 July he was buried in Westminster Abbey on the mound of earth from the Holy Land behind the high altar, within a few paces of Saint Edward the Confessor's tomb, the most sacred spot in the building. King Charles, though at this moment his soldiery were at Lewes looting and burning English homes, held a requiem Mass for Edward in the Sainte Chapelle, as he had done for the Black Prince.[1]

The coronation, of which detailed accounts have come down to us, was considered at the time a very splendid occasion. On 15 July, the day before it took place, there was a royal progress through the city, starting from the Tower, where Richard, complying with ancient custom, was staying in the palace which then stood between the central keep and the river. The nobility attended in force. Gascon lords and their retinues took part, as did the mayor and aldermen. The route was thickly lined with spectators. The Duke and Lord Henry Percy, mounted on massive horses and accompanied by their suites, rode by. 'It was quite remarkable,' writes the St. Albans' monk sarcastically, 'how polite they were to people who blocked their way; they requested them to give room in a pleasant and civil tone.' Young Richard rode in the middle of the procession, 'mounted on a great destrier, looking perfectly the part and holding himself like a king'. The Chronicler, Adam of Usk, says he resembled Absalom with his long golden hair. He was dressed in white, as were all the nobility and gentry. In front of him Sir Simon Burley held up the sword of state. Another knight, Sir Nicholas Bond, who like Burley had fought at Nájera, walked beside him holding his bridle. Saluted by music and the blare of trumpets they reached Cheap, where red and white wine was flowing from painted water pipes into huge

[1] The effigy of Edward III lying on his tomb in Westminster Abbey is a stylised likeness of the King as he looked as an elderly man. In the Abbey museum there is the funeral effigy head, recently discovered to be a death mask. See illustrations.

barrels. Anyone could drink as much as he liked. (The day was hot, it is stated.) In the middle of Cheap was a tower of painted canvas, in which were four pretty girls in their best clothes, who threw down golden leaves on the Prince and his horse. The crowd was delighted, too, with an angel above the tower 'which carried a crown and seemed to show it to the said Prince to comfort him',[1] as if to suggest that the crown which next day he would receive was sent down to him from heaven. The procession passed out of the city by Ludgate, and along Fleet Street to the palace of Westminster, where Richard was sleeping the night. With his extreme youth, his beauty, grace and charm he had evidently captivated the citizens. His progress through the city made them feel that they were sending him to be crowned or, at least, that he could not do without their approbation.

The account of the coronation in the two chronicles[2] contains some interesting and curious facts. Richard had a ceremonial bath on the evening of his arrival at Westminster Palace. Next morning he was dressed in new robes. When he was ready, the lords of the household took him first to Westminster Hall, where Archbishop Sudbury, Bishop Courtenay and the Abbot of Westminster with his monks, who had walked over from the Abbey, were awaiting him. There he performed the ceremony, symbolical of the fact that he was the fount of justice, of sitting for a short time on the King's Bench at the top of the hall, in what was called the Marble Chair. The Abbey procession was then formed. Richard was placed on a litter which four Earls raised to their shoulders. The litter moved off under a canopy of golden cloth borne by special officers of the household. In front were carried the three swords of state. The Duke as Seneschal of the Realm had the right to bear the first, and it was not denied him. His rival, the Earl of March, carried the second, and the Earl of Warwick the third. The sceptre and the rod were entrusted to the royal uncles the Earls of

[1] Like this touch, some of the most intimate come from the *Anonimalle Chronicle*, whose French seems more suited to express them than the *Chronicon Angliae's* Latin. The latter, however, has as full an account and I draw on it equally with the other.

[2] The authors of the *Anonimalle Chronicle* and *Chronicon Angliae* had access to the *Liber Regalis*, an early fourteenth-century book of the coronation service. (It has been edited by Wickham Legg in his *English Coronation Records*.) Richard's coronation was carried out in accordance with the ritual described in the *Liber Regalis*. But the chroniclers add incidents within their knowledge peculiar to the occasion.

Photo: Howgrave-Graham

13. Portrait of Richard II in Westminster Abbey

14. Troops crossing a bridge of boats

Cambridge and Buckingham. Thus, in the one party were the three men, John, Duke of Lancaster, Edmund Mortimer, Earl of March and Edmund, Earl of Cambridge (later Duke of York) whose descendants combined to produce the Lancastrian, Yorkist and Tudor royal houses.

The procession, headed by the ecclesiastics, crossed over to the Abbey, whose interior, though architecturally as it is today, must have looked very different without the tombs and inscriptions of a later date which are now its most distinctive feature. We cannot tell how it was decorated nor with what furnishings it was supplied, though it is stated that for the present occasion a dais had been put in the choir. Richard was placed in a chair upon it, where he was in full view.

The ceremony began with an anthem and a psalm. These over, Richard was led to the high altar where he made what was called the Recognition, an offering of a pall of cloth of gold and of a pound of gold. On his return to the seat on the dais, Archbishop Sudbury asked him in a loud voice to declare that he would keep the laws, temper justice with mercy and guard the church, to which he replied: 'Jeo les fra.' (Except for the Latin office, the language used appears to have been French.) When this assurance had been given, the Archbishop cried to the people crowding the nave and aisles, demanding whether they would have Richard as their King. With a loud shout they answered: 'Oïl, nous le voilloms.'

After the litany and appropriate psalms the anointment began. This was a more elaborate ceremony than it is nowadays. Archbishop Sudbury came to Richard, whose clothes he took off except his undervest. So that the disrobing should not be seen, the Earls covered him from view with a cloth of gold. His hands were then anointed with the sacred oil. This oil came from Canterbury and was associated with Thomas à Becket who was believed to have received it from the Virgin Mary with instructions for it to be used for royal unction. The sacring continued with the anointment of Richard's breast, shoulders and elbows. The unction of the head followed. Here an additional oil was introduced called the chrism, a compound of olive oil and balsam which was consecrated on Maundy Thursday. Richard's head was first anointed with the Virgin's oil and then signed on the top in a cross with the chrism.

The rest of the ceremony was a no less curious mixture of

religion and folklore. The ritual of the *Liber Regalis* was not evolved in England, but followed closely the French, which in its turn was derived from very ancient precedents. Unction was followed by enrobing. Sudbury raised up Richard and first put on him the tunic of the Abbey's saint, Edward the Confessor. On top of this were put other garments, the wide-sleeved vestment called a dalmatic, then a stole reaching to the ankles, and lastly the royal mantle cut four square to symbolize the four quarters of the world and their subjection to the four quarters of the sky. This done, he was girt by two Earls with the sword of justice, and on his wrists were clasped the bracelets, signifying the encompassing presence of God which would protect him against enemies visible and invisible. Next he was shod with Edward the Confessor's shoes, and spurs were strapped on his heels.

The placing of the crown, first censed and sprinkled with holy water, on his head followed the enrobement and the arming. The *Anonimalle* chronicler adds: 'They put the crown on his head, the Archbishop holding it on the right hand and the Earl of March on the left'. The Earl of March, not the Duke of Lancaster, had this important privilege, because he now was heir to the throne. The ring was then placed on Richard's wedding finger, the sceptre in the form of an orb with a cross on top in his right hand, and the rod in his left. Thus he was enthroned King of England and Ireland and claimant to the crown of France. The bishops kissed him and he kissed the earls. A mass followed and he confessed and was given absolution.

This ended the coronation. Richard was carried by the earls back to the palace, the litter preceded by a large number of actors or clowns, a curious detail (preserved in the *Chronicon Angliae*) which reflects the Middle Ages. There he had a light meal and rested, for he was exhausted by the long ceremony.

The banquet in Westminster Hall took place later. It was opened by the King creating new knights and earls. One of the latter was Lord Henry Percy, who was made Earl of Northumberland, in which region his future adventures were to lie and where he came at last to his death at the age of sixty-four at Bramham Moor.[1] Another of the new earls was Guichard d'Angle, the Gascon

[1] In 1408 Percy rebelled against the Duke's son, King Henry IV. He was defeated at the battle of Bramham Moor by the Sheriff of Yorkshire, Sir Thomas Rokeby. Percy's head was exposed on London Bridge. Its venerable grey hair made the people weep, it is said. (*Dict. Nat. Biog.*) However, in

nobleman who had fought on the Black Prince's side at Nájera and remained faithful to him when so many lords of Aquitaine went over to the French king. He had been living in England for the past three years and held for a time the appointment of tutor to Richard. Now he was made Earl of Huntingdon, for a foreigner an unusual honour, of which sort had more been bestowed the nobility of Aquitaine might have stood by England.[1]

Of the banquet itself there are some intimate glimpses in the *Anonimalle Chronicle*; for instance Richard's losing of one of St. Edward's shoes, held most unlucky, a sure portent of future misfortune. The Chronicler says he lost it before dinner in the middle of the Hall. It was much too big for him and fell off, and was never found.[2] When seated at dinner he felt the crown too heavy for him. The Earl of March held it up or supported it, so that it did not press so much. The Princess, who no doubt had witnessed the coronation, had a seat in a gallery overlooking the banquet. The floor was packed with people, for the Londoners, rich and poor, were allowed in to watch. The *Chronicon Angliae* declares that the servants could not have reached the table with the dishes, had it not been that the Duke and Percy, who were riding their great horses inside the Hall, made an alley for the food through the onlookers. People who could not push their way in did not do badly because a hollow pillar in the courtyard was spouting wine. 'Nobody, not even the very poorest man, was prevented from drinking his full.'

And one last incident, too curious to omit, concerns the King's Champion. Certain knights were proud of the fact that they held land on condition of rendering the King service at his coronation. Such a tenure was known as grand sergeantry. Thus, in 1377 Sir William Furnivall held the manor of Farnham Royal in Bucks on condition that he found the King a red glove and supported his right arm when he held the sceptre. The Mayor of London, by

1461 the tables were turned at Towton (only four miles from Bramham Moor) where the House of Lancaster went down.

[1] Guichard d'Angle died three years later in 1380. Froissart sums up his character as follows (Berners' translation): 'Truely this gentyll knight was well worthy to have honoure, for in his time he had all noble vertues that a knight ought to have; he was mery, true, amorous, sage, secrete, large, prewe, hardy, adventurous and chyvalrous.'

[2] A Westminister document quoted by Galbraith on p. 187 of his edition of the *Anonimalle Chronicle*, gives a different version but it seems impossible to reconcile it with the probabilities of the case.

right of a special sergeantry inherent in his office, was entitled to serve the King at the banquet from a golden cup. In the same way the King's Champion was a knight who by right of land held in grand sergeantry had the privilege of riding into Westminster Hall during the banquet and flinging down his gauntlet in challenge of anyone who might dispute the King's title to the throne. The manor of Scrivelsby, Lincolnshire, obliged the owner to give the service of Champion. In 1377 the manor was held by Sir John Dymoke. This knight had reason for wanting to be first on the scene, because he knew that a connection of his, Sir Baldwin de Freville, would dispute his right. Accordingly he arrived outside the Abbey before the mass which concluded the coronation was over and waited by the door. He had borrowed the finest horse he could select in the royal stables and the best suit of armour from the royal armoury, which custom entitled him to do, according to the *Chronicon Angliae* from where this story is taken. On the Abbey service being over, there appeared on horseback in the courtyard the Duke, the two Percys, Henry and Thomas, and one of the King's uncles, who started to clear a passage through the spectators, so that King Richard, who was about to come out, might cross conveniently to the palace. They were surprised to see Sir John Dymoke in full armour with his esquires. 'What are you doing here at this hour?' said the Duke. 'You are not due till dinner-time in the Hall. Go and take off that armour and keep quiet till then.' Sir John complied and withdrew. It is stated that later when his rival, Sir Baldwin de Freville, appeared in the Hall, a dispute ensued which was settled in favour of Sir John. From that day till the coronation of George IV a Dymoke invariably rode into Westminster Hall as King's Champion. The challenge as an item of the coronation ceremonies was then abolished, but the Dymokes, understandably proud of the family's long service, have managed to retain the style of King's Champion till today and in that titular capacity have attended the last five coronations.

One cannot help wondering how Richard was affected as an individual by being crowned at the age of ten and a half. Brought up in the country at Berkhamsted, an only child, much with his mother, how did he conduct himself, what was his mood? There is no evidence to found a guess on. Yet children adapt themselves easily even to what they do not fully understand. One has only to read of the coronation of a Dalai Lama (generally aged about four) to be amazed at how a child can take the central place in a great ceremonial with solemn propriety, as if absorbed in a world of make-believe. Richard may have felt, also, a surge of self-confidence. His father had been a great man; he must show that he was a great man too.

But this is surmise. What is known, however, is his appearance, for two contemporary paintings of him as a boy have survived, the large portrait now hanging at the entrance to the nave in Westminster Abbey and the small Wilton Diptych in the National Gallery where he appears with other figures. The exact date of these paintings is much disputed, but clearly in both he is quite young; in the Abbey portrait he looks about twelve and in the other about fifteen.[1] The former tells near enough how he must have appeared at his coronation. We see him seated in a chair of state, not, indeed, in his coronation robes, but in ceremonial dress, crowned and holding the sceptre and rod. The face is boyish and bright in general, but the eyes are strangely withdrawn and introvert, haughty, humourless, and overbearing. There is also a lurking sadness. It is the face of a clever person, very conscious of self and of high position, assured, not easily daunted, petulant, sudden in mood and unpredictable, altogether a difficult boy. One has the impression that his mother, famous ex-beauty, leader of fashion, gay, sensible and good natured, cannot have had much influence over him.

[1] For a discussion of the dates, meanings and attributions of these pictures see *English Art* by Joan Evans (1949), p. 101 seq.

Invasion of England

The day after the coronation a council of eight lords and four knights was set up. A compromise was sought. One sees here the Princess's influence. She was always in favour of moderation. She and her small boy must try to be on good terms with everyone. Hence, among the eight lords were four who were friends of the Duke: in particular, Lord Latimer, his old associate, and Ralph Erghum, Bishop of Salisbury till recently the head of his Chancery in the Savoy. These two were balanced by Bishop Courtenay and the Earl of March, his leading opponents. Indeed, the Council was so balanced that it was unlikely to take a strong line. It had no common leader.

Yet a man behind whom the nation could unite was urgently needed. In this same month of July 1377 the French followed up their savage incursion to Lewes by sacking Folkestone, Portsmouth, Plymouth and Dartmouth. In August, after failing at Winchelsea and Southampton, where their attacks were driven off, as troops happened to be ready there, they landed on the Isle of Wight and overran the whole of it. Of this incursion the *Chronicon Angliae* has: 'The French marched about the isle, slaughtering the local people, burning the towns and making away with property. They collected all the booty they could and compelled the islanders to raise a thousand marks from their friends on the mainland to ransom their houses from burning and what goods remained to them from seizure.' (One recalls that the English condottieri captains in France had provided many precedents for this sort of brigand warfare.)

The remedy for these evils was not in doubt. Command of the Channel must be regained. The Council advised the Crown to summon parliament. The money raised by the poll tax was all spent. Indeed, the Council had had to borrow £5,000 from the city and pledge some of the crown jewels as security.[1]

Parliament assembled in Westminster on 13 October. The commons consisted of the same knights (or men of the same stamp) who had been returned for the Good Parliament of 1376. Peter de la Mare was back again as speaker. The Duke, who had spent the previous two months at his castle of Kenilworth, now came to London. As in the Good Parliament the commons first asked for a committee of lords to advise them. In the list they submitted was included the Duke's name. Considering what had passed, this was surprising. But the emergency was such that it was felt impossible to do without the benefit of his experience. On hearing his name announced he at once rose in his place and, bowing to Richard who was presiding, said that he could not accept the nomination unless the commons dissociated themselves from the gross slanders levelled against him the previous year and still being repeated. He was one of the greatest lords in the realm, he declared. If what was alleged against him were true, he would be guilty of treason. 'None of my ancestors,' he went on with feeling, 'of one side or the other, was ever a traitor, and it would be a strange thing if I turned aside from the conduct they showed.'[2] Let any man come forward and charge him with treason, and he would know how to defend himself as a gentleman should.

The Duke's speech seems to have embarrassed the members. 'All the prelates and lords rose and with one voice excused themselves, entreating the Duke to cease, for they thought there was no man living who would say such a thing. And the commons said it was evident and notorious that they held him excused of all reproach and ill report, since they had chosen him to be their principal aid, comforter and counsellor.'

The Duke replied that every sort of lie about him had been

[1] In Riley's *Memorials of London*, p. 410, the deed of pawn is given in full with a detailed description of the articles pledged, some of which were jewelled clothes. Thus: 'One coat of cloth of gold with a green ground, buttoned with balls of gold and embroidered with large pearls around the collar and sleeves.'

[2] The whole episode is recorded in the Rolls of Parliament and is no mere anecdote retailed by a chronicler. The extract here is quoted in *Illustrations of Chaucer's England* by Dorothy Hughes, p. 216.

going round the country. The people who told them were the traitors; it was they who endangered the stability of the realm. He sincerely hoped that they would be punished.

There was not much chance of that; there were too many of them. The lower classes had got into the way of calling him a traitor and openly declaring he aimed at the throne, though his behaviour after his father's death could not have been more correct. The commons, of course, knew the charge was baseless or they would not have asked for his advice. They were well aware of his real shortcomings. He was blustering, tactless, overbearing, quarrelsome. They would not let him have any power. But it would be imprudent to leave him out altogether. And perhaps he might be tried again in some active capacity. What a pity it was that his two brothers, Edmund and Thomas, were no good.

Parliament's main duty was to vote supplies. It was decided not to repeat the poll tax. The usual tax on moveables, estimated to bring in £40,000, was voted. To make sure that the money was all spent on the navy and the coast fortresses, two aldermen, both members of the commons, the John Philpot already mentioned and William Walworth, head of the London fishmongers' company, were appointed treasurers and informed that they would have to account to parliament for every penny. Action was immediately taken. A naval force was fitted out. The *Anonimalle Chronicle* puts it clearly: 'Certain lords were chosen to search the sea for the French and Spanish, since great damage had been done by these enemies and a great number of merchant ships had been captured. The lords chosen to lead the fleet were . . .' and there follows a list of names, mostly of men we already know. Lord Latimer was one; he was transferred from the Council. Lord John Arundel, the Earl's brother, who had succeeded Percy as Marshal of England, was another. Sir Robert Knollys, the old condottiere of few words, appears on the list, as does Sir Baldwin de Freville, the would-be champion of England, and Thomas, Earl of Buckingham, the Duke's brother. Finally, there is a man not yet met with, but who has a melancholy part to play, Sir Robert Hales, Prior of the Hospital of St. John of Jerusalem, the master of the Knights Hospitallers in England. The force of men-at-arms and archers mustered by these lords embarked on 7 November in thirty ships and put out. The following night they were nearly lost in a gale but managed to find shelter. Making a fresh start they searched the Channel during the rest of 1377 and into January

1378, but could not find the enemy fleets. The Spanish had gone home and the French dared not leave their river mouths. The naval sortie was at least partially successful. The enemy had not been defeated but he had been prevented from raiding England.

Sir Hugh Calveley, the most famous of the condottieri captains of Companies, was now Captain of Calais. In January 1378 he made a sortie by land and took Etaples which he held to ransom, as well as two other smaller towns. He also made a naval sortie and took thirty little fishing boats and trading vessels at Boulogne, on which he raised a ransom. After causing his chaplain to celebrate mass in the cathedral, he marched back to Calais, capturing *en route* such a quantity of cattle and sheep that the inhabitants of Calais were able to buy a cow for four shillings and a sheep for sixpence. This was only a small success, yet was something because it made the French less sure of themselves.

On the lords' return from scouring the Channel in February 1378, the Duke offered to do better. At the end of the month he was given the command of a new naval expedition which was to make a determined effort to bring the enemy fleets to action. As the treasury was again short of money, for the last expedition had been very expensive, the bishops and the earls lent substantial sums. The muster was in the Isle of Wight in March. The Duke is said to have collected 4,000 men-at-arms and 8,000 archers. He had with him such well-known lords as Sir John Arundel, the Marshal; the Earl of Salisbury, of Poitiers fame; members of the great houses of Warwick and Pembroke; and Aubrey de Vere, uncle of the young Earl of Oxford. The embarkation was delayed for one reason and another. The *Chronicon Angliae*, always so hostile to the Duke, alleges that his men, their supplies having run out, started looting the neighbourhood 'where short of burning towns and killing people, they did as much harm as the French would have done'. Evidently some story of the kind was currently believed and revived the unpopularity which the Duke had begun to live down. Finally, when he put to sea in June 1378 he was no more fortunate than had been the previous expedition in bringing the French fleet to battle. In August he abandoned the attempt but, reluctant to return with nothing accomplished, and conceiving there was a chance of surprising St. Malo, led the fleet thither. He miscalculated both the chance and the difficulties. The venture was unsuccessful and he put back to England with nothing to show for the money expended.

One feels that the Duke was an unlucky commander. But even with better luck it would have been hard for him to be as versatile as was required. Soldier, statesman, pretender, magnate, he was expected also to be admiral. It was too much for one man. Nevertheless, his failure was laid against him.

While the Duke was at St. Malo an occurrence in Westminster Abbey, connected with the battle of Nájera, whose eleventh anniversary was just passed, greatly excited and shocked the public. The edifice, so sacred because it housed the shrine of St. Edward, was desecrated by a deed of violence. As was stated in its place, the great Aragonese magnate, the Count of Denia, was captured at Nájera by Robert Hauley and Richard Chamberlain. These two esquires had a right to a share in his ransom, which the Prince fixed at £29,000. At an early stage Chamberlain sold his right to another esquire, John Shakell. Hauley and Shakell were now living in London. Ransoms of this importance belonged to the Crown, which allowed the captors a percentage. So far, Count Denia, who had sent his son to England as a hostage, had paid little or nothing. The Black Prince and King Edward, despairing of seeing their money, preferred to sell their prospects to Hauley and Shakell for a small sum in cash down. The young Count then passed into the keeping of the two esquires. Their attempts to recover the ransom were no more successful than had been the Crown's. In 1378 Richard's new council asked for the hostage back. The government was interesting itself again in the collection of the ransom and negotiating direct with Aragon. Hauley and Shakell, afraid to lose their security, refused to give up young Denia and hid him.[1] Thereupon the council ordered, in the King's name, their arrest and imprisonment in the Tower until they produced their captive. They were duly locked up, but escaped, and made their way to Westminster Abbey where they took sanctuary.

The idea that a holy place gave sanctuary existed in Europe in classical times and was later adopted by the Christian church. Various sanctuaries existed under the Anglo-Saxon kings of England. In Norman times the custom became regulated by charter; Westminster Abbey was one of some twenty churches with a charter confirming its right to give sanctuary to persons escaping

[1] The settlement of accounts between the Crown and the esquires was of quite extraordinary complication. It is elucidated at length in 'L'Affaire du Comte de Denia', by Edouard Perroy in *Mélanges d'Histoire du Moyen Age offerts* à L. Halphen (1951), chap. lxvi, p. 573.

from civil justice. In London this became somewhat of a scandal, for with the increase of the city population, numerous malefactors were harboured and justice was delayed. But the Church, supported by public opinion, was strong enough to maintain its privilege.

With tradition, public feeling and a charter in their support, Hauley and Shakell felt quite safe in the Abbey. Runaways of all sorts were there, including convicted criminals or criminals evading arrest. They themselves were not criminals, but men whose right to what they could collect of Denia's ransom had been formally recognized by the Crown. True, they had refused to obey the government's order to surrender their surety. But even if their recalcitrance could be construed as petty treason, they believed themselves to be covered. As long as they remained in the Abbey they could not be touched.

The Council members, however (or such of them as were handling the business) were so enraged at being baulked that they decided to risk the scandal which an arrest in the Abbey would be sure to cause, and ordered Sir Alan Buxhall, the Lieutenant of the Tower, to recover his prisoners. Accordingly on 11 August (1378) he went to the Abbey accompanied by Sir Ralph Ferrers, and a posse of men-at-arms. They arrived unexpectedly and by some stratagem managed to lay hands quietly on John Shakell before he guessed their intention. But they could not so easily apprehend Robert Hauley. He saw the arrest of his companion, and, when they called on him to surrender, refused to do so. Buxhall attempted to seize him, but he resisted. A fight ensued in the nave. Hauley drew a sword which he had hidden under his clothes and defended himself vigorously, for he was an experienced soldier. But with so many against him he was soon wounded and retreated into the choir. Mass was in progress and the monks were in the stalls. Nevertheless, Buxhall and his men pursued him, though the monks called on them urgently to desist, and cut him down in front of the altar. A sacristan who intervened was also killed. Hauley's dead body was then dragged down the nave by the feet, his blood leaving a track on the pavement. In short, it was an aggravated case of desecration.

On the matter being reported to Archbishop Sudbury, he consulted Bishop Courtenay. With his support, and urged on by the Abbot of Westminster, he took a bolder line than was usual with him and 'solemnly excommunicated all those who had participated in the villainy and all those who had instigated it' (*Anonimalle Chronicle*). This meant that besides Buxhall, Ferrers and their men, some members of the Council were also excommunicated.

Two months later (20 October) a parliament met at Gloucester. The sacrilege was discussed. The Council sought to show that the Abbot had exceeded his rights under the Abbey's charter by sheltering Hauley and Shakell when the King in Council was proceeding against them. For that he deserved to be deprived of his temporalities. To answer this accusation the Abbot asked time to consult his lawyers, a request which was granted. During the time allowed he went to the chapter house of Gloucester Abbey where the commons were assembled, put his case to them and asked them to right the wrong which had been done to his church and also to Shakell who had been taken back to the Tower. His attempt to enlist the sympathies of the commons annoyed the Council. Their rejoinder was to call in Wycliffe, the church's greatest critic, to prove the Abbot wrong. Since the quarrel in St. Paul's between the Duke and Courtenay, the Church had made two attempts to suppress Wycliffe. In December 1377 the Pope ordered Oxford University to arrest him, but it evaded the order. In March 1378 he appeared before Sudbury at Lambeth for questioning. The Princess, perhaps at the instance of the Duke, sent word asking the Archbishop to come to no finding on his case. At a later stage of the inquiry, a section of the London mob which favoured him burst in and put an end to the proceedings. To the backing of the Princess, the University and his London admirers, Wycliffe now added the recognition of the Council. At its behest he came before the commons, supported by Thomas Percy[1] and by Sir Simon Burley, who had succeeded D'Angle as Richard's tutor. His arguments in support of the Council were unanswerable. At least, nobody present was clever enough to counter his vast learning and the subtlety of his dialectic. The Abbot, he declared, had indeed exceeded his rights; and in any case the contention that the Church could give sanctuary to the detriment of the civil power was contradicted by his theory of dominion as developed in his book on the subject and which no one had refuted.

[1] Thomas Percy had commanded the left wing of the Black Prince's midward at the battle of Nájera, the wing on which Hauley and Shakell had fought. So he knew all about the matter from the start. So did Burley, who had also been at the battle.

But though, thanks to the learned Doctor, the Council got the better of the Abbot in argument, it was uncomfortable over what had occurred in the Abbey and wanted to reach a settlement. Negotiations took place. Finally Shakell was offered release from the Tower, an estate and a settlement of his claim to ransom money, if he told where he had hidden young Denia. The King offered to endow a chantry where in perpetuity five priests would sing masses to shorten the time in Purgatory which the souls of Hauley and the sacristan might have to spend. Buxhall and Ferrers paid the Abbot compensation. On their side the Church called off the excommunication. To everyone's surprise Shakell now revealed that Denia had been with him all the time in the Tower, disguised as his personal servant. The young Spaniard's honourable behaviour was thought extraordinary and made a deep impression. The author of the *Chronicon Angliae* declares that his conduct set an example which the nobility of England would do well to copy.[1]

The episode of the Abbey desecration demonstrates the lack of unity prevailing at a crisis when union was indispensable. Sudbury, backed by Courtenay, excommunicates councillors, who turn for support to the great heresiarch Wycliffe, at the very moment when the French and Spanish fleets were renewing their attacks, this time on the Cornish ports. Public confidence in the Government's ability to meet the danger from the sea was shaken. Besides the enemy ships of war off Cornwall, French pirates were operating in the Channel. A Scottish corsair named John Mercer was in command. While the Duke was attempting to take St. Malo in August, Mercer captured a number of English merchant ships. On complaint being made to the Council, answer was returned that it was for the Duke and his fleet to take action. London was dissatisfied with this reply. Alderman John Philpot, a man of great independence of character, resolved to punish the pirates himself. 'The lords were neglecting their duty of defending the realm and the people were suffering in consequence.' Thus the *Chronicon Angliae* for his high motives. His eye, however, may have been on the mayoralty, for which he was standing the next month. Without informing the authorities, he hired several

[1] From Edouard Perroy's detailed sifting of l'affaire du Comte Denia, it transpires that the young Count was not as straightforward as appears, for he borrowed no less than £23,000 from various London merchants, who afterwards sued Shakell. It does not seem that Shakell finally got any profit from the capture of Denia.

vessels, engaged a thousand men, sailors and men-at-arms, sallied out, brought Mercer to battle, captured him and the ships under his command, also the English ships he had taken, and returned in triumph to port. His reception in London was tumultuous. On learning of his exploit, the Council was ill pleased. He was informed by the Earl of Stafford that he had had no business to wage war without the Council's permission. To which remonstrance he replied: 'Since none of you lords were raising a hand to defend the country, it was left for me to do so.' He had not spent his money, he said, and exposed his men to the perils of the sea in order to put the nobility to shame, and himself to win a great reputation, but only because there was no other way of assuring his countrymen's safety and the kingdom's freedom. He was elected Mayor of London immediately afterwards.

The episode is as good an illustration of the power, wealth and independence of London as it is of the incapacity of the government to cope with a situation where there was a boy King, no leading personalities, a lost war, danger of invasion, no money, and growing popular discontent.

The Gloucester parliament, which had debated the Abbey affair, was dissolved on 16 November 1378 after making small and inadequate grants, though Philpot and Walworth produced accounts to prove that the money voted by the last parliament had all been spent on the war. A new parliament had to be called in April 1379, to the disgust of the shire knights and burgesses, who did not relish having to find more money. When, as expected, they were asked to do this, they resolved to impose another poll tax, the second of its kind. The one of January 1377 had been a flat rate of 4d. all round. This time, while keeping 4d. for the populace, higher rates were fixed for the classes above.

The *Anominalle Chronicle* has an interesting list of the rates, which shows the standing of the various classes in fourteenth century England. The Duke, as the richest layman in the country, is assessed at £6 13s. 4d., the earls at £4, and the barons, baronets and knights who had the income of barons, at £2. A knight bachelor and an esquire whose estates were equal to a knight's, paid £1, but an esquire of medium estate 6s. 8d., and one in employ, as the servant or armed retainer of a knight, only 3s. 4d. So much for the landed gentry. There follow rates for men holding particular posts. Thus the Prior of the Hospitallers, Sir Robert Hales, paid the same as a baron, £2, while the brethren of the

Order paid the same as retainer esquires, 3s. 4d. The judges of the King's Bench were rated above earls with £5. The Mayor of London was assessed as an earl at £4 and an alderman as a baron at £2. The bigger merchants paid £1 like a knight, the lesser 3s. 4d., and small shopkeepers and craftsmen 6d. A landholder of lesser rank than a knight was assessed according to the acreage of his land, at 2s., 1s., or 6d. The 6d. class was composed of small freeholders. The unfree holders, the villeins of the manors, paid 4d. each, both men and women, if over fourteen, as also did the free labourers, the people who worked for wages on land belonging to others. These two classes composed the bulk of the agricultural population, indeed of the whole population, for agriculturists far outnumbered all the rest. The rates for the clergy and ecclesiastical orders are also given in the list, with assessments ranging from £6 13s. 4d. for the senior bishops (same as the Duke) down to 4d. for the poorest monks. The *Anonimalle Chronicle* calls the tax with its gradations 'the most extraordinary that was ever seen or heard of'. It was certainly worked out with care and with the intention of being fair to all. The poll tax of January 1377, when rich and poor paid the flat rate of 4d., had caused resentment in the shires. Whether the proportions fixed now were fair enough is impossible to say. But one may at least attempt to see whether 4d. for workers on the land and 6d. for craftsmen and small retailers were reasonable sums. There is extant a contemporary bill of accounts put in by a carpenter, William Sunning, which shows the wages he had to pay workmen for repairs to a house in Cornhill, London.[1] Tilers got 7d. a day, and their men 5d., with 1d. each extra for drink. Carpenters and painters were also paid 7d. a day and their men 5d. Thus, this sort of skilled labour, rated for poll tax at 6d., had to pay about a day's wages.

The price of some articles of food in London in 1363 is given in a Mayor's proclamation of that date.[2] A hen cost 4d., a pheasant 2d., a shoulder of roast mutton 2½d., a roast goose 7d., the best carcass of mutton 2s. In 1378, the year before the poll tax, an Ordinance[3] for cooks gives similar prices. A whole roast pig of the best quality was 8d. and a lamb 7d., a roast chicken 4d., roast snipe 1½d., roast woodcock 2½d. and ten eggs went for a penny.

[1] See Riley, *Memorials of London*, translation from Latin of the account dated Ed, III, 1359 (p. 305).

[2] Ibid., p. 312.

[3] Ibid., p. 426.

These are London prices for country produce. The villagers certainly paid less.

The London workman who had a trade could evidently afford these prices and must have had plenty to eat. It is not so easy to show the peasantry's income. The majority of them were not paid money wages. As villeins bound to a manor they made their living from cultivating the fields allotted them by the lord of the manor. They could, however, make money by keeping hens, bees, pigs and sheep. The sale of one hen would pay the poll tax. The landless free labourers such as shepherds, ditchers, cattle and pig herdsmen, carters, woodsmen and cultivators generally had, despite the Statute of Labourers, succeeded in getting higher wages than before, as has been explained. 3d. or 4d. a day with dinner was not unusual.[1] For such people the tax also represented about one day's wages.

These were some of the factors taken into consideration by the framers of the poll tax of April 1379 and which led them to believe that the demand of 4d. from the general population was reasonable. But though the second poll tax was fairer than the first, the people had similar objections to paying; it was an extra tax imposed on them contrary to custom, without their consent and for the second time in two years.

An attempt has been made to estimate what the tax yielded and the figure of £27,000 has been given.[2] On the assumption that £5,000 came in from the higher rates, the balance of £22,000 represents a payment of 4d. by 1,320,000 people over fourteen. Such then, at a guess, was the adult peasant population of England at that date. The total population has been estimated at about 2,200,000.[3] The difference of 880,000 represents the classes paying over 4d. and the children under fourteen of all classes. The government, whose statistics were imperfect, expected a larger yield and was disappointed. But in funds for the moment, they redeemed the King's jewels and prepared to fit out another expedition against the French mainland.

A chance of delivering a strong blow offered; the Duke of Brittany, King Charles' feudatory, had quarrelled with him and asked for English help. Lord John Arundel, the Marshal, was

[1] See the paper in *The Economic History Review*, vol. iv, no. 4 of 1934, 'Labour Conditions in Essex in the reign of Richard II' by Nora Kenyon.

[2] Sir James Ramsay, *The Genesis of Lancaster*, vol. ii, p. 132 (1913).

[3] *British Medieval Population*, Josiah Cox Russell (1948).

15. The Earl of Buckingham crossing the Channel

16. Troops of the Count of Flanders in action

appointed to bring it. With him were some famous knights who each raised his own troop, the most notable being Hugh Calveley and Thomas Percy. It took time to muster the various contingents but by the end of November 1379 they were ready to sail from Southampton when the wind allowed. While waiting, the soldiers of Arundel's troop misbehaved themselves, as had the Duke's men before his expedition the previous year. So outrageous was their conduct, that it would be hard to believe they treated the people of their own country so badly, were it not that the two principal chronicles[1] are agreed on the facts. The *Chronicon Angliae* gives the story in greater detail. One day Arundel accompanied by some of his men went to a nunnery in the neighbourhood and asked to see the Abbess. On her coming out he asked permission for himself and his men to lodge in the nunnery pending their departure. The Abbess excused herself as best she could, pointing out that for men to stay in a nunnery was altogether against the rules. Arundel professed surprise at her refusal. Surely she did not suspect him and his men? But the Abbess begged him to go elsewhere: 'There is plenty of other accommodation in the neighbourhood.' Sir John was not to be put off. Turning to his men he ordered them to enter the nunnery and occupy the rooms, both public and private. His soldiers were a very rough lot, soldiers of fortune who had been on raids into France. They now treated the inmates of the nunnery as if it were a French house. Besides the nuns, some poor widows were living there and also married women, who, as the custom was, were making a stay for devotional reasons. All these women were forced by the soldiery. The Abbess tried to get help in the vicinity but though the local people were extremely shocked they dared not come to the rescue. This timidity encouraged the soldiers still further and they began looting the farmhouses. Arundel was either unwilling or unable to control them. Calveley and Percy dissociated themselves from these excesses and warned their contingents that any man who molested the local population would be severely punished.

On the wind becoming favourable the order was given to embark. Arundel's soldiers obliged the women in the nunnery to accompany them. On the way to the harbour they also kidnapped a bride whom they met coming out of a church. Nor was this all,

[1] The *Anonimalle Chronicle*, p. 131 and *Chronicon Angliae*, p. 247. Froissart describes the fate of the expedition, but does not mention the outrages.

for 'one of them entered the church and snatching the chalice from the altar ran off with his booty as fast as he could to the ship. The priest, dressed as he still was in alb and stole hurried after him, calling on him to give the chalice back under threat of eternal damnation.' The thief paid no attention, but the priest did not give up and before the ships sailed brought other priests to the pier and there 'with candles, censers, bells and books . . . excommunicated everyone and threw the candle into the sea to extinguish it'.

After relating this story the author of the *Chronicon Angliae* shows himself heartily glad that divine punishment soon overtook Arundel and his men. In his description of what befell he is tediously rhetorical and I will let Froissart, in Berners' translation, tell the sequel. After the fleet put to sea to cross to Cherbourg 'the first day the wynde was reasonable good for them, but agaynst night the wynde tourned contrary to them, and whyder they wolde or nat, they were driven on the cost of Cornwall. The wynde was so sore and streynable that they coulde caste none ancre, nor also they durst nat. In the mornyng the wynde brought them into the Yrisshe see, and by the rage of the tempest thre of their shyppes brast and wente to wrake, wherein was Sir Johan Arundell . . . sir Hughe Caurell (Calveley) and a hundred men at armes, of the whiche hundred fourscore were drowned, and Sir Johan Arundell their capitayne was their perysshed, which was greate domage. And sir Hugh Caurell was never in his lyfe before soo nyghe his dethe; for all that ever was in his shyppe, except hymselfe and sevyn maryners, were all drowned; for he and the sevyn maryners that were saved toke holde of cables and mastes, and the strength of the wynde brought them to the sandes; howebeit, they had dronke waterr ynoughe, wherof they were ryght sicke and yvell at ease.'

The *Chronicon Angliae* states that altogether twenty-five ships were sunk or wrecked, and most of the men and horses aboard were drowned. Arundel, who was a very rich and elegant courtier, had gone on the expedition 'fitted out like a king. He had with him fifty-two new suits of clothes embroidered with gold. These with his horses and destriers, to the total value of £7,000, were swallowed by the sea.'[1] As we have seen, it was customary to dress up in your best for a battle. But Arundel going off to fight in Brittany with fifty-two suits in cloth of gold, even if his intention were to outshine the gorgeous chivalry of France, seems to have

[1] *Chronicon Angliae*, op. cit., p. 253.

been a bit crazy. Some of the stories about him which went the round after his death are given in the *Chronicon Angliae*. To help his ship to ride the waves, he was said to have ordered all the kidnapped women to be thrown overboard. At the height of the storm, when the navigating officer wanted to steer clear of the coast, he commanded him to stand in, and, when he demurred, cut him down.[1]

When the news of the disaster reached London at the end of December 1379, the government summoned a new parliament to discuss what was to be done. It met at Westminster in January 1380. The members were in a critical frame of mind. While the Council could not be blamed for the storm, it was blamed for failure, the accumulated failure of the many previous reverses. All the money raised by the poll tax of the previous April had been spent with nothing to show for it. How to mend matters was not easy to determine. But one thing was clear. The existing Council would have to go. But where to get better men? After long debate, it seemed best to dispense altogether with a Council. Let the King carry on the government with the five principal officers of state (or ministers as they were sometimes termed), the Chancellor, the Treasurer, the Guardian of the Privy Seal, the Chief Chamberlain and the Seneschal of the Household, heads of the departments whose offices were in the precincts of Westminster Palace. No new Council need be nominated for the present. Richard, young though he was, could manage without one. He had come on well lately, 'was of good discretion and quite grown up looking considering his age'.[2] This may well have been the case, though he was only thirteen. Clever boys of thirteen are often very grown up in manner. Since his coronation two and a half years back he had carried out public duties, such as presiding at each of the parliaments. There were signs that he had inherited the precocity of his father, who at sixteen had made his reputation at Crécy. That his self-possession was astonishing, the next year would demonstrate most dramatically. Parliament now gave him a new tutor in place of Simon Burley by appointing the Earl of Warwick to that post.

Besides abolishing the council, parliament appointed a new

[1] There can be no doubt that these disgraceful stories about Lord John Arundel the Marshal were circulating in England. They appear also in the Monk of Evesham's *Vita*. But in the telling they may have become much exaggerated. As stated, Froissart includes none of them. On the contrary, he declares Arundel to have been 'a valiant knight, bold, courteous, amorous and enterprising'. (Page 214, vol. 9, Lettenhove edn., 1869.)

[2] Rot. Parl., vol. iii, p. 73.

Chancellor in the person of Archbishop Sudbury. He was good at accounts. The previous year he had been on a commission to examine the expenditure of the last subsidy. In the present financial crisis his expert knowledge would be useful. Nevertheless, it was a curious choice and puzzled his contemporaries. As the *Chronicon Angliae* puts it: 'Many people thought the appointment of the Archbishop of Canterbury to the office of Chancellor was hardly in keeping with his dignity. Whether he procured it for himself or was offered it and accepted, God knows.' There is the suggestion here that the ways of God are past understanding, for the writer has in mind the terrible death Sudbury was to die the next year, which would not have overtaken him had he not been Chancellor.

Before dissolving in March 1380 parliament granted a subsidy, not a poll tax but the customary tax on moveables which did not affect the peasantry. The grant was made conditional on no parliament being summoned again for a year. It was not, however, large enough to put the finances on a sound footing, if the war with France were to continue. But not a word was said about coming to terms with that country.

That all might be retrieved abroad remained the general opinion. In spite of the reverses, it continued to be true that an English army could enter France via Calais and, thanks to the longbow, march at will through the country. For twenty years such raids had effected little because the French refused to expose themselves to a second Poitiers. But the situation now was more favourable. The revolted Duke of Brittany still awaited the help which the Arundel expedition had failed to bring him. If a new expedition were sent, it might be possible to provoke a pitched battle because the French would be so very unwilling to allow reinforcements to reach Brittany. A decisive defeat of their army might force King Charles to cede again a substantial part of France. Such were the considerations behind the government's resolve to make a further try to regain what Edward III had won and lost.

The decision to send an army to France was contrary to the advice tendered by the Duke. As Pretender to the crown of Castile he sought to persuade parliament to campaign in Gascony. His chancery in the Savoy had been hard at work corresponding with the kingdoms in Spain. Aragon had been led to think that he would arrive in Gascony one day soon with an army large enough to drive the French back and thereafter cross into Spain, as he had hoped to do in 1373 after his march from Calais to Bordeaux. He had also been secretly corresponding with Portugal to urge a second front, a revival of the earlier project to carve up Castile with the help of Aragon and Portugal. The advice he tendered to the English government was that to stop the south coast raids one should strike at the root, advice he had given ever since his marriage to Don Pedro's daughter, Constance. Castile was the source of the evil. If his countrymen put him on its throne, they could sleep safely in their beds. As his negotiations with Portugal were secret, he did not take the government fully into his confidence, but said enough to make it clear that to send an army to Gascony rather than to northern France was in his view the sounder policy. Parliament, however, decided against him.

A compact little army, said to have numbered 3,000 men-at-arms and 3,000 archers, under the command of the Duke's younger brother, Thomas, Earl of Buckingham, was landed at Calais in the spring of 1380. The chief generals were the well-known veterans, Thomas Percy, Hugh Calveley, Robert Knollys and Latimer, the last remembered as a courtier of doubtful honesty, but who had, in fact, a military record going back to the battle of Auray (1364).[1] The expedition's object was to join forces with the Duke of Brittany, as had been Arundel's. Instead, however, of marching there via Rouen, Buckingham followed the precedent of the many previous raids and made a wide sweep through metropolitan France, in the hope, as explained, of provoking a pitched battle, but also of obtaining valuable loot, a great attraction for his veteran mercenaries. But King Charles' orders to his generals were unchanged—follow, harass, but do not attack in force. Buckingham 'burnt the towns and crops and slaughtered the inhabitants without mercy', says the *Chronicon Angliae*. He collected a quantity of plunder. But like the commanders of previous raids, he achieved no military decision. In October he reached Brittany, to find that the French political situation had changed to his detriment. King Charles had just died.[2] It now

[1] He died soon after his return from the present expedition. In his will he founded a chantry with six priests to pray for the repose of his soul and the soul of Edward III, by whose complacence he had been able to make his fortune. (*Engl. Const. Doc.*, p. 192, Lodge and Thornton.)

[2] King Charles died on 16 September 1380. He had been predeceased by Bertrand du Guesclin, whose death occurred on 14 July 1380. Du Guesclin was buried in St. Denis beside the Kings of France. His work was done. He had delivered his country.

appeared that the Duke of Brittany's revolt had not been against the French crown but against King Charles as a person. He had no quarrel with his successor. He was faced with having to explain this to Buckingham as best he could. It was exceedingly awkward to be obliged to tell a man, who had come to help you at your own request, that you did not want him. In fact, he had not the courage to do so at once. It was evident to Buckingham, however, that something was wrong. The army was not given proper quarters and supplies were curtailed. The men fell ill, their horses died. The Duke became more difficult to see and would not answer letters. Eventually he told Buckingham flatly that he must leave. The Earl was very angry. 'There were great words between them,' says Froissart, 'but the Duke humbled himself and made what excuses he could.' Buckingham had to comply and set about hiring ships. When at last on board and ready to start (by this time it was March 1381) the Duke, who had come to see him off, sent word he would like to bid him goodbye. But, says Froissart, Buckingham refused to go ashore, for he 'desired no more parleying with the Duke, and said to his mariners, "draw up your anchors and spread your sails, and let us be gone"'. The *Anonimalle Chronicle* sums up: 'They left the land of Brittany and repaired to England without having accomplished any notable exploit, to their great discomfort and to the great discomfort of the whole English nation.'

The Third Poll Tax

The English nation had suffered nothing but reverses for ten years. Though their army had never been defeated, their French dominion had dissolved. Their diplomacy had failed to take advantage of the victory at Nájera with the consequence that they lost command of the Channel. During the Buckingham expedition the Castilian and French fleets had become active again. Buckingham had hardly landed at Calais when Winchelsea and other towns in its vicinity were burnt. In August while he was marching uselessly through metropolitan France, they threatened metropolitan England, when on the 24th they sailed up the Thames and burnt Gravesend.

The general population of the south had borne the brunt of the invasion and had become increasingly disaffected towards the government. They, not the nobility, had had their homes burnt, their womenfolk slaughtered or carried away by invaders. The government, composed of a set of church and lay magnates, had shown itself incompetent to protect them. Indeed, as we have seen, the Duke and Arundel had plundered them. In this mood of criticism and disillusion, they reflected on other long-standing grievances. A nobility, which had been worsted in the war and had exposed the country to ravage, denied the population its rights. For twenty years free labour had been oppressed by the Statute of Labourers and had had the greatest difficulty in securing the higher wages which were its due. Unfree labour, bound to the lords of the manors, was treated as an inferior caste. On top of all this, labour in general had been asked to foot the bill for the government's failures.

In the fourteenth century people said out what they thought more forcibly than nowadays. It is astonishing to read the homilies delivered in churches by preachers of the Middle Ages. They described the shortcomings of society, high and low, in terms which would not now be tolerated.[1] Nevertheless, though it was customary to denounce the nobility and gentry in the most scathing terms, a preacher's intention was not the overthrow of society, but the admonishment of evil-doers. Now, however, at this moment of grave dissatisfaction with the government, a different sort of preaching made its appearance, whose purport was political and subversive. Its object was not admonishment, but to rouse popular indignation against the upper classes, lay and clerical, and the whole social order, and incite to revolution. A preacher of this sort was the priest, John Ball, a fanatic of remarkable eloquence. Of his activities Froissart says: 'On Sundays after Mass, when the people came out of church, John Ball used to address them in the churchyard in such terms as the following: "My good people, things can't go well in England and will never go well until all property is in common and there are neither villeins nor gentlemen but one united people. What advantage is it to us that the men we call lords are our masters? Do they deserve to be so? What ground have they for holding us in servitude? We are all descended from the same father and mother, Adam and Eve. Their claim to be more truly lords than are we rests only on their power to force us to labour and produce in order that they may spend."' Froissart continues that in speeches of this sort, which Ball made all over Kent and Essex, he urged that the peasantry unite and put their grievances before the King, since no one else would listen to their appeal; and that he made this veiled threat: 'We will tell him that we wish things to be different or we ourselves will find the remedy.' Froissart adds that Ball's words were repeated up and down the countryside. 'Thus and thus said John Ball and it is true.' Men whispered them in the fields and at home and carried them from village to village. Froissart calls him the mad priest, and indeed, his sentiments must have seemed those of a madman to such an admirer of chivalric society. His preaching had started some years back and he had been arrested more than

[1] *Literature and Pulpit in Medieval England* by G. R. Owst (1933) and *Preaching in Medieval England* by the same writer (1926).

once. In the spring of 1381 he was to be arrested again by order of Sudbury, whom, it appears, he reviled, and to be imprisoned in Maidstone gaol. The lower classes of London knew of and shared his opinions and, writes Froissart, 'commenced to say among themselves that the kingdom of England was too badly governed and that the nobles were embezzling the public funds'. Certain Londoners were in communication with Ball's followers in the eastern counties and had come to an understanding with them.

In November 1380, with dangerous talk humming in the villages and some kind of insurrection in the making, parliament met again. In March of that year, when it had dispersed, Sudbury had promised not to summon it for twelve months. But the news from the Earl of Buckingham that Brittany had refused to co-operate and that his expedition could have no result, created a new situation. During the summer of 1380 Duke John had been continuing his secret negotiations in Spain in the hope that eventually he could persuade parliament to finance an expedition there. Portugal had agreed that if the Earl of Cambridge were sent over with an army, she would assist in an invasion of Castile. Now that Buckingham's expedition, against which the Duke had advised, was seen to be a failure, the moment seemed propitious for broaching the other scheme and informing parliament of the Portuguese alliance. The Duke raised the question with Sudbury. But Sudbury was averse to an open discussion in parliament of an expedition to Portugal. The Duke's unpopularity was the difficulty. The commons would refuse a grant if put to them in that way. Nevertheless, he would summon parliament and so handle it that a grant sufficient for the plan would be passed. The venue was fixed at Northampton, inconveniently distant in winter, but selected because the Londoners were in so angry a mood over a sensational murder trial that it was feared their mob might cause a disturbance at Westminster. No doubt, also, Sudbury thought he could manage his bit of deception better if he had parliament to himself in the depths of the country.

In his opening speech, the Chancellor-Archbishop dwelt on the heavy expense of the Buckingham expedition, which unfortunately had proved a failure. The last subsidy was exhausted. The soldiers, stranded in Brittany, had not been paid for months. Had the customs revenue been normal it might have sufficed, but it had shown an unexpected deficit. The crown jewels had had to be pawned again. The garrison at Calais was clamouring for its pay.

These claims must immediately be met. And other defensive measures required to be taken, which would cost money. He himself had gone into the whole question of the revenue. The truth was that it was insufficient to meet present-day expenditure. Malversation and extravagance had been alleged at the end of the late King's reign. But he could assure members that during his time the public's money had been scrupulously used. There had not been enough of it, however. And he would have to obtain their sanction to another grant.

Thus far Sudbury explained his requirements. He made no mention whatever of the Portuguese alliance nor of the projected expedition against Castile. The Duke, in fact, had two expeditions in mind, for he planned also to lead an army from Gascony and with Aragonese help attack Castile from the east, while his brother and Portugal attacked from the west. Needless to say, Sudbury kept quiet also in this matter.

The commons, moved by his description of the government's penury, and accepting his assurance that the last subsidy had been carefully expended, asked him to name the sum he required. Bearing in mind the two armies the Duke had in view, he replied that to pay off outstanding debts and budget confidently for the future he would require £160,000.[1]

This was a bombshell. The Chancellor was asking for about six times as much money as the last poll tax had yielded.

A long wrangle ensued. The demand was first cut to £100,000. Parliament agreed to find two-thirds of this if the church, voting in convocation, found the other third. What form the tax should take had then to be decided. The commons favoured another poll tax. But it was not proposed to repeat the 1379 graduated tax. There should be a flat rate, as in 1377, but to get the required sum of £66,000 the tax would have to be raised from fourpence to a shilling. Parliament knew very well that the general population would make a fuss at having to pay three times as heavy a tax as before. If they had objected to fourpence, the outcry over a shilling was bound to be loud. But it was not believed that popular indignation would boil over. Most of the labouring

[1] For a very detailed exposition of the Duke's negotiations in Spain see P. E. Russell, op. cit., chap. xiii. The facts brought to light in the chapter establish for the first time the close connection between the Duke's pretensions to the crown of Castile and the poll tax of 1380/1, and hence the responsibility of the Duke for the insurrection which followed.

population could afford a shilling (or so it was said). To meet the case of the comparatively few who were really poor, local authorities would be authorized to encourage residents of substantial means to pay a bit more than a shilling, so that fourpence, sixpence or eightpence from the least well-off would yet suffice to bring the total for the locality to what a shilling all round would give. And over fifteen years, not over fourteen, would be the lowest age for assessment. With the tax tempered in this way it would not be unfair. There would be an element of grading, though it was not compulsory and depended, if it were to be a relief, on there being enough well-to-do people in each neighbourhood to balance the reduced tax on its poor.

But nothing could have been more inopportune than to inflict a third poll tax, and that three times as heavy as the previous two, on a labouring class which was already disaffected and contemplating insurrection.

The levy of the tax started in January 1381. To effect it the revenue departments of each shire court sent out collectors to get in touch with such rural functionaries as constables, bailiffs and, in larger towns, mayors, and obtain lists of the inhabitants in their locality. With the help of sub-collectors it would then be possible to make a house-to-house demand or, if the people could be relied upon to appear, to assemble them on the village green or in the church, and there collect the money.

Anyone who has had practical acquaintance with the collection of taxes in the late eastern possessions of the crown of England, will recognize the opportunity which this poll tax gave the various collectors to make money. The local functionaries and their assistants knew well enough who were taxable. They also knew that everyone would try to avoid full payment. For their part the people knew that the collectors could be bribed. Agreement between collectors and people was easily reached. So perfectly did the two sides understand each other that the taxable adult lay population of the shires, whose number had been disclosed by the 1377 poll tax, fell mysteriously by about 360,000, representing a loss to the revenue of £18,000, more than a quarter of the expected £66,000. The collectors had omitted such dependants as unmarried sisters, aunts, old people past their work, and many children over fifteen. It may be that the omissions were in a few cases due to negligence, such as the acceptance without proper check of a householder's statement of the number of his dependants. There may also have been collusion out of sympathy, when, as sometimes happened, there were no richer people in a village to volunteer to take over part of the tax and everybody, no matter how poor, had to pay a shilling. But one suspects that in general, even in an extreme case where a poor man was supporting his parents and his wife's parents, had maiden aunts or sisters and among his children one who was just over fifteen, he did not get them written off without making it worth a collector's while. Though these considerations explain the low return, they do not explain how it was that the peasantry all over the kingdom were of the same mind. To account for this, one is obliged to postulate a conspiracy of a sort. Word must have been whispered from village to village. It is impossible not to see here the existence of some kind of inter-county understanding. The peasants of one part were already in secret touch with those of another on the possibility of a general rising. The agreement to resist the tax was part of the wider conspiracy. The population had not quite reached the point of breaking out but were sufficiently organized to combine to reduce the tax.

The Start of the Insurrection, 30 May to 7 June

When by March 1381 the returns were in, the government realized that the tax had not been properly collected. Instead of getting £66,000, they had only £48,000. They reacted as would any government. On 18 March they issued a writ to the exchequer directing that the balance due must be collected. The tax officials, it was declared, had either 'voluntarily, negligently, or by showing favour omitted to assess many people'. Commissioners were appointed to travel the shires and compel payment by imprisoning resisters.[1] They got to work in April. A careful check was made, and the aunts, sisters, old people, etcetera, were called upon to pay up.

For a population already provoked to the verge of rebellion, it was not tolerable to be asked to make good the deficit. The authorities had no idea of the delicacy of the situation. A government never knows what is in the popular mind. To make matters worse the commissioners used no tact. More than one chronicle has it on record that their men handled defaulters roughly. It is alleged that in certain cases, to find out whether a girl was under or over fifteen, they insisted on examining her person. Additional shillings were extracted under strong pressure, while resentment rose higher and higher.

In the *Chronicon Angliae* and Knighton's *Chronicle* are preserved examples of curious letters in English which about this time were

[1] Copy of latin writ given p. 182 of Charles Oman's *The Great Revolt of 1381* (1906).

being sent round the villages. They take the form of warnings and admonitions addressed by leaders to their following, and hint at the close approach of an event for which the peasantry must carefully prepare. Two of the letters are attributed to John Ball, though at this moment he was in Maidstone gaol. In one of them he uses the pseudonym John Sheep. The other letters, purporting to be written by peasants called Jack Straw, Jack Milner, Jack Carter and Jack Trueman, may also be by him. But it is more reasonable to suppose that letters of the sort were being distributed by several local leaders; a Jack Straw, for instance, later appeared as second in command of the Essex rebels. In the letter attributed to John Ball by the *Chronicon Angliae* are to be found the following admonitions. 'John Sheep bids John Nameless and John the Miller and John Carter to beware of guile and stand together in God's name. He bids Piers Ploughman go to his work and chastise well Hob the Robber. Take with you John Trueman and all his fellows and no more and look you shape you to one head and no more.' And it contains the statement: 'John the Miller has ground small, small, small.' Such phrases, says the chronicle, are full of enigmas. But the meaning is clear enough; in fact a copy of the letter, said to have been found later in the possession of one of the insurgents, was put in evidence at John Ball's trial and helped to convict him. In Langland's poem Piers Plowman is a synonym for everyman. It is unnecessary to suppose, as sometimes suggested, that the writer of this letter had read the poem. The term, no doubt, was in common use. Some modern writers have supposed that by Hob the Robber is meant Robert Hales who, as Treasurer, was responsible for collecting the poll tax, but the name is more likely to stand for the lords in general, as do the other names for classes of people. John Trueman would appear to represent all those who could be relied on to support the cause. The phrase 'shape you to one head' may mean that the leader of the revolt had already been chosen; or it might suggest that at the top there was a revolutionary council whose orders were to be obeyed. Some writers see here a reference to Wat Tyler, the leader of the revolt. There is no evidence that Wat Tyler was secretly directing affairs before the revolt broke out, but he may have been doing so. All we know is that he was publicly declared leader some days after the outbreak. The letter can hardly date from that time, as it refers to a revolt in contemplation rather than to one in being. As for John the Miller having ground small, there appears a connection with the biblical sentence: 'The mills of God grind exceeding small.' The people, likewise, will do their work thoroughly. In the Jack Milner letter, the writer, as if a real miller, is represented as asking his followers to help him turn his mill aright. By mill the cause is meant, for he goes on: 'Look thy mill go aright with the four sailes, and the post stand in steadfastness.' And he tells his followers that they have right with might to back it and will with skill to give it effect. The Jack Carter letter contains the phrases: 'Make a good end of that you have begun. . . . For if the end be well, all is well. . . . You have great need to take God with you in all your deeds. For now is time to beware.' In the Jack Trueman letter is: 'Falseness and guile have reigned too long. Truth has been set under a lock and falseness reigns in every flock. . . . Sin fares as wild flood, true love is away. . . . God give redress, for now is time.' And finally in the second letter ascribed definitely to John Ball is the sentence: 'John Ball greets you well all and does give you to understand he has rung your bell.' The tocsin of the revolt is sounded.

These letters, their jingles making them easy to learn by heart and pass on by word of mouth, so pious and resolute, solemn at a moment full of fate, are authentic reflections of the popular mind in May 1381 when the commissioners from the treasury were at work collecting shillings from the people who had not paid. The insurrection, however, did not begin as a movement concerted from a centre and deliberately set going, but flared up suddenly following a riotous assault on a particular commissioner and his men in an Essex town. It spread thence with great rapidity because the people were waiting for a signal to rise.

How the Essex riot acted as the spark which set all alight can shortly be related. On 30 May a commissioner named Thomas Bampton was sitting at Brentwood, twenty miles north-east of London. He had summoned the inhabitants of Fobbing, Corringham and Stanford, poor marshland villages on the Thames estuary nine miles to the south. The villagers arrived in a sullen mood. When Bampton, after inquiry, informed them that they were liable for further payments, the Fobbing people, says the *Anonimalle Chronicle*, 'made answer that they would not pay a penny more'. They held receipts from the authorities which showed that they had paid the tax demanded of them. On Bampton pointing out that the payments did not correspond with the known population of Fobbing, he received the same answer. 'On which the said Thomas threatened them angrily.' The men of Fobbing consulted with those of Corringham and Stanford, who promised to back them up. About a hundred of them entered Bampton's court and again flatly refused to pay. Bampton then ordered two sergeants-at-arms,[1] the only force he had with him, to arrest the ringleaders. When the sergeants attempted to obey, the villagers suddenly attacked them and Bampton. 'On which the said Thomas fled down the London road.' The villagers alarmed at what they had done, hid in the woods for a while. Too hungry to stay there long, they emerged to ask for support. People in the neighbouring villages received them with enthusiasm for daring to stand up to Bampton. On 31 May and 1 June they and the peasants who joined them went from place to place rousing the countryside. It is on record that a man called William Roger of South Ockendon and a John Smyth of Rainham, both villagers of the neighbourhood, were particularly active. 'Riding with an armed band they compelled the men of the said villages to join them.'[2] Significant of the liaison which already existed between the London working class and the Essex peasantry was the arrival at this very time of two London butchers, Adam Attewell and Roger Harry. News had reached them of the outbreak in Essex and they hastened to seek out the Fobbing men and their supporters in order to fan the flame. For a long time the London proletariat had been hoping to hear that the peasantry had risen. Now the two butchers made the Essex men all sorts of promises and invited them to come to London.[3]

[1] Sergeants-at-arms were a sort of military police on the staff of the Household. They carried a mace inscribed with the royal arms and were authorized to arrest persons in the King's name without a warrant from a criminal court. They were in no sense a civil police force but, rather, members of the King's retinue with special powers of arrest, whose services might on occasion be placed at the disposal of members of the Household, as in the case of Burley, or of an official like Bampton on the King's business.

[2] See document quoted on p. 189 of André Réville's *Le Soulèvement du Travailleurs d'Angleterre* (1898).

[3] The authority for these statements, which support the view that a widespread conspiracy to rebel existed and that the lower classes in town and country were cognisant of it, is the two inquests (Latin) of 4 and 20 November 1382, printed in App. II of Réville, op. cit. The butchers' 'ipsos insurrectores ad veniendum ad dictam civitatem excitaverunt et procuraverunt, et multa super hoc eis promiserunt'. And also the sentence which suggests that contemporaries believed the peasants' revolt to be the outcome of longstanding discontent: 'Ut mala per eosdem longe ante precogitata facilius ad finem ducerent, in diversas et magnas turmas se congregaverunt.'

Meanwhile the government had not been inactive, though it underrated the gravity of the situation. After hearing Bampton's story, it sent down to Brentwood no less a dignitary than Sir Robert Belknap, Chief Justice of the King's Bench, with special powers to try and punish those guilty of driving Bampton away. He arrived on 2 June, three days after the outbreak. Hardly had he opened his court and empanelled a grand jury to present the rioters, when an armed mob invaded the premises. The *Anonimalle Chronicle* gives the sequel. 'They took and made him swear on the Bible that never again would he hold such a session. And they made him give a list of the jurors, and they took all they could catch and cut off their heads and cast their houses to the ground. So the said Sir Robert took his way home without delay.' Three of his clerks were also executed and their heads carried on poles by men who shouted that thus would be punished those who opposed the true commons of England.

This was naked insurrection, far exceeding the riot which put an end to Bampton's taxation inquiry. Already are signs that the rising is not purely the outbreak of peasants labouring under agrarian disabilities, who have been provoked by an unjust tax. Something political is apparent; to oppose the true commons in their designs is declared punishable with death. The *Anonimalle* inserts here a sentence defining their designs at this early stage: 'It was their purpose to slay all lawyers and all jurors[1] and all servants of the King whom they could find.' How far the revolt was the work of revolutionaries, how far of persons seeking to revenge wrongs and appeal for redress, reforms, concessions, and how far the criminals who joined influenced its course, will appear as the narrative proceeds.

The government had full information at once of what had happened from Sir Robert Belknap and also from the gentry of Esssex, some of whom hastened to London with their families, afraid of being murdered or robbed or forced to join the insurgents. It was twenty-three years since the Jacquerie in France and not a few will have remembered what happened then. The English peasants did not seem as savage as the French had been, but there was no telling what they might do. The government, however, though certainly pressed to take energetic measures, seems to have remained incredulous that a national emergency had arisen. Peasant

[1] The jurors meant are not jurymen in the modern sense, but delators chosen in a locality who charged residents thereof with crimes.

outbreaks of violence were not infrequent. Peasants often made trouble; but were easily suppressed by the local authorities.

It is to be recalled that the previous year the council had been abolished, and the conduct of affairs left in the hands of the great officers of state, notably the Chancellor, Archbishop Sudbury, and the Treasurer, Sir Robert Hales, Prior of the Hospitallers. Besides these, the lords of the royal household, influential magnates many of whom have been mentioned, were in immediate attendance on the King, now aged fourteen. Among these was Sir Simon Burley, Richard's tutor till succeeded recently by the Earl of Warwick. The Earl was now a man of thirty-seven. The *Dictionary of National Biography* describes him as being of retiring and indolent disposition, unsuited to his great station among the nobles. The Chamberlain of the Household was Aubrey de Vere, forty-one years old, an inoffensive grandee. His nephew, Robert de Vere, Earl of Oxford, was also at court, a handsome youth of nineteen, of whom the young King was very fond and whose later influence over his master was ascribed to magic. The most distinguished member of the royal suite was William Montagu, Earl of Salisbury, famous as the commander of the rear battle at Poitiers, an elder statesman of fifty-three, who was intimately connected with the royal house on account of his marriage long ago to the Fair Maid of Kent, now, as the King's mother, the leading female personage at court. Among others of that society were Lord Thomas Percy, whose brother, the Earl, was at this moment on his estates in Northumberland; Henry of Derby, aged fifteen, Duke John of Lancaster's son by his first marriage, the later Henry IV; and the Earl of Kent (thirty) and his brother, Sir John Holland (twenty-eight), King Richard's half-brothers, neither of them men of stable character. The three chief members of the royal family, the King's uncles, were not in London in June. On 16 March Duke John had left for the Border to negotiate with the Scots; Thomas, Earl of Buckingham, after returning in March from his useless campaign in France, had gone to his estates in Wales; and Edmund, Earl of Cambridge,.was embarking the army at Plymouth and Dartmouth, destined for the Spanish campaign which was to place Duke John on the throne of Castile.

The expedition was occupying the whole attention of the government, which was using the poll tax to finance it. That Sudbury had not been frank with parliament about the use to which he intended to put the money, had, of course, come out by now and served to discredit him; he appeared to many as a mere creature of the Duke. Cambridge, ambitious to distinguish himself, was anxious to get to sea as soon as possible, in case opposition to the venture developed; in fact most of his men were on board by the first of June.

Such was the situation in London when the revolt started. A government busied with a big overseas venture on which it was lavishing its resources in money and troops, was suddenly called upon to deal with a rebellion. But to their minds, distracted by the other business, it did not seem more than a peasant commotion. At least, they hoped so, because the troops were two weeks' march away in Devonshire. There was no standing police force. It was true that in London they had available Sir Robert Knollys, a man of vast military experience, one time supreme commander in France, who maintained in his mansion in Seething Lane near the Tower a large retinue of men-at-arms and archers. But to send him to Essex could not be done in a moment. He would require money and additional soldiers. And his consent had to be obtained. Moreover, for him to remain in London might be more prudent, for the lower grades of citizens were known to be disaffected. The same reason precluded an approach to London's three top men, Walworth, now mayor, and Brembre and Philpot. They had money and armed men at call. But it would have been quite without precedent to expect any of them to march into Essex. As for the lords of the Household, there was Salisbury, of course, but he did not come forward with an offer. Oxford and his uncle de Vere were hardly military men, except in so far that all lords were more or less trained to arms. Warwick was not a person to suggest energetic measures. Than Sudbury, bureaucrat, churchman, timid, unassertive, no one was less likely to give a military lead.

In sum, lack of resources to hand, lack of decision, weakness of character, misjudgment, explain why the government took no steps to nip the revolt in the bud.

Meanwhile the news from Essex became more alarming. The insurgents, who on 2 June when they broke up Belknap's court only numbered a few hundreds, were now to be counted in thousands. Their mobs were marching about the country, knocking down and setting fire to the houses of persons who refused to join them. Their leaders sent letters into Kent and East Anglia calling on the peasantry of those counties to rise. The letters can hardly have been couched in the enigmatic terms of those cited above, which would seem to belong more to the period of conspiracy when secrecy was important. The leaders were now too deeply involved to bother about concealment, and no doubt sent plain incitements to rebel. Their appeals met with instant response, for the peasantry over wide areas was only awaiting a signal. The people of Kent rose on 4 June. Sir Simon Burley of the Household is stated to have contributed to that event. A villein called Robert Belling ran away from one of his manors, probably in an attempt to throw off servile status and become a wage-earning labourer, as was a common practice. Two of Burley's sergeants-at-arms, one of them called Legge, pursued him to Gravesend on 3 June, arrested him, in spite of efforts by the townspeople to buy him off, and sent him bound to Rochester Castle. As the abolition of villeinage was the main concern of some of the insurgents, Burley's assertion of his rights was very provocative, coming as it did when Kent had been summoned by Essex to rise. Burley himself was out of England at this time.

Kent was ablaze next day. A large body of peasants assembled at Dartford and discussed plans for the future. The *Anonimalle Chronicle*, which I have been following closely, declares that they were anxious lest the French should take advantage of the revolt to make one of their grievous raids, and issued a proclamation that no one residing along the coast should come out to join them. That at such a moment of excitement they should have been thus careful, suggests that they were directed by some sort of a council; and furthermore that they intended to leave Kent and march to London, as the Essex men had been asked to do. Before proceeding to other action, however, they conceived it to be their first duty to liberate Robert Belling, Burley's villein, from Rochester Castle. So, next day, 6 June, they marched to Rochester, where men from Essex, who had crossed the river joined them. By now they were becoming a formidable host. Their chief arm was what had made the English armies invincible on the Continent, the longbow, the weapon peculiar to the English countryside, in whose use all ablebodied men were practised. Its cheapness made it widely available. The authorities had no better missile weapon. In other respects the insurgents were poorly armed compared with regular mercenaries. Some had swords, or agricultural implements approximating thereto, and some had axes. Among the better to do was a certain amount of armour, not the full panoply of a knight's plate, but such as the archer wore, or old-fashioned mail. The bulk of them were countrymen with no experience of war, but they were stiffened by a percentage of ex-mercenaries, some of them veterans of Poitiers and Nájera, perhaps, others who had looted and burnt on the many raids into France. For the attack on the castle they had a leader, Robert Cave, a man from Dartford, a baker by trade, but no doubt chosen for his military experience.

Rochester Castle was held by Sir John Newton, a knight of whom nothing is known now. But we do know what the castle was like, for a great part of it is still standing. On its bluff over the river Medway, it gives an impression of immense strength. Strongholds of the sort in France were bypassed by the English armies as impossible to take without a siege-train. Sir John Newton had every reason to think himself safe. How could a mob take his castle? But the peasants managed it, and very rapidly. The *Anonimalle* has: 'They laid strong siege to the castle, and the constable defended himself vigorously for half a day, but at length for fear that he had of such tumult, and because of the mad multitude of folks from Essex and Kent, he yielded the castle to them.'

Their numbers and ferocity must have been very terrifying to cause Sir John Newton to surrender so soon. This first victory of the insurgents augured well for them; if the spectacle of them raging below could strike such fear that one of the strongest castles in England fell, what place could stand up to them? John Belling was released, as were all other prisoners found. Next day, 7 June, the victorious multitude moved to Maidstone, the county capital, and was welcomed by the labouring class of citizens. Two of the rich merchants, however, dared to cross them by not showing a lively enough compliance with their wishes. One they executed on the spot; the houses of both were sacked.

It was on the seventh day of June 1381 at Maidstone that Wat Tyler steps into history. He was appointed commander in chief of the rebel army of Kent. In exactly six days he was master of England.

The March on London

Among the extraordinary figures in the annals of England Wat Tyler stands unique in that his public career is contained in only nine days, from 7 June 1381, when he appeared, until 15 June 1381, when he was killed; yet in that short span he rose from nonentity to dictatorship. As we shall see, he behaved and regarded himself as a regnant being during the last three days of his life. He had overcome by force the rulers of England, its aristocracy, gentry and burgesses. His end came, not because he was defeated, but by reason of a blow received when at a parley; thinking he was safe to be as insolent as he pleased, he created a situation so intolerable that to strike him down, though seemingly a desperate course, was the only one open to his opponents.

The chronicles tell little of his antecedents, but what they do tell is sufficient. It comes out in the *Anonimalle* that he was known to have been a Kentish highwayman. Froissart supplies the information that at one time he had been abroad with the army in the retinue of Richard Lyons, the financial adviser of the court party, whose frauds on the revenue were exposed in 1377. Without necessarily accepting that he had been one of Lyons' men, or Froissart's further assertion that he had suffered at Lyons' hands, it is very likely that he had active military experience, since the insurgents chose him as their military chief. As to the assertion that he was a highwayman, there is nothing inherently improbable about it, for a career of robbery on the roads attracted not a few of those who returned to England after robbing in France. In the records of the period he is variously described as of Essex or Kent, and he may well have operated in both. As a robber of the rich, the poor will not have disliked him, nor thought him disqualified to command them.

The chronicles, however, make it clear that he was no ordinary footpad. The writer of the *Chronicon Angliae*, who considered him an utter scoundrel, feels bound to admit that he was a very gifted man, 'astute and of great intelligence'. It transpires also that he was a good public speaker. As a man of his sort could only have acquired this reputation by being an agitator, it may be that he was one of those who, along with John Ball, spread the idea of insurrection. It is, in fact, improbable that he would have been elected leader of the revolt unless he was already known as an advocate of the cause. When, therefore, we come on the phrase in the *Chronicon Angliae*—'he was the idol of the populace'—we understand it. Ex-soldier, ex-highwayman, he had become a mob orator.

What he conceived to be the object of the rebellion will appear as its story unfolds. Suffice it to repeat here that his followers had a variety of intentions. Redress of grievances by appeal to King Richard was certainly the cry of the main body. They rose to establish the right of every Englishman to sell his labour in the open market, to work where he liked, to call himself a free man, to share in the timber and game of the woods, and not to have to pay poll taxes. It was hoped that the young King would grant all these requests. As the peasantry was not represented in parliament, their only way of making their desires known was by going in a body to him. A rising of some sort was essential for them, as a mass deputation, if feasible at all, would not have given practical results.

But from the start of the revolt it is evident that such moderate aspirations did not account for what the insurgents were actually doing. With the decapitation of Belknap's jurors, they had entered on a course far more extreme than petitioning the crown. The explanation would appear to be that the leaders were revolutionaries, who were using rural discontent to further political aims of the most sweeping kind. Their programme was the total overthrow of the established order and the substitution of another with themselves as rulers. Wat Tyler, who must be thought of as the head of the revolutionary party, hastened to assemble an overwhelming host and strike.

When he assumed the command of the Kentish men on 7 June at Maidstone, reinforcements were arriving from all parts of the county. On their way in, the bands had been knocking down the houses of officials, lawyers and lords of manors, seizing their cattle and selling them, and burning all papers which related to tenures, law cases, taxation or the like. On the 8th and 9th this anarchy continued. Gaols were opened and all prisoners released. Surprising to relate, few if any people were killed, though some country gentlemen were seized and held as hostages. Persons met with on the roads, such as pilgrims to Canterbury, were stopped and compelled to take an oath of loyalty to 'King Richard and the commons of England'. The meaning of the oath was that the King and his commons were the whole government and that lords, lay and spiritual, knights and burgesses (that is to say, parliament) were deposed from authority.

It was now rumoured that Chancellor Sudbury was not in London but at his see of Canterbury near by. Sudbury, as head of the government, was first on a list of magnates to be executed, which the leaders had drawn up. It was a good opportunity to carry out the sentence of death. At dawn on 10 June Wat Tyler left Maidstone for Canterbury with a force of 4,000 men. On arrival he called on the citizens to admit him within the walls. To this demand the mayor and aldermen had to comply, because the whole working population insisted. The mob rushed to the great cathedral. Mass was in progress when they entered the nave and called ferociously for Sudbury. But he was not there, he was in London. The monks sat trembling in their stalls. The insurgents, however, did them no harm. No matter, they said. We are going to London and will get him there. As he is as good as dead, you had better elect one of yourselves to succeed him. And after a reverence towards the altar and the tomb of St. Thomas à Becket behind it, they took themselves off.

Disappointed at having failed to seize the first minister, Wat Tyler decided to march on London at once. The strategy of his campaign (for the rising had become a civil war) demanded that he should enter the capital before the authorities had rallied. So far they had done nothing. No armed force had been mustered and sent down to fight him. It had been known for some time that, like the general population of Canterbury, the mass of Londoners were for the insurgents. He should present himself there without further delay. The Essex leaders were in communication with him. There is little doubt that they had already agreed to march parallel with him north of the river, while he approached south of it. During the last few days they had been busy, like him, in doing as much mischief as possible, short of murder, to the upper classes, and on this very day, 10 June, had attacked the great manor or hospice of the Knights Hospitallers at Cressing Temple belonging, as their head, to Sir Robert Hales, the hated Treasurer. It was well stocked with wine and provisions. They had a great feast, 'ate the food, drank three barrels of good wine, and pulled down the manor and set it on fire'.[1]

The march on London was fixed for next day, Tuesday 11 June. During the rest of the 10th Wat Tyler remained in Canterbury. He sent for the mayor and aldermen and obliged them to take the oath of allegiance to King and commons in the form given above. Sudbury's episcopal palace was sacked and certain persons, declared traitors to the cause, were beheaded. Altogether it was a frightening visitation, a foretaste of what was to happen in London.

By dawn Wat Tyler was on the move towards the capital. As he marched westwards his army increased in size; large bands, already marshalled *en route*, joined his ranks. The chronicles put the total number of his followers at 60,000. When one considers that English armies in France rarely, if ever, exceeded 15,000 men, we must take it that the first figure is exaggerated. Nevertheless, he had certainly a great host, so great, says the *Chronicon Angliae*, that it could not be counted and so confident that its numbers would prove irresistible that the conquest of the whole realm seemed a certainty. 'It was a conglomeration of the lower classes, larger than ever seen or heard of before.' And John Malverne,[2] the Benedictine, writes: 'They hastened like mad dogs through Kent,' and also uses the simile: 'They were like Bacchants dancing through the country.' John Gower, the poet, who viewed them with horror and contempt, as did all contemporary writers, thus pictures them on the march, a multitude of clownish louts:[3] 'Wat calls on Thomas to follow and Simon does not linger. They tell Gib and Hickey to join. Colley has a mad look, Geoffrey is in hilarious mood. Says Willie, I'll back you whatever the crime. Grig steals while Dawey shouts. Lorkin is happy to be right in the swim. Hudd strikes, Jubb smashes, Cobb threatens, Jack snatches. Hudd

[1] *Anonimalle Chronicle*, p. 135.

[2] In his *Continuation of the Polychronicon*.

[3] In his latin poem *Vox Clamantis*, first published 1390. The effigy of John Gower may be seen today in Southwark Cathedral, its head on three volumes, one inscribed *Vox Clamantis*.

boasts himself better than any lord. Ball prophesies as if possessed by a devil.' How different, continues Gower, from this hideous rout was the countryside that lovely June day, with the flowers in full bloom, the cows dotting the meadows, the woods in their glory! And he shows us Wat Tyler, as he conceived him, 'a man of wild voice, master of the harangue, grim of feature, the very image of death'. He makes him climb a tree and bellow to his following: 'Poor fellows, oppressed so long, now the time is come when the labourer will prevail. The law that kept you down will yield place to your law.'

Thus the poet, a moralist who saw the revolt as an uprush of evil, while we see it now as an uprush of that energy which in later years was to give the English people mastery in their country and overlordship of a great part of the world beside.

The insurgent army was too large to advance on London by one road. Part went by Rochester, part by Maidstone. John Ball joined them at Maidstone. The archbishop's prison in that town was opened on the 10th (or perhaps a few days earlier) and he was taken out. A free man again, he had the happiness of seeing how his preaching had born fruit. He took his place among the leaders, a fanatical adjutant after Wat Tyler's heart. It began to be said that he would succeed Sudbury as Archbishop of Canterbury as soon as they had cut that traitor's throat.

On Wednesday 12 June when the Kentish forces were on their second day of the march which was to take them to the neighbourhood of London that evening, they had a strange meeting, if Froissart has his facts right. Whom should they come across but the Fair Maid of Kent herself, Princess of Wales, mother of the King, widow of the national hero! She had been, says Froissart, to Canterbury, no doubt to visit the Black Prince's tomb and make an offering to St. Thomas. She may or may not have been in the town during the disturbances of 10 June. At any rate here she was on 12 June travelling back to London, perhaps making a detour to avoid trouble. As luck would have it, she ran into an armed party which surrounded her carriage. Their mood appeared so ugly that she was much alarmed. For the moment it looked as if she and her ladies-in-waiting were lost, says Froissart. However, no violence was offered and she got away safely, though much shaken. The temper of a mob is incalculable and it is possible that she was in danger; but it is not probable, for unlike the Jacques, who were brutal to the wives of the nobles they caught, there is no record of the English insurgents having harmed a single woman. Besides the Princess Joan was widely popular, as was her son, King Richard.

On the evening of 12 June the rebel army reached the hill of Blackheath where they encamped, with London in sight over the river to the north-west. It had been a rapid march for Wat Tyler who had done fifty-two miles at least in the two days, though the bulk of his army, joining *en route*, had not walked so far. The Essex men arrived the same evening in comparable numbers on the other side of the river and camped outside the city a mile or so from Aldgate at Mile End, where at that time there was a park much frequented on holidays by the Londoners. Thus the city was threatened on two sides by rebel armies of great size, the Essex men with only a wall between them and the city, the men of Kent with London Bridge to cross before they could enter.

Though the government had sent no troops to halt the rebels' advance and disperse them, it had tried negotiation. As the insurgents were credibly reported not ill disposed towards King Richard, the best course would be for him to meet them. If he listened sympathetically to their demands and promised redress, there was a good chance of their going home. A messenger was first sent on Tuesday 11 June to intercept them on the road and ask for what reason they were assembled. Wat Tyler sent back answer that they were coming to London to deliver the King from the traitors who surrounded him.[1] A second messenger was sent to say that the King was ready to parley with them and would make reasonable amendment where they had suffered wrong. Wat Tyler replied that they would soon be at Blackheath and would gladly have speech with him there. By a third messenger it was arranged that the meeting should take place after their arrival on Thursday 13 June.[2]

During this exchange of messages on the Tuesday and Wednesday, King Richard had moved from Windsor to his palace in the Tower of London, where he would be nearer the scene and more accessible. It has generally been supposed that his safety was the chief reason for the transfer, as the Tower was the strongest fortress in England. But it would obviously have been safer for him

[1] It will be recalled that in 1377 Peter de la Mare and the commons expressed similar intentions. They carried them out constitutionally, as they had the means to do so, but the peasants had no constitutional means available.

[2] The authority for this exchange of letters, which throws much light both on the government's policy and the insurgents' intentions, is *Anonimalle Chronicle*, p. 138.

to remain at Windsor well away from the storm centre. One sees in the move a deliberate policy to make all the use possible of him in what was now realized to be a desperate crisis. Wat Tyler in his first letter had plainly said that the chief object of the insurgents was to punish traitors. The extreme unpopularity of the government, if not previously known to its members, was now no longer in doubt. But the King, an innocent and charming boy, shared none of this unpopularity and, though only fourteen, would make an excellent negotiator. It is highly significant of the agitation prevailing that Sudbury resigned the chancellorship on this very day, Wednesday 12 June. His motive may have been partly fear. The hatred he felt in the air must have been unnerving. But it may also have been that he saw himself as an embarrassment and opined that his resignation would appease the insurgents, rendering it easier for the King to calm them with promises. It was going to require the utmost tact and adroitness to induce the two hosts to disperse to their villages. The situation, already bad enough in all conscience, was likely, moreover, to grow worse, for news was coming in that Kent and Essex were not the only counties involved, but that the inhabitants of all East Anglia, and much of the midlands and the south, were joining the revolt.

Thus by Wednesday the King's advisers had their plan. It might not be possible to appease the extremists, but if a promise were given to redress the grievances of the rank and file, the revolt should subside, when the yokels who had risen to secure emancipation or better wages, and who constituted the great mass of the insurgents, were detached from the movement.

Though the government intended to trust to diplomacy rather than risk a fight, it remained highly desirable to prevent the rebels from entering London. The defence of the city was the responsibility of the mayor, William Walworth. He had already taken the obvious precautions. The drawbridge which at that time divided the northern and southern sections of London Bridge,[1] had been raised. He had closed the gates in the city walls

[1] In the fourteenth century, London Bridge was not exactly where it now is but lay a short distance nearer the Tower. It was the only bridge. At the south end there was a gateway with tower. One third of the way over was the drawbridge with its tower. There was no gateway at the north end. In the middle was a chapel dedicated to St. Thomas à Becket. Along the whole length on both sides were houses used as shops, totalling 132. The roadway was twelve feet wide. The rents of the houses were used for the maintenance of the bridge,

and directed the aldermen concerned to post guards. He did not, however, attempt to muster the armed men available in each ward. The King and his lords were guarded by retinues said to have numbered 600 men-at-arms and archers. But this force was no protection to the city; it was inside the Tower, not at the city gates.

Walworth should not, however, be charged with timidity or negligence for not calling the citizens to arms. On paper there might be 4,000 men available; the trouble was that he could not be sure of them. The city government was almost as unpopular with its working class as the King's government with the general population. The city workers, as we have seen, had actually invited the insurgents to London and promised to rise in their favour. The activities in Essex of the London butchers Attewell and Harry, have been mentioned. Other London emissaries there had also been, in particular a certain Thomas Farringdon, who, promising to lead the Essex men into the city, had been appointed captain by them and at this minute was at their head at Mile End. In such circumstances one can understand what a gamble it would have been for Walworth to muster the ward militia. Some of them were no doubt dependable, but how many were not?

He could not even depend on his aldermen, or not on all of them, though they belonged to the capitalist class, and for the purposes of the 1378 poll tax were put in the same category as barons. That Wednesday evening he thought it worthwhile to send three of them to Blackheath to warn the Kentish men to stay where they were and not attempt to enter the city; perhaps he hoped to make Wat Tyler wonder whether London was as well disposed towards him as he thought. One of the three aldermen, Horn by name, did not, however, do what he was told; in fact he did exactly the opposite and let Wat Tyler know confidentially that if he brought his men to London Bridge, the citizens would welcome them in 'like friends and relations'.[1] Furthermore, he took back to his house in London three of Tyler's lieutenants and during the night introduced them to persons ready to facilitate the entry of the rebel army, and generally discussed with them how this might best be done.

which is the reason houses were allowed. For the whole subject see *Old London Bridge* by Gordon Home (1931).

[1] See the latin documents known as the Reports of the Sheriffs, dated 4 and 20 November 1382, given on pp. 190 seq. in Réville's *Soulèvement des Travailleurs d'Angleterre*.

It appears that Horn took this course because he thought it sounder policy to welcome the insurgents than to resist them. The government of the city was not strong enough to keep them out, when the populace wanted them in. An attempt to stop them might lead to a massacre of the upper class. Horn's view has a resemblance to the court's that negotiation was preferable to a fight. Confident that he had acted for the best, he did not hesitate to inform Walworth that same night what he had done. When the Mayor appeared gravely disquieted by the prospect of two vast mobs, which had turned Kent and Essex upside down, entering London, he promised to be responsible that no harm was done.[1]

Such was the posture of affairs late at night on Wednesday 12 June. The rebels expected to enter London next day. But it was understood that King Richard would first come and speak to them early in the morning, the meeting place to be the south bank in the vicinity of Greenwich, immediately at the base of the hill of Blackheath.

[1] After the rebellion Horn was tried for collusion with the rebels but acquitted. It would appear that he was able to prove his bona fides, or at least establish that suspicion of his motives was not based on sufficient evidence to warrant a conviction.

King Richard on the River

Froissart relates in his anecdotal style how the final arrangements were made for the parley. Sir John Newton, the captain of Rochester Castle, whom the insurgents had held prisoner since they took it on 6 June, was sent across the river to the Tower by Wat Tyler. The King and his train are depicted looking over the water from the fortress, anxious for news. They descry Sir John Newton's boat. He lands at the Tower steps and is hastily conducted into the palace. The King awaits him with his mother, the Princess, his half brothers, the Earl of Kent and Sir John Holland, the Earls of Salisbury, Warwick and Oxford, Archbishop Sudbury and Sir Robert Hales, William Walworth and other notabilities.[1] 'The knight knelt before the King and said: "My lord, please do not take my message badly, for I was obliged to bring it." "You are excused," said the King. "Tell us what you are charged to say."'

Sir John then asks for what amounted to an assurance that the time and place of the meeting next day be confirmed. He adds: 'The commons do not want dealings with anyone but you. They desire me to state that you have no reason to be alarmed for your safety, for they hold you, and will hold you, for their King.' He is unable to say what matters Wat Tyler intends to raise. And ends: 'Please let me have a reply, so that I may appease them with the news that really you are coming. They have my children as hostages and will murder them if I do not return.' The time and place were then definitely fixed.

[1] Including Duke John's son, Henry, Earl of Derby, the future King Henry IV, a boy of about Richard's age.

The commons of England were hungry on Blackheath. No arrangements had been made to feed them. They had what they carried and most of them had already eaten that. During the summer night, so short in June, parties of them prowled about the suburbs on the south bank. Southwark was quite a considerable place. It was here that the famous Tabard Inn was situated, from which the pilgrims to Canterbury started. There was St. Olave's church, now Southwark cathedral. In its vicinity the prostitutes lived. Close by was the Marshalsea prison, whose governor was Sir Richard Imworth, a man hated by the Londoners on account of his cruelty to prisoners. The insurgents attacked it in the twilight of late Wednesday or early Thursday, liberated the prisoners and burnt it. It is said that some Londoners crossed the river by boat and helped. Sir Richard Imworth, in fear of his life, fled for sanctuary to Westminster Abbey. Another party went to Lambeth, where Sudbury had a mansion, again perhaps in the hope of catching him. Failing in that, they burnt, says the chronicler John Malverne, 'his books, clothes, table napkins and other possessions, and broke his cooking pots. They broached his barrels of wine and drank them, emptying out what they could not finish. They were in great spirits, shouting and revelling.'

Early on Thursday morning King Richard embarked for Greenwich in his barge to meet the rebels after attending Mass at the chapel inside the White Tower. He had with him Sudbury, who though he had resigned was still acting as Chancellor, Hales, the Treasurer, and the earls, Salisbury, Warwick and Oxford. His retinue of knights followed in four other barges. One would like to have a notion of how the boy king held himself on this day when the others expected so much of him. The authorities are silent. All we know is that he was advanced for his age. Four years on the throne had given him poise. No doubt he had been carefully coached in the part he was to play.

As the barges approached Greenwich the spectacle on the bank startled the royal party. Says Froissart: 'Some ten thousand of the rebels had come down from Blackheath and were waiting. As soon as they saw the King's barge they began to shout. They made as much noise as if possessed by devils. Sir John Newton was there. Had the King not come they would have cut him to pieces.'

Though the lords were desirous that the King should land, parley with Tyler and use the magic of his office, it now seemed too risky to let him go ashore. 'The people were in such a mad state,' says Froissart. 'They were like men without power to reason or sense to behave,' as the *Anonimalle* puts it. To get off the barge would be folly, advised the lords. 'Orders were given,' says Froissart, 'to row the barge up and down a short distance off shore. The King called out: "I have come for a talk with you. Tell me what is it you want." The rebels shouted back in chorus: "We can't say to you what we've got to say like this. We want you to land." But it looked far too dangerous. The Earl of Salisbury announced on Richard's behalf: "You are in no state for the King to go and speak to you."' The oarsmen were directed to row back to the Tower.

It is not stated where Tyler was. He may have been standing on the meridian where the disused observatory now is, a position a little up the hill of Blackheath and commanding a good view of the river. Watching the King depart, he considered the moment opportune to send a letter after him, an alarming, extreme letter. He had already in the first of his letters, as mentioned, declared that his object was to destroy the traitors round the throne. His people, very angry at the King's refusal to land, were in the mood to endorse extreme demands. They had already condemned Sudbury to death. He would now send the King a list of all the traitors and ask for their heads to be delivered to him. The *Anonimalle* gives the list. Sudbury, of course, was on it, but it was headed by a more famous name than the Archbishop of Canterbury's. John Duke of Lancaster, the King's uncle, Pretender of Castile, was to be beheaded first. Mixed up in the financial scandal of Edward's last days, hated for having undone the work of the Good Parliament, still suspected of having designs on the throne, held in despite as an unsuccessful commander, and, if not definitely known to have asked for the huge sum for his Castilian venture which necessitated the third poll tax, supposed to exercise great influence over Sudbury, his unpopularity was confined no longer to London and Westminster but was universal. Wat Tyler could count on the support of a big majority in demanding his head. Besides his name and Sudbury's, the list contained those of Hales, Courtenay, Bishop of London, Sir John Fordham, Clerk of the Privy Seal, Sir Robert Plessington, Chief Baron of the Exchequer, Sir Robert Belknap, the Chief Justice of the King's Bench, Thomas Brampton, the poll tax commissioner, John Legge, a royal sergeant-at-arms attached to the King's Bench, and seven more persons connected with the higher administration. Such was the formidable letter addressed by Wat Tyler to the King.

The *Anonimalle Chronicle* relates that an informer at this time gave the King intelligence that the rebel leader had yet darker designs. He said that Tyler was contemplating a general massacre of the lords, lay and spiritual; it would be imprudent for the King to put himself in the insurgents' power, as would have happened that morning had he landed, for their plan was to take him with them round England and force him to grant whatever executions and spoilations they might require until 'all the land was lost'. That was the inner meaning of their form of oath, 'The King and the commons of England'.

If this intelligence was true and Richard had landed at Greenwich, he would have fallen into the kind of trap where safe conduct for a parley is given but disregarded. The two of his train on the list, Sudbury and Haldes, would have been immediately executed, others perhaps also. And he would have been seized and proclaimed King of the commons of England. Yet it is possible that Wat Tyler was not ready on Thursday 13 June to go quite so far. The events of Friday were to show that he meant what he said about the proscribed persons, but do not show that he conceived the moment had come to seize the King, for in fact, the King did place himself in his power that day. The events of Friday will also show that, if the King received the secret intelligence which the *Anonimalle* claims, he did not believe it or else that his lords gambled with fate in exposing him to the danger. As for Saturday 15 June, the drama is carried to a high pitch of intensity and, indeed, of mystery, when all is suddenly resolved by a blow.

London is occupied by the Insurgents

The *Chronicon Angliae* states that at this time, the early hours of Thursday 13 June, John Ball harangued the insurgents on the top of Blackheath hill, a wide, open, flat space. Wat Tyler wanted the passions of his followers whipped up. It was not enough for them to demand redress of grievances, to require the heads of traitors in the government. There was the more drastic programme for which he wished to prepare them. John Ball was therefore told to make the most inflammatory speech he could and represent that what had been done so far was only the first step in a plan to substitute a peasant state for the existing order. The *Chronicon Angliae* records his oration as follows: 'He exhorted the peasants to be prudent and to hasten like good farmers to destroy the weeds which were choking the crops. First the leading magnates must be killed; then all persons connected with the law; and finally everyone harmful to the people. Not until there was equal liberty for all, each man having the same degree of power and rank and standing, would there be peace and security.'

When formerly Ball had addressed rustic audiences in churchyards, he had dwelt on the workers' wrongs and advised resort to the King. Now he declared that a massacre must come first, a clean sweep of the upper classes. It is not difficult to debauch a mob. His hearers had already indulged in the dark excitements of destruction. They had had a taste of power. To whet their appetite for murder was easy. The more extreme among them were ready for anything. So much did this element relish his advocacy of a general massacre that they swore to make him Archbishop of Canterbury.

That he made no mention of seizure of the King is not to say that the project was not in Tyler's mind, but only that the time had not come to reveal it to the rank and file.

The royal party, back in the Tower, having seen with their own eyes what the Kentish mob was like, and knowing that the Essex mob of like dimensions was assembled at Mile End, had to decide what next to do. The receipt of Tyler's letter must have increased their consternation. How were they to save the lives of those on the list? Well, at least Duke John was out of harm's way on the Scottish border.[1] But some of the others were in the Tower. Considering the enormous strength of the fortress, surely they were safe? Yet Rochester castle, a place hardly less strong, had fallen to the mob, then not so large. Perhaps it would be better for the proscribed men to move elsewhere. Archbishop Sudbury, Sir Robert Hales and John Legge, the sergeant-at-arms, decided to stay. The rest seem to have left and gone into hiding. Theirs was the wiser choice, for none of them came to hurt.

The royal party had by now, one supposes, been told by Walworth what Horn had told him that night: the populace was set on welcoming the rebels and to resist their wish would be highly dangerous and probably impossible, as the mayor and aldermen of Canterbury had found. Their entry might be expected any moment. What then was the best course? If the King and his train stayed in the Tower they would be surrounded and cut off from outside support. Would it not be more prudent to leave London while there was yet time and rally the lords and gentry of the home counties to the westward? The decision taken, however, was to remain and trust to the plan of conciliating the rebels. The popular boy King was the government's best card. Sir John Newton had assured them the rebels meant him no harm. There was every indication that they desired to put their grievances before him. The informer's report of the plot to seize him clashed with Sir John's assurance. Yet there were reasonable grounds for holding that if the King in person listened sympathetically to their grievances, the great majority of the rebels would go home, satisfied that what they had risen for had been granted.

[1] The paradox here is one of those which show history as high comedy. All the government's available money and soldiers were being used to make Duke John King of Castile. All the resources of the people were mobilized to behead him. Nothing could illustrate better the fundamental nature of the differences dividing government and people.

In fact, no other plan was possible, for already the insurgents were beginning to enter the city. The top of the Tower commanded a full view of London Bridge and Aldgate. The Kentish men were crossing the bridge, the Essex men were being let in at Aldgate by the alderman in charge, William Tonge.[1]

Wat Tyler had set his legions in motion soon after the King left Greenwich. They had gone a little way towards London, when they were met by Horn, riding under a standard with the royal arms, which he had procured so as to make it appear that he had the King's authority for what he was doing. He led the insurgents through Southwark towards London Bridge. The Marshalsea was billowing smoke, as also the brothels, to which fire had been put, as they were known to be Walworth's property. The bridge was in charge of Alderman Walter Sybyle, who agreed with Horn that it was less dangerous to let the rebels in than to try to keep them out. It is recorded that at the time, when the rebel van arrived on the south bank, a certain Thomas Cornewayles, who was in favour of opposing their entry, came up with an armed party and offered his help. Sybyle refused it, and gave orders for the drawbridge to be lowered. The bridge gate was also opened. When Wat Tyler and his men crossed into the city, it was about midday.

It seems that Tyler had enforced a degree of discipline. The insurgent forces were no longer like Bacchants or mad dogs; orders had been given that there was to be no stealing. Yet their good behaviour was partly the response to the welcome they got. The populace was delighted to see them; the more well-to-do citizens, led to believe that they would depart as soon as they had put to death those declared to be traitors, hoped that by receiving them with hospitality their ill-will could be avoided. Food and drink in plenty were offered them. For the moment quiet reigned as the Kentish men, joined now by the multitude from Essex, satisfied their hunger, which was great as most of them had had nothing to eat for twenty-four hours. Wine flowed. It is said that some were humbly grateful and offered to pay. All were mollified. The better-class citizens were relieved to find that for the moment they had nothing to fear. It appeared that the rebels' immediate intention

[1] See Reports of the Sheriffs. The finding on Tonge stated: 'We do not know whether Tonge opened the gate by malice, or because he was in league with Horn, or because of his fear of the rebels and their threats against the city.'

was to kill Duke John at the Savoy and Sir Robert Hales at the Priory of St. John of Jerusalem at Clerkenwell, the headquarters of the Knights Hospitallers in London, if they could find them at those addresses, and to destroy both places. The London mob was particularly delighted by the prospect of the first, recalling that they themselves had intended the same a couple of years before.

It is necessary to suppose that Wat Tyler and his captains, the most prominent of whom was Jack Straw, established some sort of a headquarters. From there orders were issued for part of the rebel forces to attack the Savoy and part the Priory of the Hospitallers. The Temple also was to be destroyed, as the centre of the legal profession, a class, as we have seen, which the rebels wished to do away with. Moreover, the Temple itself was the property of the Hospitallers, to whom it had been granted after the suppression of the Knights Templar in 1314.

The rebels deputed for the Savoy left the city by Ludgate, went up Fleet Street, a suburb under the Mayor's jurisdiction, passed on their left the Bishop of Salisbury's town house and the convent of the White Friars, each standing in very large grounds, and reached the Temple. There some of them turned aside to attack it, while the main body hurried on over Temple Bar[1] into the Strand, where, on its present site, the Savoy stood, a magnificent Gothic structure on which the two Dukes of Lancaster, Duke John and his father-in-law, Duke Henry, had spent huge sums of money. Besides being Duke John's private residence, it contained his Castilian secretariat and accommodated numerous Castilian legitimist lords, their wives, children, ladies-in-waiting and servants. It had been splendidly furnished and its appointments were of the best, much of the plate, tapestries, carpets, curtains, being loot from France or purchased there. The chroniclers insist that no other palace in the kingdom compared with it. Tyler's men had probably learnt by this time that the Duke was in Scotland and his wife, Constance, Don Pedro's daughter, in Hertford castle. Their object remained to destroy his palace. As to the Duke's Castilian household, it is not on record whether they were in residence or had fled.

As stated a little back, Wat Tyler had enforced discipline to

[1] Temple Bar marked the boundary of the extra-mural jurisdiction of the city government. On more than one of the main roads entering London there was a bar or chain to mark the extra-mural boundary. The bar at the Temple is mentioned in 1301, but may have existed earlier.

some extent. A sack of the Savoy was a great temptation, but he had ordered that nothing be taken, all destroyed, even jewels, coin and plate. For this order he had at least one good reason. If his first act in London was to loot the Savoy, it would make his revolution look too like banditry. There were, no doubt, many other reasons of a practical kind. It was too soon to start sacking London. That would come later.

The Duke had only left doorkeepers, porters, watchmen or the like on duty at the Savoy. The rebels made short work of them, burst in the gates and doors and swarmed into the building. The *Anonimalle* has: 'They took what torches they could find . . . and burnt all the sheets and coverlets and beds. . . . And all the napery and other things they could find they carried to the hall and set on fire. Then they burnt the hall and the chambers. They found three barrels of gunpowder and threw it onto the fire; when it exploded, the hall blazed the more.' The other chroniclers speak of them breaking up the silver plate with axes and throwing it into the Thames, tearing up the silks and grinding the precious stones in mortars. Such a profusion of wealth was too tantalizing for some. It is interesting that a woman seems to have got away with the Duke's cash chest. She was a Mrs. Joanna Ferrour of Rochester and the records[1] describe her as one of the leaders. The chest contained £1,000, a dazzling sum in the fourteenth century. She transported it over the river to Southwark and divided the money among her followers. No orders had been issued against getting drunk. A party, leaving it to their comrades to do the work of smashing and burning, made their way to the Duke's cellars, where they found wine more delicious than they had ever tasted. Neglecting to keep a proper look out, they were blown up or buried when the building collapsed.

While this was happening at the Savoy, the insurgents who had invaded the Temple were engaged on similar work. It is not stated that they killed any of the residents, who perhaps had escaped before they broke in. But the law books and parchments, deeds and charters, were burnt.

The destruction of the Hospitallers' Priory of St. John at Clerkenwell was the third major event of Thursday afternoon. The rebel force mustered for this expedition was commanded by Farringdon, the London leader of the Essex men. It left the city

[1] See the extract from the Coram Rege Rolls quoted on p. 199 of Réville's *Soulèvement des Travailleurs.*

by Aldersgate, crossed the Smithfield cattle market in the northern suburbs and came to the Priory in the open country beyond. If they hoped to find and kill the Prior, Sir Robert Hales, they were disappointed, for he was in the Tower. But they did not fail to set fire to the buildings, which burnt for days and were destroyed, 'a great and horrible piece of damage for all time to come'.[1] It was here that the insurgents first showed their hatred of Flemings, seven of whom had taken sanctuary in the Priory church and were dragged out and killed. Murders of Flemings became frequent after this. When anarchy prevails foreigners are less safe than natives, because, never popular and always suspected of sharp practice and unfair competition, they seem enemies of the people.

By late afternoon Wat Tyler saw himself master of London. His bands had destroyed three of the principal groups of buildings with their valuable contents. No one had dared to say him nay. Not a hand was raised to resist. The government of the city was mum. The King and his lords were huddled in the Tower. The rich had barricaded themselves in their houses and, if they had retainers, had armed and posted them. Even the formidable Sir Robert Knollys was not showing his face. It was unsafe for anyone in the streets. Not only Flemings were murdered, but also the Italian bankers, the Lombards. As these murders were outside the programme of the peasant rebels one must attribute them to the animosity of the London mob. Many criminals, moreover, were loose in the city, for both the Newgate and Fleet prisons had been broken open. All sorts of ruffians came into their own. They would suddenly accuse innocent persons of crimes against the commons of England and threaten them with decapitation if they did not pay a ransom.

Alderman Horn's assurance to Walworth that no harm would come to the citizens was seen to be nonsense. It was true that, broadly speaking, Wat Tyler had so far confined himself to striking against two of the persons on his list of traitors. Nevertheless, his actions had brought a degree of anarchy in their train. All propertied citizens might well feel extremely nervous that complete anarchy was on the way.

Tyler most certainly did not want this to happen. The more

[1] *Anonimalle Chronicle*, op. cit., p. 142. The gate and gatehouse of the Priory still stand. One comes on them unexpectedly in a side street off St. John's Street, about 200 yards north of Smithfield market.

anarchy, the less his power. He must hold the insurgents together and direct their united will against the government. There was first to oblige the King to deliver the heads which had been demanded. So we find Tyler on Thursday evening concentrating his forces against the Tower. He had one camp on Tower Hill to the north and west of the fortress and another on the east side in the space between the Hospital of St. Catherine and the moat. Though it was very warm, he caused great fires to be lit in order to illuminate the approaches during the night. The men he wanted were, he hoped, still inside the Tower. He would see to it that they did not escape under cover of darkness.

The Tower today is sufficiently like what it was in the fourteenth century to make it easy for us to visualize the scene on the evening of Thursday 13 June 1381. The moat, of course, was full of water and the approach to the main gate was over more than one drawbridge and not by a causeway as at present. Some of the buildings in the interior now are of post-medieval date, and the palace has disappeared, but the visitor as he walks, say, between the inner and outer curtains or in the circular stairways of the White Tower, has a good impression of the stronghold as it was. Professionals properly equipped for the purpose might storm it after a protracted siege. It could not be rushed by peasants. But there are more ways of taking a castle than by siege or assault. If not defended by the garrison it may be entered at will.

Wat Tyler had a means of entry to the Tower. He occupied a metropolis whose proletariat acknowledged him as their leader. The property and lives of the whole upper class were at his mercy. If the King refused his demand for the heads of the Archbishop of Canterbury and the Treasurer, known for certain to be in the Tower, trusting that its moat and walls would keep the rebels out, Tyler could force him to open by threatening to destroy London. The explanation follows of how this impasse was resolved. It was of the utmost importance that the King should meet the rebels and by conceding all their demands, including that for the heads, induce them to go home. But how could a King, who was a boy of fourteen, hand over to death the ministers of his government, when he was by the nature of things advised and directed by the said ministers?

Thursday Night at the Tower

News that the rebels had entered London, blockaded the King and government in the Tower, and were destroying the Savoy and the Priory of the Hospitallers, spread rapidly through south-east England and greatly heartened the peasantry who in several counties had already risen. Wat Tyler began to be viewed as a national leader and his orders were awaited. That he was in touch with events outside London is shown by the message he sent on Thursday afternoon to the inhabitants of Barnet and St. Albans, eleven and twenty-one miles to the northward, ordering them to despatch an armed contingent to join him in the city. It is probable that he sent similar messages through the counties, for on the Saturday he is reported as expecting contingents from several counties to reach London the next day.[1] But while there was prospect of his already large forces being augmented, there was no news that the county lords and gentry were marching to the government's assistance. They had, indeed, as much as they could do to secure their own safety at home.

As the summer evening wore on, the rebels surrounding the Tower clamoured for the King to come out and speak to them. They shouted that if he refused to do so they would overrun the Tower and kill everyone inside. This may not have been such an empty boast as the strength of the fortress might lead one to suppose, for the garrison was small,[2] its morale was low and some of

[1] Froissart, Lettenhove edn., p. 410.

[2] A fortress could be taken by scaling ladders, if the attacking force greatly outnumbered the defenders.

its members may have been in league with the London populace or, at least, have held opinions similar to Horn's.

The King, warned as he had been that it would be imprudent to put himself in the rebels' power, was in no hurry to comply with their wishes. An attempt was first made to address them from the wall. He went into a turret at the south-east corner towards St. Catherine's, where a great number of them were encamped. There an announcement was made, presumably by a herald, that if they returned peaceably home no proceedings would be taken against them for the damage, arsons and murders they had committed. But the herald was shouted down; they would not budge an inch until the traitors had been delivered to them and until the reforms they desired, such as the abolition of serfdom, had been granted in charters under the royal seal.

The King, that is to say his ministers and advisers, had hoped from the start, as we have seen, to calm the insurgents and disperse them by fair words. If they wanted charters, why, they should have them, as many as ever they liked. Provided they believed the promises therein and went home, the government had won. So now the King, through the herald, announced that charters would be granted and an undertaking in writing immediately given to that effect. The rebels looking up at the turret then saw a clerk write out the undertaking and the King seal it. To make its contents the more public, two knights were sent down with it to St. Catherine's wharf. There one of them stood on an old chair, it is said, and read it out in a loud voice. The promise of complete indemnity was repeated. Let the good commons go home, put their grievances on paper, and submit them. On their receipt, the King and his council would sympathetically consider them.

The rebels greeted the reading with jeers. Their demand for the traitors had been ignored. And they were asked to believe that if they gave up the advantages they held, these same traitors could be trusted to consider petitions sympathetically! It was ludicrous. So angry was the crowd at the duplicity of the writing that some of them hastened away through the streets, shouting that all lawyers and clerks be killed at sight and the country rid of a tribe whose sole skill was the production of such plausible documents. Late though it was the cry was taken up and men started burning private houses.

The *Anonimalle* describes how the King and his advisers watched these fires and the more distant glow of the burning

Priory and Savoy, and despairingly wondered what they should do next. Some of them, headed by Walworth, were for bolder action. They had been cautious long enough, he said. True, to have used in daylight what forces they had to attack the rebels would perhaps have been too risky. But now, with the June night at last closing in, why not make a sally? The rebels were expecting nothing of the kind. They had taken no particular precautions. Many were asleep, many others very drunk.[1] The retinues in the Tower, Walworth went on, made a compact little body of professional soldiers. Sir Robert Knollys, whose house in Seething Lane was only a bow shot away, had a retinue there of 140 veterans. He would join in, as would several other leading citizens who had armed retainers in their courtyards. The rebels, taken unawares, 'could be killed like flies'. Sir Bertucat d'Albret, a Gascon condottiere of Nájera fame, who was the King's guest at this time, backed up the Mayor, saying he was sure they could muster between them 7,000 men.[2]

The proposal, however, seemed too risky to the Earl of Salisbury, the most experienced military lord they had in the Tower. Famous as the commander who had broken the opening charge of the French cavalry at Poitiers twenty-five years back he could hardly be accused of timidity. 'If we commence a thing we can't carry through, we're done for,' he is reported to have said. The decisive factor was that the London populace was against them. What could a small force like theirs do, scattered as they would be in the narrow streets with the people hurling things from the houses? Best to stick to their original plan, and think of ways of appeasing the rebels.

It looked as if King Richard would have to go out and parley with them. If he did, their first demand would be for the heads of Sudbury and Hales. He would not be able to refuse, for by going out he placed himself in their power. A discussion followed on how this dilemma could be avoided, as not unnaturally Sudbury and Hales, the two chief people at the table, did not want to sign their own death warrants. At last someone suggested—the *Anonimalle* says it was Richard himself—that if the parley were fixed at a place some little way off and all the insurgents were induced to go there, the Tower would be left unwatched. That would provide

[1] The Knighton *Chronicle* has: 'You saw them lying about in the squares and under walls as unconscious as slaughtered pigs.'

[2] Froissart is the only chronicler who records this discussion, but that is not a reason to disbelieve what is so likely to have taken place.

Sudbury and Hales with a chance of escaping. The suggestion was thought very good. Besides giving the proscribed men a chance, it had other advantages. If the King were to detach those rebels who only wanted redress of grievances from the section who were revolutionaries, he must speak directly to them. That he could best do if they all assembled in an open space, where he could address the rank and file and invite them to petition him. There would be the demand, of course, for the heads of traitors and, he would have to concede that. But if Sudbury and Hales were safely out of the Tower in hiding, what matter? Charters redressing all grievances could be liberally issued. Clerks should be taken to write them out on the spot. The betting was that most of the insurgents would then go home. All they had risen for would have been granted. The extreme section would be left in the air. The only objection was the risk of the King being seized. But this seemed unlikely. The rebel rank and file were not against him. They looked to him for relief and if he granted the relief, it would not be an opportune moment for the extremist leaders to arrest him.

The plan was a gamble, but it was adopted and Mile End fixed for the parley. Mile End was a mile and a half north-east of the Tower. It was not too far, not too near. The park there afforded room for the rebel army. A proclamation was sent out and means found for circulating it rapidly through the city. It announced the King's intention of being at Mile End next morning at 7 a.m. and impressed on the insurgents that all of them without exception should meet him there. It is to be noted that the method adopted was a summons to the people over the head of Wat Tyler, Jack Straw and John Ball, to whom no direct communication was addressed.

What will have been Wat Tyler's reaction? We have it on record that he was an astute man. He knew where his weakness lay. He had to carry with him a horde of rustics on a revolutionary course beyond anything they had originally conceived. He had carried them a certain distance. He had involved them in many criminal acts. They had felt the exhilaration of being masters of London. But they still held to the idea of petitioning the King. If the King won their hearts by his graciousness, they might cool towards the total revolution. He, Tyler, had gone so far already, that it was all or nothing for him, but a percentage of his followers did not see that it was all or nothing for them. Despite the hold he had over their emotions, he could not count on their obedience if he forbade them to see the King. Nevertheless, though he ran the risk of their succumbing to the royal fascination, he perceived how he could turn the Mile End parley to good account. He saw how it was bound to result in Sudbury and Hales falling into his hands. By beheading these two grandees, he would commit his followers irrevocably, for they would have gone beyond the limits of indemnity, and, moreover, have come under the spell of total revolution. Some might fall away, but enough would remain; and they would be men to go any lengths. The moment would then come to seize the King and begin the general massacre.

All we know suggests that such was Wat Tyler's estimate of the prospects for the following day. It is said that he spent the evening in Thomas Farringdon's house, where with his lieutenants and advisers he drew up 'a list of citizens to be executed and of their houses to be destroyed'.[1]

[1] The Report of the Sheriffs in op. cit., p. 195.

The Meeting at Mile End

At first light on Friday, 14 June, 'the commons of the country and the commons of London mustered in very hideous power to the number of 100,000 or more,' says the *Anonimalle*. Some of them went off under Thomas Farringdon and Jack Straw to burn Sir Robert Hales' private house at Highbury two or three miles up the St. Albans road. Most of the rest moved out to Mile End, but a few remained about the Tower. To get them to leave, an urgent message was sent out 'asking them to join their friends at Mile End and saying that the King would soon be with them there'. It would seem that the majority of them went.

Some time about seven, though it may well have been later, the royal party rode out of the Tower by the main western gate. The leading personages have often been mentioned. In front of the King was Aubrey de Vere, Chamberlain of the Household, bearing the sword of state. Behind were the Princess's sons by her former marriage: Thomas Holland, Earl of Kent, and John Holland. Thomas Holland as a very young man had fought at Nájera under the Black Prince, his stepfather, and now at thirty-one was Marshal of England. The eldest grandee present was the Earl of Salisbury, who was fifty-three, and the youngest, Robert de Vere, Earl of Oxford and Hereditary Grand Chamberlain, who was nineteen. Others were Lord Thomas Percy, the Earl of Warwick and William Walworth. Sir Robert Knollys may have joined when the cavalcade passed his house in Seething Lane. Two contemporary accounts state that the Princess (now fifty-three) accompanied her son in a carriage. If so, she can only have been seeing him off, as far perhaps as Aldgate, for she was certainly in the Tower a little later, as will appear. How many men-at-arms or archers went with the King is nowhere stated, though one is given to understand that the party was unarmed. As to Richard's demeanour on this alarming occasion, no one mentions it except the Monk of Evesham in his *Vita Ricardi II*, who says he was very nervous. As settled the previous evening, Sudbury and Hales remained behind, ready to slip out, when they could do so unobserved, by the Little Water Gate and, embarking in a waiting boat, row for their lives. There seemed every hope of their accomplishing this; a few of the insurgents were hanging about the precincts but the rest had either gone on to Mile End or now came along with the royal party.

To assess correctly what follows one should have it clear that Sudbury and Hales were the government. Sudbury had submitted his resignation of the Chancellorship two days before, but as no one had yet been appointed to succeed him, he remained Chancellor pending relief. He and Sir Robert Hales, as the two professional ministers, must have taken a leading part in determining that the King should go to Mile End. They must also have decided on the time and method of their own escape from the Tower. On the departure of the royal party, everything was left in their hands. Sudbury, whose career had been that of an indoor churchman, had no military experience whatever, but Hales, as a knight and head of the Knights Hospitallers in England, was fully competent to take charge, give the Tower garrison what orders he liked and, when the coast was clear, make a dash for it with Sudbury. Little seems to be known about his past history, but one has the impression that he was an irresolute character, as certainly was Sudbury. The Tower's Little Water Gate opened on the Thames; why did they not slip out in the darkness after the Mile End parley was fixed? The garrison could have made a diversion of some sort to cover the escape. Duke John and Lord Henry Percy had evaded the London mob when it was harder for them to get to their boat. But perhaps one underestimates the terror of the occasion. Sudbury and Hales were being hunted by a host of implacable enemies. Their nerve had gone.

Nevertheless, they did make an attempt to escape some time after the departure of the King.[1] But Wat Tyler had his watchers well posted. There was such a hue and cry when Sudbury and

[1] The chroniclers are vague about the time and even give the impression that their attempted escape took place before the King left. That cannot have been so because for the King to have left the Tower knowing they could not

Hales were seen leaving, that they hesitated and then rushed back into the Tower.

The King and his lords, oblivious of this, rode towards Mile End to carry out their part of the plan. Before they were clear of the city, they ran into Thomas Farringdon. He was already back from Highbury where his men were burning Hales' manor, and was making for Mile End. According to the Sheriffs' Report, on seeing the King he boldly seized his bridle and began screeching in a demented way: 'Avenge me on that false traitor, the Prior, who has fraudulently seized houses belonging to me! Do me justice! If not, I am strong enough to take the law into my own hands.' So he shouted, like a man grievously wronged, in spite of having just set fire to the Prior's house. Richard, playing his part of the benevolent young king, replied: 'You shall have justice' and so got rid of him.

The royal cavalcade issued from the city by the Aldgate. On top of the gate was a dwelling-house which in 1374 the mayor and corporation had granted Chaucer the free use of for the rest of his life. It is not improbable that the poet was at home, since the streets were so unsafe, and may well have looked down from his window and seen the little King riding below. In his *Nun's Priest's Tale* there is a short allusion to Jack Straw and the Flemish weavers murdered by the rebels that very Friday, but otherwise the vast canvas of *The Canterbury Tales* contains not a hint of the rebellion.

When the cavalcade was passing through Whitechapel fields the insurgents crowding along with it became threatening. It would seem that they directed their threats against the two Hollands, the King's stepbrothers. It is not known why. But the whims of a mob are incalculable. The Hollands became frightened and turning their horses off the road galloped away over the fields as fast as they could. Froissart thought their desertion deplorable, particularly the elder Holland's, the veteran of Nájera, the Marshal of England, but his loss of nerve is the clearest proof of the terrifying nature of the rising. The author of the *Vita Ricardi II* says of this time: 'The King looked like a lamb among wolves.' It was, in fact, touch and go.

At Mile End, however, a more respectable section of the

escape would have been to condemn them to death. It is impossible to suppose that he and the other lords would have gone on with the plan if it involved the certain murder of the Archbishop of Canterbury. Nor is there any evidence that Sudbury and Hales offered to sacrifice themselves.

peasantry was drawn up in expectation of the visit. The *Anonimalle* states that as soon as the King arrived 'all the commons knelt down to him, crying: "Welcome to our Lord, King Richard" and they said: "May it please you, we want no other King than you."' The people who spoke thus were the men who had risen to secure rights and put an end to oppressions. They wanted to make it clear straight off that they had not risen to depose the King. On the contrary, their watchword was 'King Richard and the commons of England'. But to secure a hearing they had had to use force. One must concede the basic soundness of their cause, though carried out of their depth on the tide of force, they had committed many violences and murders. Yet they saw clearly the limit. The ministers held responsible for their ills and who would never redress them, must be punished with death. But that was as far as they intended to go. In their simplicity they thought they could stop there. But Wat Tyler was under no such delusion.

Some students of the period have not been convinced that he was present at Mile End. The *Anonimalle* is emphatic that he was and that it was he who spoke on behalf of his men. He had drawn them up in some kind of formation under banners and pennons, and when he spoke was standing under a banner like the commander of an army. He repeated his demand for the heads of the proscribed men. As for the other requests which his followers desired to make—the abolition of the serf manor and the repeal of the Statute of Labourers—he put them forward also, though it was not essential for him to do so, because in the total subversion of the state which he intended, their realization would follow as a matter of course. He put first, however, the matter of the proscribed ministers, and asked the King's sanction to take and deal with them.

King Richard, supported by his lords and prompted by their whispered admonitions, did not at once give the plain answer desired. He replied that they had his authority to catch traitors where they liked, but should bring them to him, when they would be tried according to law. As this answer was not explicit enough, Wat Tyler insisted that the traitors should be his to deal with. Whereupon 'our Lord the King granted that they might take those who were traitors against him and put them to death, wheresoever they might be found'.[1]

[1] This comes, not from the *Anonimalle Chronicle*, the chief source here, but from the Letter Books of the City of London (H. fol. 133, Latin). The Letter

When the King uttered these words there can be little doubt that he and his train believed that Sudbury and Hales had made good their escape and were safely in hiding, as there was no reason to think that the plan of escape worked out before he left the Tower had failed.

Though not explicitly stated, it would seem reasonable to suppose that Wat Tyler asked the King to put in writing the grant of authority to deal with the traitors. The King was not in a position to refuse anything. His plan hinged upon his granting in a frank and spontaneous manner whatever was demanded of him. It was essential, as we shall see, for Wat Tyler to have in his hand written authority or similar proof of the King's grant to him, and we may be sure that, since to obtain it he had only to ask for it, he did ask and got it.

Having obtained what he wanted, Wat Tyler left Mile End. The King and his lords remained. There was a good deal to be done. The contingents from the various localities had come provided with written petitions, in response to the King's orders at the Tower that they should put their grievances on paper. These he now invited them to present. When they did so, he received them graciously, agreed to everything asked, and directed the clerks who had accompanied his party to start writing out charters at once. A copy is extant[1] of one of these, granting complete manumission, thereby at a stroke of the pen abolishing the manorial system, the basis of rural economy and the main source of income of the aristocracy and gentry. The plan of appeasement seemed to be working well. The peasants were mollified. Their anger and desperation subsided. They believed the King's word. They did not doubt the validity of the charters. It did not occur to them that they must be bogus, for the obvious reason that the King had not the power to abolish the rights of the aristocracy and gentry, who constituted parliament, without their assent in parliament. So satisfied were many that, as the hours passed, they prepared to return home. They were anxious, it is said, about their wives and families, and were eager to get back at once to take possession of their new and exciting rights. There was nothing more they need stay for. Wat Tyler would execute the traitors and

Book cited contains the account of the insurrection which was drawn up immediately afterwards by the corporation for their records. It is given in translation on p. 449 of Riley's *Memorials of London*.

[1] Given on p. 298 of the *Chronicon Angliae* (Rolls edn.).

see that better ministers were appointed. All would be well for ever in the villages. To please them further the King distributed a number of royal banners, to indicate that he accepted them as loyal subjects engaged on their lawful occasions. In short, he played his role to perfection. His advisers could congratulate themselves that their plan to end the revolt by fair words was beginning to work.

The Murders at the Tower

While the business of granting the charters was proceeding at Mile End, Wat Tyler, as we have seen, returned to London, armed with the royal authority to exterminate the traitors. He had with him only a few hundred men, as he knew that he would not have to use force. It would seem that before he reached the Tower he met with the men of St. Albans and Barnet, whom he had summoned the previous day. A big company of peasants and townspeople, they had come in via Highbury, where they had halted a moment to watch Hales's manor as it blazed, and to inquire where Wat Tyler was to be found. On being informed that he was at Mile End and that the King was issuing charters there, they set out for the place and, so, met him on the road. After explaining how things stood at St. Albans, they asked him for his support against the Abbot, from whose jurisdiction the townspeople had been trying to free themselves for years. Their unbounded admiration for Tyler and the height to which his reputation had risen, is shown by the following from the Chronicle[1] of the St. Albans monastery, where it describes the meeting: 'They thought that there would never be a greater man in the kingdom nor would the laws of the land have validity but from him, because he had already destroyed the greater part of the lawyers and the rest, in their opinion, would be rightly destroyed.' They worshipped him, in fact, the writer adds. In reply to their request for help, he

[1] *Gesta Abbatum Monasterii Sancti Albani*, by the monk Thomas Walsingham, vol. iii, p. 299 (Rolls edn.).

promised to come to St. Albans, if they sent for him, with 20,000 men and shave the beards of the Abbot and his monks, a jocular way of saying, explains the writer, that he would cut off their heads. The episode is indicative of the influence which he was beginning to exert over the movement as a whole.

But his immediate business was inside the Tower. It begins to be plain how he will get in. All he has to do is to inform the guards at the entrance that he has authority from the King to enter and take certain persons declared to be traitors. The garrison was, as has been suggested, somewhat lukewarm. It should not be forgotten that the traitors, headed by Duke John, were, apart from the hatred felt for them by the rebels, generally unpopular. Duke John had few friends in any class and Sudbury, his adherent, hardly more. There is no reason to suppose that the soldiers in the Tower were better disposed towards Sudbury than the generality. We do not know exactly their attitude to the rebels, but the probability is that some of them, for reasons of fear, discretion or sympathy, had no desire to come to blows with them. Salisbury's caution cannot otherwise be wholly explained. We do not hear of them having made even a minor sally or demonstration against the besiegers; it is not said that they let fly arrows from the walls. They seem to have been quite unnaturally passive. One suspects that, when Sudbury and Hales made their attempt at escape, some of them even passed the news out to the watchers. These suspicions will be seen to be supported by their behaviour afterwards.

With the garrison in this frame of mind, Tyler had little difficulty in getting them to open the several gates[1] by displaying the royal authority to take the traitors. For the majority this was good enough; they did not look beyond it. If any inquired the reason, there was the cynical explanation that the King and his party were deliberately handing over the wanted men to save their own lives. (The author of the *Chronicon Angliae* believed this to be true.) If there was any hesitation, Tyler only had to say that the King was in his power and that a refusal to open would expose him to grave danger. With so many ways of getting in, it hardly matters which

[1] The Lion Gate at the first drawbridge, the Middle Gate in the middle of the Moat, the gate in the outer curtain and the gate in the inner curtain. The zoo was located in the Lion Tower. At that time the animals were mostly carnivora and bears. The yelling of the mob on Thursday night may well have excited the lions to add their roars to the din.

he used. Sufficient to record that the garrison opened the gates and Tyler, followed by the small force which accompanied him, entered the fortress. The time is given by John Malverne,[1] the chronicler, as 11 a.m.

What happened now goes a long way to show that the rebels and the garrison had some previous understanding. They began fraternizing. The passage in the *Chronicon Angliae* which describes the scene has not hitherto, perhaps, been fully understood. The author says: 'The peasants stroked the beards even of the knights and talked to them familiarly as if they were all comrades together who had sworn to hunt down the traitors.' He goes on to declare that some of the rebels were in a rollicking mood. While Wat Tyler and a party entered the White Tower, guided by an inmate who said the Archbishop and Hales were in the chapel, these others entered the palace, perhaps to search for wanted lords[2] in the royal apartments, and were shown the King's bed, on which they 'sat or lay joking', says the monkish author, who is profoundly shocked. The Princess's bedroom was next door. They walked in and found her there. They seem to have indulged in rustic horseplay, for her bed was upset. Though she had nothing worse to fear than impertinence, she became seriously alarmed. When one of them asked her for a kiss, she fainted. Says Froissart: 'Her ladies-in-waiting and squires carried her to a postern on the bank (the Little Water Gate) and put her in a boat. She was taken to the mansion called the King's Wardrobe (in Carter Lane by St. Paul's) and lay there in a state of collapse.'

Meanwhile Wat Tyler and his retinue were engaged on their more sinister business. Archbishop Sudbury and Sir Robert Hales, after their failure to escape, had given themselves up for lost. By the plan they themselves had helped to draw up, the King was to agree to their surrender. The rebels would shortly be arriving and could not by any manner of means be kept out. That the two unfortunates did not attempt to hide inside the Tower, which had many secret chambers, shows either that they were too dazed with fright to think or, more probably, that they deemed it useless to

[1] John Malverne, besides being a Benedictine monk of Worcester, was a Fellow of Oriel College, Oxford. He continued Ranulf Higden's *Polychronicon*, bringing it up to 1394.

[2] The Duke's son, Henry Earl of Derby, was still in the Tower. Though his name was not on the list of prescribed persons, as he was only a boy, he was certainly in some danger as the hated Duke's son. It is recorded that he was smuggled out of the Tower after the entry of the rebels.

hide, as someone would be sure to give them away. There was nothing to be done but prepare for death. They went upstairs to the chapel in the White Tower.[1] There, says the *Anonimalle*, 'the Archbishop sang the mass devoutly, and shrived the Prior of the Hospitallers and others. Then he heard two masses or three, and chanted the *Commendacione*, the *Placebo*, the *Dirige*, the Seven Psalms and a Litany. He was at the words "Omnes sancti orate pro nobis", when the commons burst in.'

The description in the *Chronicon Angliae* of the murders which followed is in the pseudo-rhetorical style favoured by the author when he attempts a dramatic scene. Parts of it, however, will stand quoting. The rebels seized the old prelate at the altar (he was sixty), dragged him down the winding stone staircase, striking and jostling him, and hurried him out to Tower Hill. 'When he got there, a most horrible yelling arose. The rebels always raised a loud clamour at all their executions and when they set fire to houses. One could not hear words in the din, but only throaty sounds with bellowing or, more exactly, what was like the demoniacal screeching of peacocks.'

Sudbury was not given even the semblance of a trial. But he made an effort to plead for his life, declaring that he was no traitor, but an entirely innocent man who had discharged his duties to the best of his ability. And he warned them that to kill an archbishop was a deadly sin. The rebels, however, were so frantic to despatch him that without further ado they forced him to his knees and began hacking at his neck. It took eight blows to sever his head. Sir Robert Hales, seized with him in the chapel, was next beheaded. Two more suffered, John Legge, the sergeant-at-arms who had been prominent over the poll tax, and one of Duke John's retinue, a well-known doctor, whose connection with the hated Duke sealed his fate. The heads were carried in procession on poles to the Confessor's shrine in Westminster Abbey, where they were as if shown to the saint. This done, the mob took them to London Bridge and put them on the spikes used for traitors' heads. Says Malverne: 'They put the Archbishop's head in the centre and

[1] The chapel in the White Tower is as it was in the fourteenth century. The earliest example of the Norman style in this country, it was built by William the Conqueror with stone imported especially from Caen where he had already built his two famous, and infinitely more beautiful, churches, the Abbaye aux Hommes and the Abbaye aux Femmes. The visitor today is shown the spot where Sudbury was kneeling when the rebels burst in.

principal place, and to make sure the people should know to whom the head belonged, they fixed his red hat on it with a nail.'[1]

In this rough and ready style the commons of England moved a vote of censure on a government which for years had mismanaged the war in France, failed to protect the shores of England, imposed new taxes, refused liberties and kept down wages.

One is reminded of how five years back the knights and burgesses of the Good Parliament under Peter de la Mare removed from about the King persons they called traitors. Their procedure was legal, though their object was similar to the insurgents. Here the parallel between Peter de la Mare and Wat Tyler ends. For Wat Tyler the execution of the traitors was not merely a punishment of individuals, but part of a conspiracy to subvert the state. How far during the thirty hours or so of life remaining to him he advanced towards that end, the remaining pages are written to show.

[1] The particular spike used was the one till then occupied by the head of Sir John Menstreworth (*Historia Vitae et Regni Ricardi II a Monacho quodam de Evesham*, p. 27 of the 1729 edn.). After the suppression of the rebellion Sudbury's body, with a leaden head, was taken to Canterbury and buried. The tomb is close to the Black Prince's. There is no effigy remaining today. The head, after being taken down from the bridge, was sent to Sudbury, the Archbishop's birthplace in Essex, according to the notice in Canterbury Cathedral at the tomb. I am informed that the head, which was embalmed, is still to be seen in Sudbury Church.

The Terror

The hour on Friday the fourteenth, when the King and the lords with him at Mile End heard of the death of Sudbury and Hales, is nowhere recorded, but as the executions took place in public only a mile and a half away, the time must have been soon after eleven, the hour given for the rebels' entry into the Tower. At the news, the issue of the charters was suspended, though it was, if possible, yet more urgent to satisfy the insurgents and induce them to leave. Yet, to linger at Mile End was clearly imprudent. But where to go? The court's base at the Tower was now in Tyler's hands. There was no advantage in returning there; and there was the disadvantage that to do so would be putting the King more entirely in the rebel hands than he already was. When it was learnt that the Princess had fled to the Wardrobe, the King decided to join her. Those who had not yet received charters were advised that the clerks would continue to write them out and the King to seal them at the Wardrobe. It would not be necessary for the whole body to assemble there. Let deputies be appointed. Meanwhile all those with charters and banners should prepare to go home; the rest also need not wait, since their deputies would be following immediately with the charters. 'This advice,' says Froissart, 'calmed the people, particularly the simple inhabitants of the country, who did not understand things very clearly. They said among themselves: "It is well spoken, well spoken. We don't want better than that."' But the more extreme elements, who knew that their leader had further designs and, in any case, wanted to take the opportunity to extort, rob, ransom, murder, when they had chance to do so, returned into the city bent on mischief.

Though the King and his retinue remained wholly at the rebels' mercy, they had no immediate reason to fear seizure, since the issue of the charters was to proceed and so many insurgents were anxious to get them. Nevertheless, after the capture of the Tower, as Wat Tyler was in full possession of London, he had the power to seize them at any moment he thought opportune. Unpleasantly aware of the delicacy of their position, which would remain precarious until they were rescued, though by whom was a very big question, they returned to London and, avoiding the Tower, crossed the city from east to west, a distance from Aldgate of about a mile and a quarter, and came safely to the Wardrobe, a royal residence with some fortifications, though but a poor protection from rebels who had found the Tower no obstacle. Their arrival must have been a great relief to the Princess, dispelling both fears for her son's safety and her own. The peasants awaiting charters followed the King, and he spent the afternoon supervising the issue of parchments granting indemnity and freedom.

But while he was quietly busy in the Wardrobe, playing his part as King of the commons, a title which the peasants had trustfully bestowed upon him, and his advisers intended him to exploit to good advantage, a terror broke out in the city. Greatly excited by their success in taking and killing the two chief ministers, the insurgents began to run amok. Wat Tyler had restrained them when they entered the previous day, though a few individuals were killed. But now on Friday afternoon and evening he let them loose. Perhaps he had little option; they were out of hand? Yet this would not appear to have been the case, for the next day we find them amenable to his authority and so dependent upon his presence that they are lost when he dies. One concludes that Friday's terror resulted as much from his incitement as their devilment.

The city letter-book, already cited from, has: 'That day there was no little slaughter within the city, as well of natives as of aliens. Richard Lyons[1] and many others were beheaded in Cheap. In the Vintry also there was a very great massacre of Flemings. In

[1] This was the financier who during Edward's last days had helped Lord Latimer and Alice Perrers to make money by defrauding the revenue. That the rebels remembered his frauds and how Duke John had annulled the Good Parliament's proceedings against him, is a further example of how they and the Good Parliament had some ideas in common.

one heap were piled some forty headless bodies of persons who had been dragged out of churches and houses. There was hardly a street in which bodies of men killed were not lying about.' The *Anonimalle* summing up reports: 'On that day there were beheaded some 140 to 160 persons.' A proclamation had been issued, presumably by Wat Tyler, that aliens be killed at sight. But anyone met with in the street was liable to be stopped, interrogated and, if what he said was unsatisfactory, despatched. Lawyers and tax collectors suffered worst. Criminals took advantage of the anarchy to kidnap and demand ransom, debtors to murder creditors, and those with old scores to settle them by dagger thrusts. 'This went on all that day and night with hideous cries and horrid tumult.' Wat Tyler had not forgotten Duke John. In an effort to kill him wherever he might be found, a strong force was sent up to search the border. His Duchess, Constance of Castile, did not feel safe in Hertford Castle where she was staying, and fled northwards to Pontefract, another of the Duke's castles. So great was the terror that the castellan refused to let her in, in case the rebels, pursuing her, wrecked the castle. Not till she reached yet another of his castles, Knaresborough by York, did she find refuge. The Duke remained on the other side of the border.

The murders in the city greatly alarmed Londoners with money or property. They had been pinning their faith on the departure of the rebels after the death of the ministers. Evidently they were mistaken. It looked as if things might get worse. They began discussing plans for resistance. Friday afternoon saw the first signs of a rally of the well-to-do against Tyler. Nevertheless, the prospect remained very dark. As Froissart points out: 'The revolutionaries, Tyler, Straw and Ball, remained in the city, still supported by 30,000 men. They did not even ask for charters. Their whole intention was to foment more trouble. Rich men and lords were marked down as victims, their houses listed for pillage and burning.'

The Scene at the Abbey

So Friday night passed. Saturday morning brought no change in the situation. Of succour from the country there was no news at all. The rich burgesses were the more convinced that they must either fight or be massacred, though it was not clear how, scattered as they were about the city, they could come together in streets infested with roving bands. Where could they muster, who should lead them, how choose where to strike, when insurgents were everywhere? These questions were discussed but remained for the moment unanswered.

Surveying the scene, the King and his advisers saw nothing for it but to continue trying to thin the rebel ranks by granting charters without reservation. Young Richard's nerve still held. Indeed, his confidence in himself seemed to be growing. Described as nervous when he set out for Mile End, on his return he had, says Froissart, enough go in him to comfort his mother and tell her not to give up hope. It was an invigorating experience for him to have charmed the multitude. The magic words he had been advised to utter—'I am your King; tell me what you require; what is it you wish to say'[1]—had worked like a spell. On a huge destrier, far too large for him but perching him up so that all could see him, his purple robe embroidered with leopards and fleurs-de-lis, a crown on his head, a golden rod in his hand, he looked so young, so innocent, such a darling prince, that when he spoke, smiling sweetly,

[1] Froissart, Lettenhove edn., p. 405. Froissart states that Richard opened the Mile End meeting with these words. The words recorded by the *Anonimalle Chronicle* (quoted further back) as spoken by the rebels may be taken as their affirmative answer. 'We want no other King but you.'

the anger of the crowd vanished. Indeed, indeed, he was their King. Had they not declared it from the first day? Had they not come to London confident that he would concede them all, when they had delivered him from the traitors who were misleading him?

No wonder finding he could touch the peasants' hearts had increased his confidence. Probably he received many compliments from his entourage. Their advice will have been to continue as he had begun. Let him repeat the phrase, 'I am your King,' whenever the occasion required it, say it with the same frank boyish air and the magic would work again.

But would it work with Tyler? No; the lords knew well that it would not. Yet, if Tyler's following was substantially reduced, the moment would come when the burgesses could counter-attack with success. It remained to induce Tyler to bring his men to another parley. The King would play his part as before. By the day after, perhaps, the rebel army would mostly have dispersed. Then they could turn on Tyler and the fanatics of the rebellion. A message was sent inviting him to meet the King at Smithfield market outside the Aldersgate some time that afternoon. It was evidently thought impracticable to summon his followers direct, as before Mile End; the meeting could only take place if he agreed.

Though not two days had passed since Tyler took possession of London, his conception of himself as a man of destiny had grown until now he thought the moment close when he could do what he had intended to do from the first, if he could bring his followers to it. He would seize the King, force him to agree to a general massacre of the governing classes, including churchmen, just as he had agreed to the execution of the ministers, and oblige him to inaugurate a new state, where there would be no upper class between King and commons. If he were unmanageable, he would be killed. Tyler himself would then become king. Was he not already king in fact? Who had more power in London, in England, than he?

The *Chronicon Angliae* puts it this way: 'It is credibly reported that Wat Tyler boasted, putting his hand to his lips, that in four days' time all the laws of England would be issuing from his mouth.'

When Tyler received the King's message asking for a parley at Smithfield he agreed. He would make sure that it took a very different course from the parley at Mile End. Rightly managed, it would give him the opportunity he required to apprehend the King and consummate the revolution.

It will be recalled that three days earlier, on the Wednesday, the King and his council had received a warning that such was Tyler's plan. Nevertheless, they had taken a gamble and gone to Mile End. The gamble had come off. An emotional loyalty had rendered the peasants harmless. Moreover, Tyler had been engaged in securing the ministers. They would be gambling again by going to Smithfield; and the risk would be greater than before. But it had to be taken. There was no other way. A further parley was essential, if the rebels were to be dispersed.

Before setting out, however, they felt the need of supernatural help. They would ride to Westminster Abbey, make offerings at the tomb of the national saint and beg him to intercede for them with God; and they would make use of whatever other divine resources the sacred edifice afforded.

During the morning negotiations by messenger were conducted with Tyler in the hope of discovering whether he would withdraw on any terms. But he made cavilling objections to whatever was proposed, for he wanted no settlement. He knew that any offer, no matter how favourable, would be a trap. He was so far committed that he could not afford to concede anything. For him to agree to any terms, short of the government's unconditional surrender, would be to give up the advantage he held in return for a promise. The government would honour a promise only as long as he was the stronger. He had no use for such kind of promises. Indeed, he dared not entertain the thought. For him to do otherwise than impose his will would be suicide. Yet he did not recede from his agreement to meet the King at Smithfield in the late afternoon. That he kept to it, afforded the government a crumb of comfort. Perhaps he might yet accept terms and go. But, as we know, he had no such purpose; he intended a coup, not a parley.

Thus it was settled. The King and his lords would first visit Westminster Abbey and, when their supplications were finished go straight to Smithfield. In view, however, of the great risk to the King's person which the parley with Tyler involved, those citizens who were preparing to strike in their own defence when opportunity offered, were warned to hold their forces in readiness, in case the King should need their help.[1]

[1] While there is no direct documentary evidence that such a message was sent, what happened later can only be explained on the assumption that it

Says the *Anonimalle*: 'At three in the afternoon the King went to the Abbey of Westminster and some 200 persons with him. The Abbot and monks of the said abbey . . . came to meet him in procession half way to Charing Cross, clothed in their copes and their feet bare.' And the *Polychronicon*: 'The King dismounted and kneeling kissed the cross borne in front of the procession, the tears running down his cheeks.' He was overcome at suddenly hearing that the Abbey had been violated by the rebels during the morning. The violation was not as bad as when Robert Hauley had been killed before the altar two years before, but was bad enough. Sir Richard Imworth, the notorious governor of the Marshalsea prison, who as mentioned further back had taken sanctuary on Wednesday night, was seized and carried away. 'He was at the shrine of St. Edward' says the *Anonimalle* 'embracing a marble pillar and beseeching the saint to preserve him from his enemies. The commons wrenched his arms away from the pillar[1] and dragged him to Cheapside, where they beheaded him.'

Mounting again the King rode slowly down what is now Whitehall, then a road through open country, and was escorted into the Abbey by the monks. They led him first to the high altar 'where he prayed devoutly and left an offering for the altar and the relics' (*Anonimalle*). Then, says the *Polychronicon*, he went to Saint Edward the Confessor's tomb on the royal burial mound behind the altar 'and remained there a long time in prayer. You could see the knights of his retinue piously contend who should be the first to make offerings to the relics and who weep the most contritely.' Here, only a few hours before, the Saint had refused to hear Sir Richard Imworth's plea for help and let him be taken away to his death. But now, says the chronicle, 'the divine help was not denied. They rose to their feet assured that all would be well.'

was, and also that Walworth was the person who sent it. It is probable that the sentence in the *Continuation of the Eulogy*, a minor chronicle of the time, refers to this: 'The Mayor ordered the city to arm and follow Robert Knollys.' The position of the sentence in the unknown monk's meagre narrative indicates that the order to arm was given before the parley began at Smithfield. The message, whatever exactly it amounted to, was of a general nature—that the citizens get ready. As later events will show, it did not, for instance, specifically state that the London force should keep a lookout on what was happening at Smithfield and come out of Aldersgate at once if the King was in danger.

[1] The shrine, as the visitor may perceive today, has two short curly pillars, of Italian design, either of which would give a good hold.

The King's devotions, however, were not yet finished. He descended from the burial mound to pray, says Froissart, before 'an image of Our Lady in a little chapel where miracles were done'. This little chapel, opposite the steps from the mound on the north side, may still be seen. The image was destroyed at the Reformation, but an outline of it is visible on the wall. The King besought the Virgin Mother to work a miracle in his case and deliver him from Wat Tyler. And, indeed, he was delivered that very afternoon in circumstances so unlikely as to appear miraculous.

Before leaving, Richard had yet another call to make. For over a hundred years there had always been a hermit attached to the Abbey. His cell was built outside the building in the angle formed by the east wall of the south transept and the main south wall, the point where inside lies St. Benedict's chapel. The cell's entrance was by a door from the chapel. In 1381 the hermit's name was Brother John Murimouth. It had become the fashion at court to confess to him. To this recluse Richard now went. 'He spoke with the anchorite, confessed to him and remained with him some time,' records the *Anonimalle*.[1]

At last all was done—prayers, offerings, confession. Everyone now felt 'more hopeful of a happy end to their troubles. They mounted their horses in good spirits and rode to Smithfield, there to hold colloquy with the rebel leader.'[2]

[1] The cell no longer exists, but the doorway to it in St. Benedict's chapel is still there. A squint-hole through the main wall which enabled the hermit to see St. Benedict's altar without leaving his cell, also remains. I am indebted to Mr. R. P. Howgrave-Graham, Assistant Keeper of the Muniments, for pointing out to me the door and the squint-hole, and also for drawing my attention to an article in *Archaeologia*, vol. xciii, 1949 (p. 151) by Mr. Lawrence Tanner, Keeper of the Muniments, entitled 'On some recent discoveries in Westminster Abbey', where all the known facts about this hermit are given.

[2] The *Continuation of the Polychronicon*.

At Smithfield on the Saturday

In the fourteenth century Smithfield market was in a suburb immediately outside the city wall at its north-west corner. As at present, its east and south sides were bounded by the close and grounds of St. Bartholemew's Church and St. Bartholemew's Hospital. On the west side were houses, though probably not so far in as at present. There were buildings, also, on the north side where the meat market is now. Beyond them lay the Priory of the Hospitallers, some two hundred yards into the open country. That is to say it was there on the previous day; by the Saturday afternoon it was a smouldering ruin except for the church. The two nearest city gates were Newgate (to the east of where is now Holborn Viaduct), about a furlong to the south-west of the market, and Aldersgate (at the south end of the present Aldersgate Street), the same distance to the south-east. The market's size was slightly greater than it is at present, as it extended farther on the western side, but does not seem to have been more than 200 yards each way. Cattle, horses and pigs were sold there; fairs were held and also tournaments. In contemporary records it is still referred to as a field, but there cannot have been much grass on it. Though probably nowhere paved, an ordinance dated 1372 shows that fees were levied to have it kept clean.

These details will explain why it was fixed for the rendezvous. It was the nearest open space of sufficient size. Besides this obvious reason, it provided other advantages for both parties. Tyler could concentrate his army there and draw it up in battle formation, a precaution he may well have thought desirable if he were to abduct the King and defeat any attempt to rescue him by the citizen militia, now become a possibility, since the citizens, as he will have heard, were beginning to organize resistance. From the King's point of view the vicinity of the two gates was an advantage, particularly Aldersgate, by which he could quickly withdraw into the city.

When the royal train reached Smithfield it was about 5 p.m. and as it was midsummer, the sun was still high. The names of the grandees with the King are not given, but presumably much the same people accompanied him as to Mile End, with the exception of Sir Robert Knollys who was inside the city, seeing to the muster of the militia. William Walworth, the Mayor, was certainly present. He may have come direct from the city to meet the King, for he was wearing armour (though hidden below an over-garment), while the rest were in the robes they wore in the Abbey. But one must suppose that the retinue contained armed men.[1]

While the King and his company had all the appearance of state dignitaries come for a parley, the rebels' aspect was belligerent. Says the *Anonimalle*: 'When the King and his train arrived at Smithfield they turned into the field to the eastward in front of St. Bartholomew's which was a house of canons. The commons arrayed themselves on the west side in great battles.' At Mile End the rebels had been in some kind of formation under banners; they were now in regular military battles, of which normally, as at Crécy or Poitiers, there were three. (One recalls that Câle, the leader of the Jacques, had also trained his peasants to form battles.) How many men Tyler had assembled at Smithfield is uncertain, though it is roundly stated to have been 20,000, a figure which strikes one as exaggerated. As to their armour, they had started from home with little and with weapons of indifferent make. But two factors are to be taken into account: the seizure of the Tower must have provided a proportion of them with good arms and armour, since it was the royal arsenal; and their archers were, some of them, professionals of the war in France and some the class of young villagers, long practised in the bow, from whom the professionals came. As has been frequently noted, archers when properly posted with a clear view, rendered an attack extremely

[1] That Walworth was wearing armour does not prove that he was expecting immediate danger. Had that been so, he would have warned Knollys to come out of Aldersgate at once with his men if things suddenly became critical. The sequel shows that he did not do this.

hazardous. The flat expanse of Smithfield market provided Tyler's archers with an effective field of vision. This affords another reason why he was content to accept the market for the parley. He may not have thought an attack likely, but in view of the preparation the citizens were making, he wished to provide against its possibility after he had seized the King.

When the royal party took their stand opposite the gate of St. Bartholemew's Church on the market's south-east corner, and saw, not more than 150 paces away, Tyler's battles, they must have been very startled, for they were covered by the archers. They were so completely in Tyler's power that a sign from him and they were all dead men. But since their object was to grant everything he demanded and they had no intention of resisting or in any way provoking him, they stood their ground. It would have required more nerve than they possessed to approach any closer, go among the rebel ranks as at Mile End, address them and invite their complaints. Instead, they would ask Wat Tyler to come across to them. Indeed, the quickest and most effective method of getting the rebels out of London was now seen to be negotiation direct with him. But this was going to be more difficult than dealing direct with his followers. In the exchange of messages earlier in the day he had evaded a clear statement of what terms he required. Yet as he had agreed to the parley he had surely demands to make. When they were all granted, it was to be hoped that he and his men would have little inclination to remain.

At this point Froissart provides us with an account of Tyler's intentions and the orders which he was giving his men. One would like to know the source of his information. As to its truth, all one can say is that it makes sense. Tyler is disclosed addressing his army while he waits for the King's arrival: 'We have done nothing so far. The charters which the King has given us are worth little if anything. The time has come for us to take united action. Let us sack this great city, this rich and powerful London; and let us do it before the commons of the other counties arrive on the scene. For they are all coming, and I can tell you that Baker and Lister are at their head. If we sack London first and gain possession of its gold and silver and riches before they do, we shall never regret it. For I assure you, if we let them, they will take all.'

Here we see Wat Tyler warning the peasantry that the charters are bogus. It was not easy to convince them of this. Those who had received them had deserted him and gone home satisfied.

Many of the rest were anxious to get them. As a bait to keep the rest together, he held out the dazzling prospect of a London sack. The city was at their mercy. There was nothing to prevent them sacking it except their respect for the King and belief in his promises. But, says Tyler, his promises are worth nothing. Come, let us make hay before others arrive who in all likelihood will not have your scruples.

Froissart does not stand alone in declaring Tyler to have had this design. The *Chronicon Angliae* has: 'As Tyler was stronger than the King and his advisers, he was resolved to put them off with cavilling objections, so that he could the better carry out his infamous plan that night. For he planned that very Saturday night to loot the city with the support of the London mob, and after massacring the burgesses, the lords, even the King, to set it on fire on the four sides.'

Some historians have been loath to credit the leader of a peasantry, who had risen against oppression and to obtain freedom, with such extreme ferocity. But a popular rising, the further it goes, the more extreme it becomes, for the leaders, having put themselves beyond the pale, dare not stop, and continue in the hope of annihilating opponents who otherwise will annihilate them.

Froissart continues that Tyler, after inciting his troops to a night of pillage, saw the King arrive and spoke to certain of his adjutants as follows: 'There is the King. I intend to go over and speak to him. Don't you move from here if I do not sign to you. But if I make this sign (and he made the sign) come across and kill everybody, except the King. Do the King no harm. He is young, he will do what we want. We will take him with us over England, and, I guarantee, thus become lords of the land.'

Here Tyler at last discloses to his following, or to the section of them whom he could depend on, the project of abducting the King, hitherto known only to the leaders. John Ball had not mentioned it in his violent harangues on Blackheath on the Thursday morning, though, as stated further back on the authority of the *Anonimalle*, a message reached the King that same Thursday that such was the leaders' intention. Now on the Saturday Tyler takes the more daredevil of his men into his confidence. As a prelude to the sack of London, he may give them a sign to seize the King. The massacre can then begin with the killing of his lords.

It is to be remarked that Tyler did not give the order at once, though there was nothing to prevent him from seizing the King there and then. At first sight it seems strange that he preferred to enter first into a parley, and one which he did not intend should come to anything. By doing so, he ran a certain risk, though perhaps an infinitesimal one since his archers covered the royal party, in going among men who were his implacable enemies. The explanation appears to be this: the feeling among the bulk of his followers was such that, before committing an act so heinous in their eyes as the seizure of the King, he had to bring about a situation which would seem to justify it. And that was what he intended to do at the parley.

The Parley

The King now sent a messenger across the market to invite Tyler to come over to him. It is not quite certain who the messenger was. Some say Walworth, others Sir John Newton, the knight who had acted as the rebels' envoy at Blackheath, but was now, it is thought, with the King and had carried the messages of the earlier part of the day. It seems likely it was he, as Tyler knew him. When he rode up and delivered his message, Tyler listened haughtily, like a sovereign, and rebuked him for entering his presence without dismounting. When Newton urged him to come at once, he said: 'It is your business to hurry, not mine. Go back to your King. I will come when I please.'[1]

It may have been during the interval before Tyler crossed the market that a tailor, says Froissart, accosted him. 'My lord,' says he, 'what about my bill for the sixty quilted surcoats I have supplied? Who's going to pay that? I'm owed 30 marks.' 'Be easy,' replied Tyler, 'You will be well paid this nightfall. Stick close to me and you have as good a pledge as you want.' There would be plenty of loot to pay for everything.

When Tyler deemed that he had kept the King waiting long enough, he called for his mount. 'Riding his little horse, he came to the King with great confidence,' says the *Anonimalle*. He was confident, not only because his archers sheltered him, but also for

[1] This is quoted from the *Chronicon Angliae* which, however, is too confused at this point to be clear. The author seems to have heard something about the royal manner which Tyler had adopted. Other chroniclers also report it, though in different contexts.

the reason that he was protected by the safe conduct attaching to an invitation to a parley, even though he did not intend it to be a real parley. As Froissart puts it, 'il ne demandoit que le rihotte,'[1] 'he was out to make trouble only'. His standard bearer and a small retinue accompanied him. Froissart continues: 'He placed himself so close to the King that the tail of his horse was under the head of the King's horse.' The *Anonimalle*[2] then has: 'He took the King by the hand and shook his arm hard and strong, saying: "Brother, cheer up, for you will have in the next fortnight 40,000 more of the commons than you have had till now, and we shall be good companions."' The meaning of this remark has not been found immediately apparent. It should, I think, be taken as a jocularity. The King, his dear brother, need not worry. He will soon have double the number of loyal commons, when the other counties arrive. In the last words the tone has hardened from jocularity to sarcasm: you will be so happy with us when we abduct you. Tyler's self-confidence was, indeed, marked. After giving little Richard a very rough handshake, he addresses, him as one king speaking to another king soon to fall, in a tone of contemptuous *bonhomie*, simulating compassion for his downcast state and reassuring him —it won't be so bad—we'll treat you proud—till we cut your throat.

To this opening gambit Richard's reply was: 'Why won't you go home to your county?' That, indeed, was the point. That was what the parley was for. To find out what more Tyler wanted before he would leave.

At this question Tyler's face became grim, says the author of the *Vita*, and Froissart reports the following conversation. '"Do you see those men over there?" "Yes," said the King, "why do you say so?" "I say so because they are all under my command and have sworn to do what I want." "Very well," said the King, "I have no objection to that." Tyler who desired only to pick a quarrel, went on: "And do you think, King, that the people over there, and as many more in London, and all under my orders, should leave you thus without having your charters?" "Certainly

[1] riot. There is the alternative reading here of *hutin*, which means disturbance, conflict or clamour, as in our *hue* and cry.

[2] As the contemporary accounts of what happened at Smithfield have been very variously interpreted, it is imperative here to give frequent references to support my interpretation, despite the cumbrous effect which a heavy annotation has on a narrative.

not," said the King, "they shall have them. I have given orders that charters are to be immediately made out and given to each section one after the other. And now, my friend, go back and ask your people to leave London quietly. For it is our intention that each of your villages and towns should have its charter, as I have said."'

How the colloquy then proceeded is told in the *Anonimalle*. Tyler, intent on picking a quarrel which would provoke, he hoped, the King's company to some act which would justify him in signalling to his men to begin the massacre, now stated, 'with a great oath' that his men would not depart until they had charters written and sealed which granted far more than the indemnity and freedom promised by the charters already issued. 'In a threatening fashion he declared that the lords of the realm would bitterly regret it if the points he would now raise were not freely conceded.' Whereupon, in the same menacing tone, he listed demands which were so extreme, so revolutionary, that he felt certain no king on earth could grant them and that in refusing them the uproar he desired would be provoked. Among the demands was one for the confiscation of all ecclesiastical property and its distribution among the commons. (A third of the country's wealth was in ecclesiastical hands at this time, it is said.) Another item was that all ranks be abolished, by the abolition of the nobility. But these demands failed to rouse the angry scene he anticipated. Richard continued to play his part unperturbably. Ridiculous though the demands were, he agreed. Some of his lords found it difficult to restrain their indignation, but 'none of them ventured to reprove Tyler for his impertinence,' says the author of the *Vita*, because they did not want to jeopardize the King's well-maintained effort to bring him to terms. Though by the time Tyler had finished, he had demanded the annulment of the main institutions of the state, Richard replied pleasantly. 'He gave an easy answer,' states the *Anonimalle*. Tyler should have everything he had asked for. Let him go back and tell his people so and take them home. But Tyler did not move.

In this way the parley ended, for what followed was no longer a parley, but an *émeute*.

The Blow

When the King and those about him (whoever they were besides Walworth—Lord Thomas Percy, perhaps, Lord de Vere, the Earl of Warwick, the Earl of Salisbury, the two Hollands if they had not fled the city, and the Earl of Arundel, now acting as Chancellor) saw that Wat Tyler did not return to his men, they knew that their plan had failed. Agreeing to his demands had had no effect. He had stated his terms and they had accepted them, but he had not taken himself off as they had hoped. Still he sat his horse before them. His forces remained in battle array. His mien had not altered. What was next to be done? To withdraw and go elsewhere would not lessen their predicament, for there was nowhere to go to be out of his power. And what would he do next? They waited.[1]

We must also conceive of Wat Tyler as nonplussed, at least for a moment. His insolence, his wild demands, had precipitated no scene. He had had no excuse to give the sign. That the King had remained unruffled, pleasant, and conceded everything with

[1] It may here be objected that if, as seems to have been the case, Knollys and the citizen militia had been warned, a message should now have been sent asking for help. To send, however, would have been to provoke a fight, when Tyler's men had the advantage of being drawn up in battle array with archers in position. Moreover, it was not certain what Tyler intended to do. Perhaps the King and his company were not in greater danger than they had been all along. There was nothing they could do but wait and see.

charming grace, had, indeed, made it more difficult to swing the mob into the desperate mood required. He was suddenly very thirsty and called for drink.

Says the *Anonimalle*: 'Presently Wat Tyler sent for a flagon of water to rinse his mouth, because of the great heat he was in. It was soon brought and he rinsed his mouth in an ugly common way in front of the King. After that they brought him a flagon of beer and he drank a great draught.'

It was after drinking that Tyler decided what he would do. His mood became darker. The spectacle of the court's helplessness had already given him deep pleasure. Like men tortured, the grandees had been ready to agree to anything if only they be delivered. What a triumph! The King had been forced to assume an air of gracious benevolence and give away his kingdom. That his advisers believed that thereby they were hoodwinking the man who had taken their capital, was good comedy, for to undo what they had done they must get out of his power, but he was going to massacre them that very hour. Before he did so, however, he must bait them further. He knew what he would do. He had been executing men for days. He would now execute one of the King's retinue, slay him before the King's very face. That would rouse the lords surely; they would have to throw off their restraint. And as soon as they did so, he would give the signal. But if terror, sense of utter weakness, held them back, and they let the blood of one of their fellows wash around their horses' hooves without raising a hand, he would, after showing his contempt for their abject state, demand another man, kill him, and then another, until the rest to save their lives broke out against him. Then at his signal the commons would come streaming over, convinced he was the victim of a treacherous attack. Says Froissart: 'Tyler now cast his eyes on one of the King's esquires, who was behind the King and carried the King's sword. The esquire had annoyed him by an abusive remark which he had overheard him to make.' The *Anonimalle* records that the esquire was a Kentish man and when he saw Tyler recognized him as a highwayman who had committed robberies in Kent, and said so out loud. When Tyler's glance now fell on him, Froissart says the following exchange occurred: '"Ha," said Tyler, "so you are here. Give me your dagger!" "I won't," said the esquire, "why should I?" The King looked down on the esquire and said: "You had better give it to him." The esquire handed it over much against his will. When Tyler had got hold of it, he began to play with it and turn it this way and that in his hand.[1] Then speaking to the esquire again, he said: "Give me your sword!" "I cannot," said the esquire, "it is the King's sword."' The *Anonimalle* continues: 'Nodding his head at the esquire, his face working with malice, Wat ordered him to come to him. But the esquire refused to go because he was afraid what the others with Tyler might do. But the lords finally got him to go, in order to see what he (Tyler) would do in front of the King.' From Tyler's expression it looked as if he intended to do violence to the esquire for having disobeyed him. But would he dare to do this in the presence of the King, in the presence of the royal retinue? They would call his bluff. Let them see what he would do. If he did a violence, they would have to resist. They had reached the end of their endurance. Which was exactly what Tyler had anticipated.

The *Anonimalle* continues: 'When Wat saw him coming, he ordered the horseman holding his banner to dismount and behead the said esquire.' At this the esquire said boldly that if he was struck, he would strike back. Whereupon Tyler, intent to precipitate the *ribotte* he desired, tried to stab him with his dagger, shouting: 'By God, I will not eat again till I have your head!'

At this, Walworth quickly moved forward on his horse and intervened, remonstrating with Tyler for his contempt in the King's presence. 'I owe the King no respect,'[2] retorted Tyler. Froissart gives Walworth's hot reply: 'Fellow, how dare you use such words before the King! You presume too far.'[3] 'What is it to you what I say or do?' rejoined Tyler and struck at the Mayor's stomach savagely with his dagger, unaware that he had armour under his robe. The point was turned aside. The King screamed: 'Arrest him! Arrest him!' But Walworth took the gamble which

[1] The way Tyler played with the dagger was a bit of news which seems to have stuck in reporters' memories, for the monk who wrote the Continuation of the Knighton Chronicle of Leicester, though his information about what happened at Smithfield was only fragmentary and is confused, has the sentence: 'Tyler held a naked dagger which he threw from one hand to the other like a boy playing.' The report he had received led him mistakenly to think that Tyler intended to stab the King with it.

[2] This sentence is one of the small contributions made by Malverne's *Polychronicon* to the general picture here, a mosaic composed from all the chronicles, but chiefly from the *Anonimalle* and Froissart, which complement each other remarkably in this case.

[3] The words are very revealing in the original French: 'Gars, comment es-tu si osés de dire tels parolles en la présence dou roy? C'est trop pour toy.'

immortalized him. Drawing his basilard[1] he shouted: 'You stinking scoundrel,' and delivered the famous blow which ended the peasants' revolt. Tyler had run it too fine. He had not left himself time to give the signal.

[1] A basilard was a broad short handy sword. It was not generally used by knights, but Sir Hugh Calveley is shown with a basilard in his tomb effigy in Bunbury Church, Cheshire. There is also a basilard on view in the London Museum.

After the Blow

The utmost confusion followed the blow, confusion which is reflected in the contemporary narratives. Everybody concerned had his story to tell of what he saw, or thought he saw. The chroniclers make what sense they can of them. Their versions vary; interpretations are not identical. Nevertheless, the main facts are in little doubt. A coherent picture, consistent with what went before, emerges. The half dozen sources supplement each other and the best effect is achieved by weaving their statements into a chronological whole.

Walworth followed up his blow by a second. The retinue immediately closed in on Tyler and an esquire called Ralph Standish ran him through. Though mortally wounded, he was not dead. 'He spurred his horse,' says the *Anonimalle*, 'crying to the commons to avenge him. The horse carried him some four score paces, when he fell to the ground half dead.'

The sudden onslaught, the wounding, and Tyler's dash for safety, must have been over in a minute. His standard bearer and retinue had no time to defend him. Too late they struck at Walworth, were beaten off and then seem to have hastened to pick up Tyler where he lay in the middle of the square. The main rebel body had been watching the parley with the closest attention, waiting for the expected signal. When Walworth drew his sword and struck, there was a cry of apprehension, says the author of the *Eulogy*: 'What is the King doing with our spokesman?' Others, however, incredulous that Tyler, whose beer they had just seen carried over, was in danger, stupidly took the flash of Walworth's sword for the King's and shouted with delight: 'Our leader is being knighted.' They were soon disillusioned, for when he appeared galloping towards them, calling on them to avenge him, and fell from his horse, it was clear that something dreadful had happened, 'though they were not quite certain how it was,' says the *Anonimalle*; it seemed too fantastic that he had been killed all in a minute. Their uncertainty did not last long. The *Chronicon Angliae* has: 'A great and sorrowful cry went up: "Our captain is dead! Our leader has been treacherously slain! Let us stand together! Let us die with him! Let us loose our arrows and avenge him!"' Froissart adds: 'They murmured among themselves: "Come, come, let us put them all to death." At these words they ranged themselves into the square in battle array, each archer with his bow before him.' 'They began to bend their bows and to shoot,' says the *Anonimalle*.

As we have seen, the blow which struck down Tyler was caused by a combination of circumstances which made it inevitable. Yet it exposed the King and his train to instant danger of death. The parley had ended in the very clash which from first to last it had been the King's effort to avoid, and Tyler's to bring on. Tyler had brought it on, but had been its first victim. By the look of things, the King was likely to be the second. Events had moved much too rapidly for Sir Robert Knollys and the citizen militia to be of any use, even if they had been drawn up ready in the city, which they were not.

Then quick as lightning Richard saved the situation. As son of the Black Prince, his ambition must have been to distinguish himself. Though two years younger[1] than his father was at Crécy, his chance had come. Arrows had begun to fly. He was commanding in a battle. Nothing could save his lords and himself but an action of the boldest sort, like the one his father instinctively took when he saw the French King's division top the ridge at Poitiers and himself advanced in defiance of all prudence. He would advance, go out alone to meet the rebels. The previous day at Mile End had given him confidence. He knew what to do, how to do it, what to say. The magic formula—I am your King—had worked yesterday; it would work now. Suddenly confident, he turned to his lords. Froissart writes: 'He said to them: "Stay here. Let no one follow me." Then he left his people and went forward by himself to where

[1] Philip, King John's fourth son, when he distinguished himself at Poitiers by warding off blows aimed at his father, was the same age as Richard now.

the mad folk were preparing to avenge their captain. His words to them were: "Sirs, what is it you require? I am your captain. I am your King. Quiet yourselves."'

As at Mile End, this address had an immediate effect. It must have been deeply moving for the peasantry to see the boy King, the crown on his head, so good looking and gracious, showing no sign of fear. That he was alone greatly augmented the effect. Many mobs since have been stayed by single men who had the nerve to face them. According to Froissart, the result of Richard's action was that the peasants of the quieter sort, those who had not looked beyond punishing traitors and winning charters, became less threatening and began to leave the ranks of their formations. But the more dangerous characters remained arrayed and gave the impression 'that they were going to do something'. For the moment, however, there was a pause. The King was not molested; no more arrows were discharged. Froissart then asserts, what seems highly probable, that Richard rejoined his lords to ask advice. Walworth is represented as saying that help from London could quickly be expected. 'Our supporters there are armed and ready in their houses.' Other chroniclers add that he offered to go and summon them in all haste. Meanwhile the attention of the rebels must be distracted. It would be advantageous if they could be induced to leave Smithfield market and assemble beyond the houses on the north side of the square in the cornfields about the Priory of the Hospitallers. A move there would break up their battle array; it would get them away from the vicinity of Aldersgate from which the London forces would issue; it would isolate them from the thousands of rebels inside London, both its disaffected proletariat and other elements which Tyler had not mustered at Smithfield; and it would also enable the London forces to approach them unobserved under cover of the houses north of the square instead of having to advance across its open space against the archers. There was certainly no time to argue these points, nor any necessity, for they were presumably quite obvious. What had to be decided without a moment's delay was how the insurgents could be persuaded to move. It seems to have been thought that just as they had gone the previous day to Mile End at the King's request when he offered to hear their complaints there, so now if he told them to assemble in the fields for that purpose they would go. It was estimated that the revolutionary core of the movement was small. The bulk of the mob at Smithfield, though led by a desperate gang, still consisted of peasants whose principal aim was to obtain charters. These people would listen to the King; had they not just now quieted down when he spoke to them? If he went forward again and offered to conduct them to the fields, they would follow. The extremists would be obliged to fall back also, as they could not remain where they were unsupported. Moreover, Tyler was no longer there to hound them on. They would be lost without their leader.

The only imponderable was whether the desire to avenge Tyler would overweigh every other consideration and render them intractable. It was this which made Richard's second attempt to dominate their minds such a dangerous gamble. One must suppose that by now they had come forward into the market-place and that there was no longer the same gap between them and the grandees. The confusion and shouting made it more difficult to achieve an effect. When the King moved out, however, he obtained a hearing. The remarks attributed to him in the *Chronicon Angliae* may well have been made at this stage: 'Do not be sad over the death of your leader, for I will go with you as your captain. If you follow me into the fields you shall have everything you choose to ask me.'

And suiting his action to the words he began to ride towards the fields north of the square, accompanied by part of his suite. The commons moved after him, as had been hoped. Yet, their minds were not made up. As the *Chronicon Angliae* puts it: 'They followed the King and his suite into the open fields, not yet sure in their minds whether they would kill him or agree to go home with charters.' Indeed, things looked so doubtful that the suite began melting away. Says the *Anonimalle*: 'At this time most of the knights and esquires of the King's household, and many others, were so frightened that they deserted their lord and went each his way.' By the time Richard reached the beech tree by the well of St. Agnes le Clair just north of the market, he had few companions left, but with wonderful courage went on into the fields.

Walworth accompanied him as far as the sacred well and then galloped back the quarter of a mile or so to Aldersgate and entered the city to summon Sir Robert Knollys. Not apprised of the dangerous turn of events in the market, he had not called out the force which he had been getting together, but acted quickly when informed by Walworth that the King was alone with the insurgents, hardly better off than if they had abducted him. Indeed, it was likely that the revolutionary section regarded him as their prisoner and would never let him go unless they were forced. There was no time to explain how he came to be there, nor did Sir Robert wait to ask. The alarm was sounded, knights came rushing up with their retinues, among them the Gascon condottiere, Bertucat d'Albret. The ex-mayors, Brembre and Philpot, headed their ward bands. In a very short while Sir Robert had drawn up a well-armed body. It was indeed fortunate that such an experienced condottiere of the French wars was available at this crisis.

While this was happening the wildest rumours flew round. It was asserted that both the King and Walworth had been killed; that a massacre had begun and at any moment the rebels would pour into the city to sack and set it on fire. John Horn and Walter Sybyle, the two aldermen who had taken it upon themselves to open the bridge on the Thursday morning, now rode about the streets, shouting: 'Shut your gates and man the walls or all is lost!' It is hard to make out what they were up to—whether they were idiotic busybodies or really believing the King dead thought a sack was imminent. The finding in the Sheriff's inquiry held later stated that: 'They caused Aldersgate to be shut and did all they could to hinder the men coming to the King's rescue, though they knew he was in great peril. If the citizen forces had not hastily set out notwithstanding, help would have come too late.'[1] But as both were acquitted when put on trial, it is probable that their behaviour was due to fright, not to treachery.

This maddening interference delayed Knollys somewhat, but he managed to reopen Aldersgate and within half an hour of receiving the call issued from the city at the head of 7,000 men-at-arms and archers.

Meanwhile in the cornfields beyond the market the little King was alone with the rebels and, as the Sheriff's Report truly says, in great peril. They remained in two minds what to do with him. Some were still for obtaining charters, but the revolutionaries were pressing for drastic courses. They had always intended to abduct the King; they had now got him. But without Tyler to tell them what to do, they were too slow at taking advantage of their opportunity. They should have attacked instantly in the market when their leader was cut down. They had not done so, had wasted time; they were still wasting time. Jack Straw, Tyler's second-in-command, was not competent to take his place. John Ball, though the chief fomenter of the rebellion, was no leader of

[1] The Sheriff's Report, as cited.

fighting men in the field. The report in the city Letter Book indicates that Richard continued his efforts to mollify the rebels by promising them what they would, 'but they refused to treat of peace except on condition that they should first have the head of the Mayor'. This demand was made by the more moderate section, since it implies a willingness to come to terms if the slayer of their chief was punished. But the rest, 'an infuriated multitude' as the Letter Book calls them, were seen to be making ready for the onslaught upon the city and the general massacre intended all along.

When Knollys led the van out of Aldersgate, Walworth went aside to look for Tyler, to learn whether he was yet dead. His retinue had taken him into St. Bartholemew's Hospital and there Walworth discovered him in bed in the Master's room. Though mortally wounded, he was still breathing. Walworth had him carried into the market at once and decapitated. His object was to confront the rebels with his head. With this fixed on a lance he arrived at the fields to find that Knollys had surrounded them and that the King was safe. Approaching under cover of the houses between Aldersgate and the Priory fields, he had taken them by surprise. This factor of surprise, together with the Londoners' greatly superior armour and professional leadership, sufficed to offset their numerical inferiority—7,000 against 20,000 men. Add to this what has already come to light, that many of the 20,000 had no desire to fight, and the success of Knollys' manoeuvre is explained. Jack Straw was unable to rally his men. When they saw themselves surrounded they lost all heart and attempted no resistance. 'The very people,' says the *Chronicon Angliae*, 'who a few minutes before had the life and death of the nobility in their hands, now began throwing down their swords, bows, axes and clubs.' Some slunk into the corn and hid. Walworth's arrival with Tyler's head was decisive. 'When the commons,' says the *Anonimalle*, 'saw their leader had died in that manner, they were utterly discomfited and fell to the ground there in the corn, crying to the King to forgive them their misdeeds.' Without their captain, who for three days had made them masters of London, they became a rabble of poor rustics. The suddenness of their collapse seemed a miracle to the writer of the *Chronicon Angliae*; a mob which had held the King prisoner till a few minutes ago was now begging him for mercy. Against this tide of moral prostration the revolutionaries were helpless.

Sir Robert Knollys, who had been slaughtering peasants in France for over thirty years and had seen the vengeance taken on the Jacques by their own lords, was anxious to close in upon and massacre the miserable people, but it was thought preferable to let them go, if they would go quietly. With a disaffected London proletariat and the many lawless persons about in the streets, the situation was still very delicate. It would pay for the present to continue the policy of conciliation, which had been followed from the first. The King was advised to grant the clemency demanded of him. Indeed, he is said to have opposed a massacre, though his father in the circumstances would have been more severe. Those who had not thrown down their arms were ordered to do so. The whole body was then marched out of London by knights appointed for the purpose. Knollys, says Froissart, was very annoyed, but the King cheered him by saying that his vengeance would follow.

Richard had had a great personal triumph. He was the hero of the hour. He had the tact, however, to declare that had it not been for the burgesses under Walworth, Brembre and Philpot coming to his aid in the nick of time, he would have perished. 'Put your bacinet on and kneel,' said he to Walworth. 'Why, sir?' asked the Mayor. 'Because I am going to knight you.' 'I am only a poor fishmonger,' protested Walworth, though one of the richest merchants in the city. 'The King made him put on his bacinet and taking a sword in both hands gave him a smart blow on the neck with lively good-will,' and did the same for Bembre and Philpot and also Ralph Standish, the esquire who had run Tyler through after Walworth had struck him. This done, says the *Anonimalle*, from which the scene is taken, 'the King made his way through London to the Wardrobe, there to rest after his great labours'.

Froissart's dramatic sense prompted him to record the meeting between Richard and his mother at the Wardrobe. 'The Princess had spent the last forty-eight hours very greatly disturbed in mind, as, indeed, she had every reason to be. On seeing her son arrive safe, she was overjoyed. "Ah, dear son," she cried, "you can imagine how anxious I have been." "Indeed, I can, Madam," said he. "But now, thank God, you may be happy, for today I have recovered the crown I had lost." '

By putting these words into Richard's mouth, Froissart repeats what was his own opinion of the rebellion: 'England was on the point of being lost beyond recovery. No kingdom was ever in such peril as was she on that occasion.' This was the general contemporary view. Thus the *Chronicon Angliae* has: 'Unless God had prevented it, the realm would have been utterly destroyed.' Richard had, indeed, lost his kingdom and he regained it by keeping his head. Whether Walworth's blow, though inevitable in the circumstances, was an aggravation of an already desperate situation or its cure, will always be debated.

The drama of Smithfield market is very complex. Perhaps the blow, though fatal if Richard had not remained cool, was the best solution, since, had Tyler not been killed, he would have massacred the royal party in the market and moved in to sack London, an onslaught in which Knollys and his men would probably have been swept away, hampered as they would have been by the streets and the savagery of the London mob.

Conclusion

After the departure from London of the Kent and Essex men, the rebellion ceased to be a serious threat. It had been destroyed as a revolution; to put it down as an agrarian rising was not difficult. The counties said to be marching on the city held off when the events of Saturday became known. In Norfolk, Suffolk and Cambridgeshire the peasantry were more troublesome than elsewhere but their suppression only took a few weeks. The rights and liberties they demanded were refused and they were punished for asking in so riotous a manner. All the charters granted at Mile End and the Wardrobe were declared null, as having been extorted under duress. Serfdom remained as before, as did all the other disabilities against which labour had risen. The government did not think it prudent to take the revenge which the French lords did on the Jacques. There was no indiscriminate slaughter. Punishments were meted out according to law. Everyone arrested had a regular trial. The number of executions was moderate. The rank and file got off lightly. Wat Tyler's two chief lieutenants, John Ball and Jack Straw, were pursued, tried and hanged.

Walworth promised Straw before his execution to pay for masses for his soul, if he made a full confession. What he confessed is preserved in two chronicles.[1] He confirmed that the rebel leaders were out and out revolutionaries, a fact which the government had reason to suspect, though not till then knew for certain. Part of what he said was: 'We intended to abduct the King and take him with us through the country. At sight of him the people

[1] The *Historia Vitae et Regni Ricardi II* and the *Chronicon Angliae*.

would have joined us *en masse*, believing we had his authority for our actions. We would have killed him later on. All members of the nobility who opposed us would have perished. Our intention was also to execute the bishops and other rulers of the Church. Having exterminated the ruling classes, we would then have enacted new laws. We had resolved to make Wat Tyler king of Kent and set other chosen men over each county. Had Tyler not been killed on the Saturday, we would have sacked and then burnt London, which we could easily have done since its working class was on our side.' The author of the *Vita* adds: 'Nor was this the only confession. Many others under sentence of death confessed to similar designs. There is no doubt that the rebels planned to destroy the state.'

In contrast with this revolutionary programme, very similar to to that of the French revolutionaries of 1789, the last recorded words of William Grindcob, the leader of the St. Albans rebels, strike a pathetic note. The ambitions of his followers did not go beyond forcing the Abbot of St. Albans monastery, the greatest landowner in those parts and who owned St. Albans town, to grant liberties which they had been striving to wring from him for a long time. At Mile End the King had granted them a charter which enjoined him to grant the liberties. Like others, it was cancelled. Grindcob was imprisoned in Hertford. Thinking that, if let out, he would calm the St. Albans people, who continued to disturb the peace, the authorities released him on bail. Instead, he addressed the townsmen as follows: 'You, who have enjoyed a taste of liberty after long oppression, stand fast while you may. Do not be anxious on my account. For I shall die happy, if I end my life as a martyr in the cause of liberty. Act as you would have, had I been beheaded yesterday in Hertford.'[1] Here spoke, not a revolutionary, but a man who believed that the government could be forced to grant agrarian reforms. Tyler did not believe this; nothing short of total revolution would suffice. But Grindcob's comparative moderation did not save him; he was re-arrested and executed.

The story had, thus, a happy ending for the nobility and gentry. They emerged unscathed from a week's terror. All was apparently lost, but in a flash all was theirs again. They were not obliged to make a single concession. Life resumed for them its normal course.

[1] *Gesta Abbatum Monasterii Sancti Albani* (Rolls series, p. 341).

For the commons, time was their only friend, and time is slow in distributing alms. With time's help, however, their descendants eventually had their way. Everything sought in 1381 they have obtained. Unlike the French Sansculottes, they had never to resort to massacre in order to win a representative government, a church subordinate to the state and equal laws for all. These were attained by economic pressure, by mutual agreement, step by step, and by, as it were, a natural evolution.

What is so remarkable about the revolt of 1381 is that the peasantry of that early date should have foreseen that government by the commons was necessary for England. By adopting as their slogan, 'The King and the commons of England', they made a basic political statement, round which the whole history of England was to revolve. At a time when the commons were not represented in parliament and had no voice in the government, the claim that they should be the ruling power was an idea of the greatest originality. Its soundness was not affected by the belief that massacre was an indispensable preliminary. That the English people, if they were to realize their destiny, must rule themselves remained the correct estimate of the future.

The question arises how they came to conceive of this idea, the greatest idea engendered during the fourteenth century. The story traced in this book provides an answer. Their experiences in France made them realize themselves. They had there a revelation of their capabilities. The battles in France were not won by the knights but by the archers. An English army with enough archers could march anywhere, without archers it could march nowhere. The archers were the commons. But not only had the commons won Crécy, Poitiers and Nájera by archery; they themselves had created archery. It was not a case of their using a superior weapon supplied to them; the weapon came from them. It was the village weapon which they had developed and perfected. Small wonder that they conceived a high notion of their capacity. From the knowledge that they had been the decisive factor in three grand victories, more spectacular than any hitherto gained, came the intuition that they were competent to be the rulers of England. Since the nobility had shown themselves singularly incompetent to conserve what the archers had won, the intuition became a yet more reasonable assumption.

That the revolutionaries were, in fact, not capable of ruling England and that they proposed to establish themselves by an atrocious massacre (which Tyler was right in thinking was the only way they could establish themselves) does not, as argued, negative the visionary truth of their idea. In propounding it they led Europe, just as in manipulating the longbow they did what Europe had not thought of and could not manage.

Another idea peculiar to England and unique in Europe which appeared at this time was Wycliffe's theory of the relation of church and state, so fecund that it paved the way for the Reformation. Wycliffe's idea was so close to the commons' demand for the dissolution of church establishments and the distribution of their revenues among the people, that it has been thought that they derived their demand from him. It seems more likely, however, that he gave philosophic form to conceptions already current in the country. If so, the commons of 1381 not only sketched the future constitution, but also adumbrated the post-medieval Anglican church.

England produced one other unique creation at this time, the perpendicular style in architecture. An art movement, so fundamental as to change all building, never originates at the top. The perpendicular style cannot be related to anything in the life and thought of the nobility, so French and florid in their tastes, and must be thought of as originating in popular sentiment. It did, in fact, represent the popular dislike of the decorated style, a French style which mirrored chivalry. The mood which brought it into existence was so strong that the upper classes were converted to it. If then the perpendicular originated in an anti-French, antichivalric impulse arising from the depths of the national spirit, it may not be too fanciful to see in the arrowy rush of its lines a symbol of the arrow-shower, the commons' great achievement in the world of action. So seen, it becomes the abstract picture of the Hurling Time.

[illegible] right in claiming [illegible] only was the [illegible] that [illegible] was [illegible] [illegible] and [illegible] manner.

Another new pressure in England and [illegible] was [illegible] the [illegible] of [illegible] was for the [illegible] countries [illegible] derived their ideas and [illegible] that [illegible] the [illegible]

[illegible] other [illegible] to change in building [illegible] style cannot be [illegible] of the [illegible] the popular [illegible] style [illegible] carved [illegible] was [illegible] that the [illegible] from the [illegible] may not [illegible] time.

Index

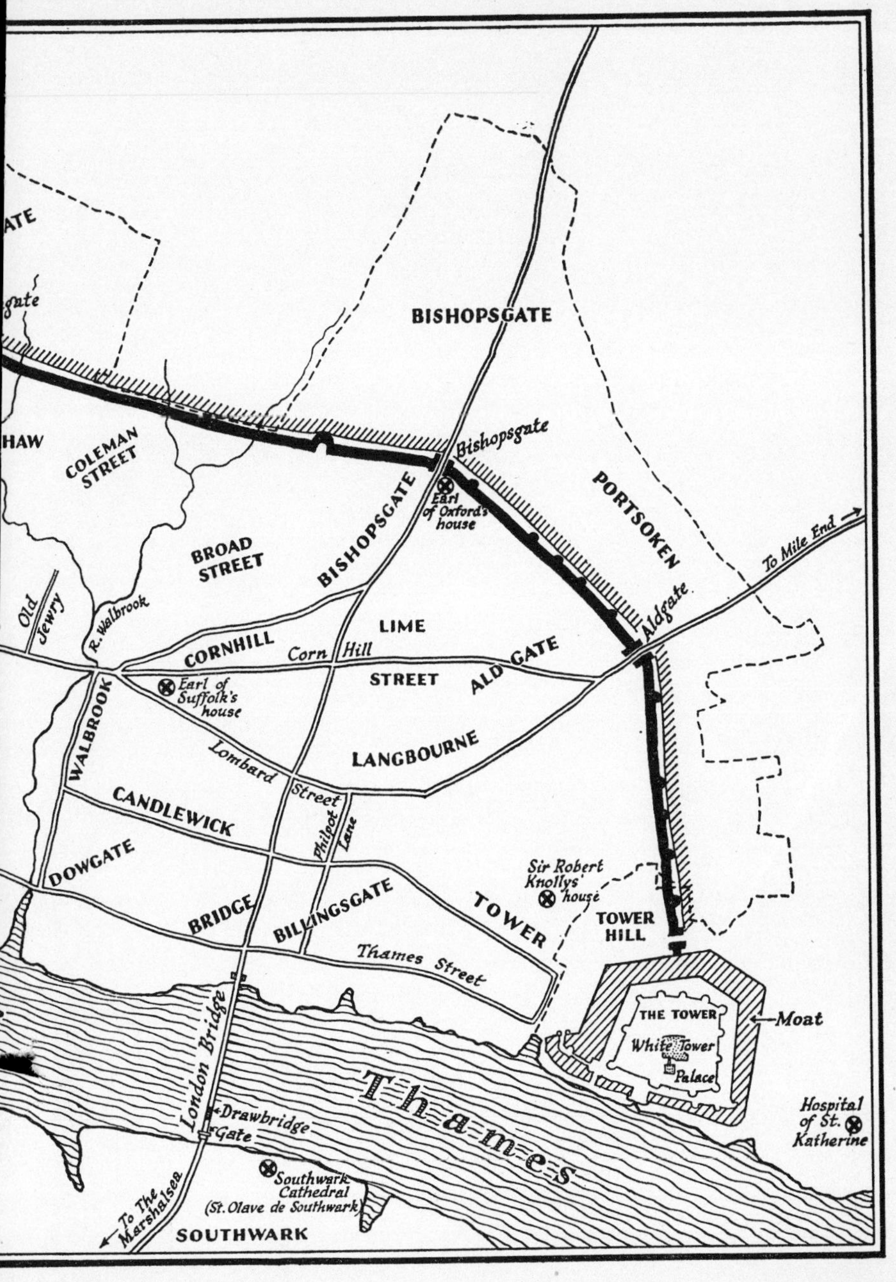

ATE
gate
BISHOPSGATE
HAW
COLEMAN STREET
Bishopsgate
Earl of Oxford's house
PORTSOKEN
BROAD STREET
BISHOPSGATE
To Mile End
Old Jewry
R. Walbrook
LIME
Aldgate
CORNHILL
Corn Hill
STREET
ALD GATE
Earl of Suffolk's house
WALBROOK
Lombard
LANGBOURNE
Street
CANDLEWICK
Philpot Lane
DOWGATE
Sir Robert Knollys' house
BRIDGE
BILLINGSGATE
TOWER
TOWER HILL
Thames Street
London Bridge
THE TOWER
White Tower
Palace
Moat
Thames
Drawbridge
Gate
Hospital of St. Katherine
Southwark Cathedral
(St. Olave de Southwark)
To The Marshalsea
SOUTHWARK